EXPEDITION TO BORNEO.

LUNDU DYAKS.

London Chapman & Hall, 180 Strand, Jan'y 15th 1846.

THE
EXPEDITION TO BORNEO

OF

H.M.S. DIDO

FOR

THE SUPPRESSION OF PIRACY:

WITH EXTRACTS FROM

THE JOURNAL OF JAMES BROOKE, ESQ.

OF SARĀWAK,

(NOW AGENT FOR THE BRITISH GOVERNMENT IN BORNEO.)

BY

CAPTAIN THE HON. HENRY KEPPEL, R.N.

IN TWO VOLUMES.

VOL. II.

Rediscovery Books

Reproduced by kind permission of the
Royal Geographical Society

Published by
Rediscovery Books Ltd
Unit 10, Ridgewood Industrial Park,
Uckfield, East Sussex,
TN22 5QE England
Tel: +44 (0) 1825 749494
Fax: +44 (0) 1825 765701

This edition © Rediscovery Books Ltd 2006

To find out more about Rediscovery Books
and its range of titles visit
www.rediscoverybooks.com

Published in association with

Royal Geographical Society
with IBG

Advancing geography
and geographical learning

The **Royal Geographical Society with IBG** was founded in 1830 to advance geographical science. Today it supports geographical research, promotes geography in schools and through outdoor learning, in society and to policy makers. Geography connects us to the world's people, places and environments.

The **Rediscovery Books** series allow us to see how previous geographers and travellers understood and recorded the world.

In reprinting in facsimile from the original, any imperfections are inevitably reproduced and the quality may fall short of modern type and cartographic standards.

CONTENTS OF VOLUME II.

CHAPTER I.

Captain Keppel's voyage in the Dido with Mr. Brooke to Sarāwak. Chase of three piratical prahus. Boat-expedition. Action with the pirates, and capture of a prahu. Arrival at Sarāwak. Mr. Brooke's reception. Captain Keppel and his officers visit the Rajah. The palace and the audience. Return royal visit to the Dido. Mr. Brooke's residence and household. Dr. Treacher's adventure with one of the ladies of Macota's harem. Another boat-affair with the pirates, and death of their chief . . . . *Page* 1

CHAPTER II.

The Dido recalled to China. Effect of her presence at Sarāwak. The Rajah's letter to Captain Keppel, and his reply. Prepares for an expedition against the Sarebus pirates. Pleasure-excursion up the river. The Chinese settlement. The Singè mountain. Interior of the residences. Dyak festival of Maugut. Relics. Sporting. Return to Sarāwak. The expedition against Sarebus. State and number of the assailing force. Ascent of the river. Beauty of the scenery 25

CHAPTER III.

Ascent of the river to Paddi. Town taken and burnt. Narrow escape of a reinforcement of friendly Dyaks. Night-attack by the pirates. Conference: they submit. Proceed against Pakoo. Dyak treatment of dead enemies. Destruction of Pakoo, and submission of the pirates. Advance upon Rembas. The town destroyed : the inhabitants yield. Satisfactory effects of the expedition. Death of Dr. Simpson. Triumphant return to Sarāwak . . *Page* 50

CHAPTER IV.

Captain Keppel sails for China. Calcutta. The Dido ordered to Borneo again. Arrival at Sarāwak. Great improvements visible. Atrocities of the Sakarran pirates. Mr. Brooke's letter. Captain Sir E. Belcher's previous visit to Sarāwak in the Samarang. Coal found. Second letter from the Rajah Muda Hassim. Expedition against the Sakarran pirates. Patusen destroyed. Macota remembered, and his retreat burnt. Further fighting, and advance. Ludicrous midnight alarm 74

CHAPTER V.

Seriff Muller's town sacked. Ascend the river in pursuit of the enemy. Gallant exploit of Lieutenant Wade. His death and funeral. Interesting anecdote of him. Ascend the Sakarran branch. Native boats hemmed in by pirates, and their crews slaughtered to a man. Karangan destroyed. Captain Sir E. Belcher arrives in the Samarang's boats. Return to Sarāwak. New expedition against Seriffs Sahib and Jaffer. Macota captured. Flight of Seriff Sahib. Conferences. Seriff Jaffer deposed. Mr. Brooke's speech in the native tongue. End of the expedition, and return to Sarāwak. The Dido sails for England 99

CHAPTER VI.

Later portion of Mr. Brooke's Journal. Departure of Captain Keppel, and arrival of Sir E. Belcher. Mr. Brooke proceeds with Muda Hassim, in the Samarang, to Borneo. Labuan examined. Returns to Sarāwak. Visit of Lingire, a Sarebus chief. The Dyaks of Tumma and Bandar Cassim. Meets an assembly of Malays and Dyaks. Arrival of Lingi, as a deputation from the Sakarran chiefs. The Malay character. Excursion up the country. Miserable effects of excess in opium-smoking. Picturesque situation of the Sow village of Ra-at. Nawang. Feast at Ra-at. Returns home. Conferences with Dyak chiefs 122

CONTENTS OF VOLUME II.

CHAPTER VII.

Arrival of Captain Bethune and Mr. Wise. Mr. Brooke appointed her Majesty's Agent in Borneo. Sails for Borneo Proper. Muda Hassim's measures for the suppression of piracy. Defied by Seriff Houseman. Audience of the Sultan, Muda Hassim, and the Pangerans. Visit to Labuan. Comparative eligibility of Labuan and Balambangan for settlement. Coal discovered in Labuan. Mr. Brooke goes to Singapore and visits Admiral Sir T. Cochrane. The upas-tree. Proceeds with the Admiral to Borneo Proper. Punishment of Pangeran Usop. The battle of Malludu. Seriff Houseman obliged to fly. Visit to Balambangan. Mr. Brooke parts with the Admiral, and goes to Borneo Proper. An attempt of Pangeran Usop defeated. His flight, and pursuit by Pangeran Budrudeen. Triumphant reception of Mr. Brooke in Borneo. Returns to Saráwak . . . . *Page* 140

CHAPTER VIII.

Borneo, its geographical bounds and leading divisions. British settlements in 1775. The province of Saráwak formally ceded by the Sultan in perpetuity to Mr. Brooke its present ruler. General view of the Dyaks, the aborigines of Borneo. The Dyaks of Saráwak, and adjoining tribes; their past oppression and present position 163

CHAPTER IX.

Mr. Brooke's memorandum on the piracy of the Malayan Archipelago. The measures requisite for its suppression, and consequent extension of British commerce in that important locality 189

CHAPTER X.

Proposed British settlement on the north-west coast of Borneo, and occupation of the island of Labuan. Governor Crawfurd's opinions thereon 209

CONCLUDING OBSERVATIONS 224

CONTENTS OF VOLUME II.

APPENDIX.

I. Proposed exploring expedition to the Asiatic Archipelago, by James Brooke, Esq. 1838 . . *Page* i
II. Sketch of Borneo, or Pulo Kalamantan, by J. Hunt, Esq. xvi
III. Treaty between his Britannic Majesty and the King of the Netherlands, respecting territory and commerce in the East Indies. Signed at London, March 17, 1824   lxv
IV. Official Letters lxxix
V. Admiral Sir Thomas Cochrane's Despatches . . lxxxv
VI. Memoir of Lieutenant Wade xcvii
VII. Memoir of Mr. George Steward ci

ILLUSTRATIONS TO VOLUME II.

Lundu Dyak	*to face the Title*
Attack on the Dido's boats off Sirhassan	8
Hall of audience, Sarāwak	13
Mr. Brooke's first residence at Sarāwak	15
War-dance of the Lundu Dyaks	35
Attack on Paddi by the boats of H.M.S. Dido . . .	52
Funeral of Lieutenant Wade	105
Mr. Wise's Plan for accelerating the Mails between Great Britain and China	220
Plan of Labuan	*at end of vol.*
Map of the River Sarebus	*ditto*
,, the Batang Lupar River	*ditto*
,, the Forts and Villages of Patusen . .	*ditto*

A

VISIT TO BORNEO.

CHAPTER I.

Captain Keppel's Voyage in the Dido with Mr. Brooke to Sarāwak. Chase of three piratical prahus. Boat-expedition. Action with the pirates, and capture of a prahu. Arrival at Sarāwak. Mr. Brooke's reception. Captain Keppel and his officers visit the Rajah. The palace and the audience. Return royal visit to the Dido. Mr. Brooke's residence and household. Dr. Treacher's adventure with one of the ladies of Macota's harem. Another boat-affair with the pirates, and death of their chief.

I HAVE already mentioned my meeting Mr. Brooke, and his accompanying me over to Sarāwak. I had not then seen my friend's Journal; and it was not until some time after, that I by degrees heard the progress of his infant government from its commencement: and it was with unfeigned pleasure that I found, while performing my duty in the suppression of piracy, I was, at the same time, rendering the greatest assistance and support to an individual in his praiseworthy, novel, and important position.

I had long felt a desire to explore the Island of Borneo, which the few travellers who have called there describe as not only one of the largest and most fertile in the world, but one of the most productive in gold and diamonds, and other rich minerals and ores; one from which the finest camphor known is brought into merchandise, and which is undoubtedly capable of supplying every kind of valuable spice, and articles of universal traffic and consumption. Yet, with all these capabilities and inducements to tempt the energetic spirit of trade, the internal condition of the country, and the dangers which beset its coasts, have hitherto prevented the interior from being explored by Europeans; and to prove how little we are acquainted even with its shores, I actually sailed by the best Admiralty chart eighty miles inland, and over the tops of mountains!

May 4th.—Passed through the Tambelans, a beautiful group of between 100 and 150 small islands. They are very extensive, and but thinly inhabited. There is good anchorage near some of them; but we had nothing less than twenty fathoms. They are placed so close together that, after passing the first, we were to all appearance completely land-locked in a magnificent and capacious harbour. The following morning we anchored off the mouth of the Sambas river, and sent the boats away to examine the creeks, islands, and rivers along the coast for traces of pirates—

which were discovered by the remains of their fires on different parts, although no clue could be obtained as to the direction in which they had gone. On the morning of the 8th I again sent the pinnace and two cutters, Mr. Partridge, Messrs. D'Aeth and Jenkins, with a week's provisions, the whole under the command of Lieutenant Wilmot Horton, Mr. Brooke kindly offering his assistance, which, from his knowledge of the Malay language, as well as of the kind of vessels used by the pirates, was thankfully accepted. I directed them to proceed to the island of Murrundum, and, after visiting the South Natunas, to rejoin the Dido at Sarāwak. In the mean time I proceeded leisurely along the coast, anchoring where convenient, and finding regular soundings all the way in from four to ten fathoms—weather remarkably fine, and water smooth. On the morning of the 9th, on rounding Tanjong Datu, we opened suddenly on a suspicious-looking boat, which, on making us out, ran for a small deep bay formed by Cape Datu and the next point to the eastward. Standing a little farther on, we discovered a second large boat in the offing, which likewise stood in shore, and afterwards a third at the bottom of the bay. From the description I had received, I easily made these out to be Illanuns, an enterprising tribe of pirates, of whose daring adventures I had heard much. They inhabit a small cluster of islands off the N.E. coast of Borneo, and go out in large fleets every year to look for prahus bound to Singapore or the Straits; and, after capturing the vessels, reduce their crews to slavery. It is of a cruel nature; for Mr. Brooke observes: "Nor is the slavery of that mild description which is often attributed to the Asiatics; for these victims are bound for months, and crowded in the bottom of the pirate-vessels, where they suffer all the miseries which could be inflicted on board an African slaver." Having fairly pinned these worthies into a corner, and knowing that the only two small boats I had left on board would stand no chance with them in pulling, to make sure of my prizes I loaded the two foremost guns on each side, and, having no proper chart of the coast, proceeded under easy sail, feeling my way into the bay with the lead. When just within musket-range, I let go the anchor, which was no sooner done than the three boats commenced making a move. I thought at first they were coming alongside to sue for pardon and peace: and my astonishment was great when I discovered that nothing was further from their intention. One pulled away, close in shore, to the eastward, and the other two to the westward. They were rowed by about forty oars each, and appeared from their swiftness to be flying, and that too from under my very nose; and what rendered it still more ridiculous and disagreeable, owing to a strong ebb-tide, the ship remained exactly in a position that no gun could be brought to bear on either side. The dingy and jolly-boat gave chase; but the pirates had the start, and it was useless; for although a few men were seen to drop from their oars in consequence of our fire of musketry from the forecastle, still their pace never slackened; and when they did come within the bearing of our guns, which they were obliged to do for a minute or two while rounding the points that formed the bay, though our thirty-two pound shot fell thickly about their heads, frequently dashing the spray all over them, not a man flinched from his oar. We could not help admiring their plan of escape, and the gallant manner in which it was effected. I saw that it would be quite unavailing to attempt to catch the boats that had pulled to windward; but we lost no time in slipping our cable and making all sail in chase of the one that had gone to leeward. But the "artful dodger" was still too fast for us: we lost sight of him at dusk close off the mouth of a river, up which, however, I do not think he went; for our two boats were there very shortly after him; and although they searched all night and next morning, they could discover no traces of the fugitive. Besides, these pirates have no friends among the inhabitants of the province of Sarāwak who would have screened them from us; on the contrary, they would have put them to death if once in their power. I certainly never made so sure of any thing in my life as of capturing the three prahus after I had seen them safe into the bottom of the little bay at Tanjong Datu: but "there is many a slip between the cup and the lip." We returned the following day to pick up the anchor and cable, and observed that it was a place well adapted as a rendezvous for pirates. The bay is studded with rocks; and to my horror, I found that I had run her Majesty's ship Dido inside two that were a-wash at low water! A mountain-stream of most delicious water runs into the bay between two rocks, and the coast abounds with oysters.

On the 13th the Dido anchored off Tanjong Poe, outside the bar at the entrance of the river leading to Mr. Brooke's residence and seat of government, at the town of Sarāwak, situated about twenty-four miles up. At half-tide on the following morning we crossed the bar, carrying no less than three and a half fathoms, and entered the beautiful river of Morotaba, which we ran up for the first fifteen miles under all sail, with a fresh leading breeze. The Dido was the first square-rigged vessel that had ever entered those waters. We came-to at the junction river which unites the two principal entrances to the Sarāwak.

In the evening our boats returned on board from their expedition, having reached Sarāwak the day previous by the western entrance. On leaving the Dido, on the morning of the 8th, they proceeded to the island of Murrundum, a favourite rendezvous for pirates, where they came on a fleet of the Illanun tribe, who, however, did not give them an opportunity of closing; but, cutting their sampans adrift, made a precipitate flight, opening fire as they ran out on the opposite side of a small bay, in which they had been watering and refitting. This, of course, led to a very exciting chase, with a running fire kept up on both sides; but the distance was too great for the range of the guns on either side; and the pirates, who, in addition to sailing well, were propelled by from forty to sixty oars each, made their escape. It was not until nearly hull-down that they (probably out of bravado) ceased to fire their stern-guns. As they went in the direction of the Natunas, our boats steered for those islands, and anchored under the south end of one of them. At daylight next morning, although in three fathoms water, the pinnace, owing to the great rise and fall of tide, grounded on a coral reef, and Lieutenant Horton and Mr. Brooke proceeded in one of the cutters to reconnoitre. As they neared the s.w. point, they were met by six prahus, beating their tom-toms as they advanced, and making every demonstration of fighting. Lieutenant Horton judiciously turned to rejoin the other boats; and the pinnace having fortunately just then floated, he formed his little squadron into line abreast, cleared for action, and prepared to meet his formidable-looking antagonists. Mr. Brooke, however, whose eye had been accustomed to the cut and rig of all the boats in these seas, discovered that those advancing were not Illanuns, and fancied there must be some mistake. The Natunas people had been trading with Sarāwak, and he was intimately acquainted with a rich and powerful chief who resided on the island; he therefore raised a white flag of truce on his spy-glass, and from the bow of the pinnace hailed, waved, and made all the signs he could to warn them of the danger into which they were running; but a discharge of small arms was the only reply he got. They then detached their three smallest vessels inshore, so as to command a crossfire and cut off the retreat of our boats; and the rest advanced, yelling, beating their tom-toms, and blazing away with all the confidence of victory, their shot cutting through the rigging, and splashing in the water all round. It was an anxious moment for the Dido's little party. Not a word was spoken. The only gun of the pinnace was loaded with grape and canister, and kept pointed on the largest prahu. The men waited, with their muskets in hand, for permission to fire; but it was not until within pistol-range that Lieutenant Horton poured into the enemy his well-prepared dose. It instantly brought them to a halt; yet they had the temerity to exchange shots for a few minutes longer, when the largest cried for quarter, and the other five made for the shore, chased by the two cutters, and keeping up a fire to the last.

G. Hawkins, lith.

Day & Haghe Lith⁰ to the Queen.

ATTACK on the DIDO'S BOATS off SIRHASSEN.

London Chapman & Hall, 180 Strand, Jan' 15th 1846.

DISPOSAL OF THE ENEMY.

The prize taken possession of by the pinnace proved to be a prahu mounting three brass guns, with a crew of thirty-six men, belonging to the Rajah of Rhio, and which had been despatched by that chief to collect tribute at and about the Natunas islands. They had on board ten men killed, and eleven (four of them mortally) wounded. They affected the greatest astonishment on discovering that our boats belonged to a British man-of-war, and protested that it was all a mistake; that the island had lately been plundered by the Illanun pirates, for whom they had taken us; that the rising sun was in their eyes, and that they could not make out the colours, &c. Lieutenant Horton thinking that their story might possibly have some foundation in truth, and taking into consideration the severe lesson they had received, directed Dr. Simpson, the assistant-surgeon, to dress their wounds; and after admonishing them to be more circumspect in future, restored them their boat, as well as the others which belonged to the island, two of them being a trifle smaller but of the same armament as the one from Rhio, and the remaining three still smaller, carrying twelve men each, armed with spears and muskets. These had been taken possession of by the cutters after they had reached the shore and landed their killed and wounded, who were borne away from the beach so smartly by the natives, that our people had not time to ascertain the number hurt. The surgeon went ashore, and dressed the wounds of several of them; an act of kindness and civilisation far beyond their comprehension. The natives, however, appeared to bear us no malice for the injury we had inflicted on their countrymen, but loaded our boats with fruit, goats, and every thing we required. It afforded some amusement to find that among the slightly wounded was Mr. Brooke's old, wealthy, and respectable friend already alluded to, who was not a little ashamed at being recognised: but piracy is so inherent in a Malay, that few can resist the temptation when a good opportunity for plunder presents itself. The fact, which I afterwards ascertained, was, that they took our boats for some coming from a wreck with whatever valuables they could collect; and not having seen any thing of the ship, rather strengthened their conjecture: and the excuse they made for continuing the fight after they had discovered their mistake was, that they expected no quarter would be given them.[1]

May 16th.—We proceeded up the river twelve miles further into the interior of this interesting country, and, with my friend Mr. Brooke on board, approached Sarāwak, his seat of government; in the reach before you near which, and off the right bank of the river, is a long and dangerous shelf of

---

[1] I am happy to say that the Lords of the Admiralty have since been pleased to promote Lieut. Wilmot Horton and Mr. W. L. Partridge, mate, who commanded the pinnace, for their gallantry on this occasion.—H. K.

rocks. The deep channel which lies between the bank and the rocks is not more than sixty or seventy feet wide, and required some little care in passing; but, with the exception of the flying jib-boom, which got nipped off in the branch of a magnificent overhanging tree, we anchored without accident in six fathoms water, and greatly astonished the natives with a royal salute in honour of Muda Hassim, the Rajah of Borneo. During the whole morning large boats, some carrying as many as two hundred people, had been coming down the river to hail Mr. Brooke's return; and one of the greatest gratifications I had was in witnessing the undisguised delight, mingled with gratitude and respect, with which each head man welcomed their newly-elected ruler back to his adopted country. And although many of the Malay chiefs had every reason to expect that in the Dido they saw the means by which their misdeeds were to be punished, they shewed their confidence in Mr. Brooke by bringing their children with them—a sign peculiar to the Malay. The scene was both novel and exciting; presenting to us, just anchored in a large fresh-water river, and surrounded by a densely-wooded jungle, the whole surface of the water covered with canoes and boats dressed out with their various-coloured silken flags, filled with natives beating their tom-toms, and playing on their wild and not unpleasant-sounding wind-instruments, with the occasional discharge of fire-arms. To them it must have been equally striking and extraordinary (as few of them had ever seen any larger vessel than their own war-boats, or a European, until Mr. Brooke's arrival), to witness the Dido anchored almost in the centre of their town, her mast-heads towering above the highest trees of their jungle; the loud report of her heavy two-and-thirty pounder guns, and the running aloft, to furl sails, of 150 seamen, in their clean white dresses, and with the band playing; all which helped to make an impression that will not easily be forgotten at Sarāwak. I was anxious that Mr. Brooke should land with all the honours due to so important a personage, which he accordingly did, under a salute. The next business was my visit of ceremony to the Rajah, which was great sport, though conducted in the most imposing manner. The band, and the marines, as a guard, having landed, we (the officers) all assembled at Mr. Brooke's house, where, having made ourselves as formidable as we could with swords and cocked hats, we marched in procession to the royal residence, his majesty having sent one of his brothers, who led me by the hand into his presence. The palace was a long low shed, built on piles, to which we ascended by a ladder. The audience-chamber was hung with red and yellow silk curtains, and round the back and one side of the platform occupied by the Rajah were ranged his ministers, warriors, and men-at-arms, bearing spears, swords,

HALL of AUDIENCE, SARAWAK.

London Chapman & Hall, 180 Strand, Jan'y 15th 1846.

shields, and other warlike weapons. Opposite to them were drawn up our royal marines; the contrast between the two body-guards being very amusing. Muda Hassim is a wretched-looking little man; still there was a courteous and gentle manner about him that prepossessed us in his favour, and made us feel that we were before an individual who had been accustomed to command. We took our seats in a semicircle, on chairs provided for the occasion, and smoked cigars and drank tea. His majesty chewed his sīrih-leaf and betel-nut, seated with one leg crossed under him, and playing with his toes. Very little is ever said during these audiences; so we sat staring at one another for half an hour with mutual astonishment; and, after the usual compliments of wishing our friendship might last as long as the moon, and my having offered him the Dido and every thing else that did not belong to me in exchange for his house, we took our leave.

May 19*th.*—This was the day fixed for the Rajah's visit to the Dido, about which he appeared very anxious, although he had seldom been known to go beyond his own threshold. For this ceremony all the boats, guns, tom-toms, flags, and population were put in requisition; and the procession to the ship was a very gorgeous and amusing spectacle. We received him on board with a royal salute. He brought in his train a whole tribe of natural brothers. His guards and followers were strange enough, and far too numerous to be admitted on the Dido's deck; so that as soon as a sufficient number had scrambled on board, the sentry had orders to prevent any more from crowding in; but, whether in so doing the most important personages of the realm were kept out, we did not ascertain. One fellow succeeded in obtaining a footing with a large yellow silk canopy, a corner of which having run into the eye of one of the midshipmen, the bearer missed his footing, and down came the whole concern,—as I was informed, by *accident!* The party assembled in my cabin; and the remarks were few, nor did they manifest great astonishment at any thing. In fact, a Malay never allows himself to be taken by surprise. I believe, however, the Rajah did not think much of my veracity, when I informed him that this was not the largest ship belonging to Her Britannic Majesty, and that she had several mounting upwards of 100 guns; though he admitted that he had seen a grander sight than any of his ancestors. There was much distress depicted in the royal countenance during his visit, which I afterwards ascertained was owing to his having been informed that he must not spit in my cabin. On leaving the ship, whether the cherry-brandy he had taken made him forget the directions he had received I do not know, but he squirted a mouthful of red betel-nut juice over the white deck, and then had the temerity to hold out his hand to the first lieutenant,

G. Hawkins, lith.   Day & Haghe Lith^{rs} to the Queen.

MR BROOKE'S FIRST RESIDENCE at SARĀWAK.

who hastily applied to him the style (not royal) of " a dirty beast," which not understanding, he smiled graciously, taking it as some compliment peculiar to the English.

This farce over, I had now some time to look about me, and to refit my ship in one of the prettiest spots on earth, and as unlike a dock-yard as any thing could be.

Mr. Brooke's then residence, although equally rude in structure with the abodes of the natives, was not without its English comforts of sofas, chairs, and bedsteads. It was larger than any other, but, like them, being built upon piles, we had to mount a ladder to get into it. It was situated on the same side of the river (the right bank), next to, but rather in the rear of, the Rajah's palace, with a clear space of about 150 yards between the back and the edge of the jungle. It was surrounded by palisades and a ditch, forming a protection to sheep, goats, occasionally bullocks, pigeons, cats, poultry, geese, monkeys, dogs, and ducks. The house consisted of but one floor. A large room in the centre, neatly ornamented with every description of fire-arms, in admirable order and ready for use, served as an audience and mess-room; and the various apartments round it as bed-rooms, most of them comfortably furnished with matted floors, easy chairs, pictures, and books, with much more taste and attention to comfort than bachelors usually display. In one corner of the square formed by the palisades were the kitchen and offices. The Europeans with Mr. Brooke consisted of Mr. Douglas, formerly in the navy, a clever young surgeon, and a gentleman of the name of Williamson, who, being master of the native language, as well as active and intelligent, made an excellent prime minister. Besides these were two others who came out in the yacht, one an old man-of-war's man, who kept the arms in first-rate condition, and another worthy character who answered to the name of Charlie, and took care of the accounts and charge of every thing. These were attended by servants of different nations. The cooking establishment was perfect, and the utmost harmony prevailed. The great feeding-time was at sunset, when Mr. Brooke took his seat at the head of the table, and all the establishment, as in days of yore, seated themselves according to their respective grades. This hospitable board was open to all the officers of the Dido; and many a jovial evening we spent there. All Mr. Brooke's party were characters—all had travelled; and never did a minute flag for want of some entertaining anecdote, good story, or song, to pass away the time. From breakfast until bed-time there was no intermission; and it was while smoking our cigars in the evening, that the natives, as well as the Chinese who had become settlers, used to drop in, and, after creeping up, according to their custom, and touching the hand of their European Rajah, retire to the further end of the room and squat down upon their haunches, and remain a couple of hours without uttering a word, and then creep out again. I have seen sixty or seventy of an evening come in and make this sort of salaam. All were armed; as it is reckoned an insult for a Malay to appear before the Rajah without his kris. I could not help remarking the manly independent bearing of the half-savage and nearly naked mountain Dyak, compared with the sneaking deportment of the Malay.

The following little adventure was told me during my stay at Sarāwak by Dr. Treacher, who had lately joined Mr. Brooke, his former medical attendant having returned to England. It appears that Dr. Treacher received a message by a confidential slave, that one of the ladies of Macota's harem desired an interview, appointing a secluded spot in the jungle as the rendezvous. The doctor, being aware of his own good looks, fancied he had made a conquest; and, having got himself up as showily as he could, was there at the appointed time. He described the poor girl as both young and pretty, but with a dignified and determined look, which at once convinced him that she was moved to take so dangerous a step by some deeper feeling than that of a mere fancy for his person. She complained of the ill-treatment she had received from Macota, and the miserable life she led; and avowed that her firm resolve was to destroy (not herself, gentle creature! but) him, for which purpose she wanted a small portion of arsenic. It was a disappointment that he could not comply with her request: so they parted—he full of pity and love for her, and she, in all probability, full of contempt for a man who felt for her wrongs, but would not aid in the very simple means she had proposed for redressing them.

While at Singapore, Mr. Whitehead had kindly offered to allow his yacht, the Emily, a schooner of about fifty tons, with a native crew, to bring our letters to Borneo, on the arrival at Singapore of the mail from England. About the time she was expected, I thought it advisable to send a boat to cruise in the vicinity of Cape Datu, in case of her falling in with any of these piratical gentry. The Dido's largest boat, the pinnace, being under repair, Mr. Brooke lent a large boat which he had had built by the natives at Sarāwak, and called the Jolly Bachelor. Having fitted her with a brass six-pounder long gun, with a volunteer crew, of a mate, two midshipmen, six marines, and twelve seamen, and a fortnight's provisions, I despatched her under the command of the second lieutenant, Mr. Hunt; Mr. Douglas, speaking the Malayan language, likewise volunteered his services. One evening, after they had been about six days absent, while we were at dinner, young Douglas made his appearance, bearing in his arms the captured colours of an Illanun pirate. It appears that the day after they had got outside, they observed three boats a long way in the offing, to which they gave chase; but soon lost sight of them, owing to their superior sailing. They, however, appeared a second and a third time after dark, but without the Jolly Bachelor being able to get near them; and it now being late, and the crew both fatigued and hungry, they pulled in shore, lighted a fire, cooked their provisions, and then hauled the boat out to her grapnel near some rocks for the night; lying down to rest with their arms by their sides, and muskets round the mast ready loaded. Having also placed sentries and look-out men, and appointed an officer of the watch, they one and all (sentries included, I suppose), owing to the fatigues of the day, fell asleep! At about three o'clock the following morning, the moon being just about to rise, Lieut. Hunt happening to awake, observed a savage brandishing a kris, and performing his war-dance on the bit of deck, in an ecstasy of delight, thinking in all probability of the ease with which he had got possession of a fine trading-boat, and calculating the cargo of slaves he had to sell, but little dreaming of the hornets' nest into which he had fallen. Lieut. Hunt's round face meeting the light of the rising moon, without a turban surmounting it, was the first notice the pirate had of his mistake. He immediately plunged overboard; and before Lieut. Hunt had sufficiently recovered his astonishment to know whether he was dreaming or not, or to rouse his crew up, a discharge from three or four cannon within a few yards, and the cutting through the rigging by the various missiles with which the guns were loaded, soon convinced him there was no mistake. It was as well the men were still lying down when this discharge took place, as not one of them was hurt; but on jumping to their legs, they found themselves closely pressed by two large war-prahus, one on each bow. To return the fire, cut the cable, man the oars, and back astern to gain room, was the work of a minute; but now came the tug of war, it was a case of life and death. Our men fought as British sailors ought to do; quarter was not expected on either side; and the quick and deadly aim of the marines prevented the pirates from reloading their guns. The Illanun prahus are built with strong bulwarks or barricades, grape-shot proof, across the fore part of the boat, through which ports are formed for working the guns; these bulwarks had to be cut away by round shot from the Jolly Bachelor before the musketry could bear effectually. This done, their grape and canister told with fearful execution. In the mean time, the prahus had been pressing forward to board, while the Jolly Bachelor backed astern; but as soon as this service was achieved, our men dropped their oars, and seizing their muskets, dashed on: the work was sharp but short, and the slaughter great. While one pirate-boat was sinking, and an effort made to secure her, the other effected her escape by rounding the point of rocks, where a third and larger prahu, hitherto unseen, came to her assistance, and putting fresh hands on board, and taking her in tow, succeeded in getting off, although chased by the Jolly Bachelor, after setting fire to the crippled prize, which blew up and sunk before the conquerors got back to the scene of action. While there, a man swam off to them from the shore, who proved to be one of the captured slaves, and had made his escape by leaping overboard during the fight. The three prahus were the same Illanun pirates we had so suddenly come upon off Cape Datu in the Dido, and they belonged to the same fleet that Lieutenant Horton had chased off the island of Murrundum. The slave-prisoner had been seized with a companion in a small fishing-canoe off Borneo Proper; his companion suffered in the general slaughter. The sight that presented itself on our people boarding the captured boat must indeed have been a frightful one; none of the pirates waited on board for even the chance of receiving either quarter or mercy, but all those capable of moving had thrown themselves into the water. In addition to the killed, some lying across the thwarts with their oars in their hands, at the bottom of the prahu, in which there was about three feet of blood and water, were seen protruding the mangled remains of eighteen or twenty bodies. During my last expedition I fell in with a slave belonging to a Malay chief, one of our allies, who informed us that he likewise had been a prisoner and pulled an oar in one of the two prahus that attacked the Jolly Bachelor; that none of the crew of the captured prahu reached the shore alive, with the exception of the lad that swam off to our people; and that there were so few who survived in the second prahu, that having separated from their consort during the night, the slaves, fifteen in number, rose and put to death the remaining pirates, and then ran the vessel into the first river they reached, which proved to be the Kaleka, where they were seized, and became the property of the governing Datu; and my informant was again sold to my companion while on a visit to his friend the Datu. Each of the attacking prahus had between fifty and sixty men, including slaves, and the larger one between ninety and a hundred. The result might have been very different to our gallant but dosy Jolly Bachelors.

I have already mentioned the slaughter committed by the fire of the pinnace, under Lieutenant Horton, into the largest Malay prahu; and the account given of the scene which presented itself on the deck of the defeated pirate, when taken possession of, affords a striking proof of the character of these fierce rovers; resembling greatly what we read of the Norsemen and Scandinavians of early ages. Among the mortally wounded lay the young commander of the prahu, one of the most noble forms of the human race; his countenance handsome as the hero of oriental romance, and his whole bearing wonderfully impressive and touching. He was shot in front and through the lungs, and his last moments were rapidly approaching. He endeavoured to speak, but the blood gushed from his mouth with the voice he vainly essayed to utter in words. Again and again he tried, but again and again the vital fluid drowned the dying effort. He looked as if he had something of importance which he desired to communicate, and a shade of disappointment and regret passed over his brow when he felt that every essay was unavailing, and that his manly strength and daring spirit were dissolving into the dark night of annihilation. The pitying conquerors raised him gently up, and he was seated in comparative ease, for the welling-out of the blood was less distressing; but the end speedily came: he folded his arms heroically across his wounded breast, fixed his eyes upon the British seamen around, and casting one last glance at the ocean—the theatre of his daring exploits, on which he had so often fought and triumphed—expired without a sigh.

The spectators, though not unused to tragical and sanguinary sights, were unanimous in speaking of the death of the pirate chief as the most affecting spectacle they had ever witnessed. A sculptor might have carved him as an Antinous in the mortal agonies of a Dying Gladiator.

The leaders of the piratical prahus are sometimes poetically addressed by their followers as *Matari*, i. e. the sun, or *Bulan*, the moon; and from his superiority in every respect, physical and intellectual, the chief whose course was here so fatally closed seemed to be worthy of either celestial name.

CHAPTER II.

The Dido recalled to China. Effect of her presence at Sarāwak. The Rajah's letter to Captain Keppel, and his reply. Prepares for an expedition against the Sarebus pirates. Pleasure excursion up the river. The Chinese settlement. The Singè mountain. Interior of the residences. Dyak festival of Mangut. Relics. Sporting. Return to Sarāwak. The expedition against Sarebus. State and number of the assailing force. Ascent of the river. Beauty of the scenery.

My stay at Sarāwak was of but short duration, as, before I had time to carry out the arrangements I had made to put down this horrid traffic, the Dido was, owing to some changes in the distribution of the fleet, recalled to China, not expecting to revisit Borneo during the period that the ship had to run before completing her usual time of commission; and it is gratifying for me to read in my friend's journal, alluding to that time: "I came myself in the Dido; and I may say that her appearance was the consummation of my enterprise." "The natives saw directly that there was a force to protect and to punish; and most of the chiefs, conscious of their evil ways, trembled; Muda Hassim was gratified, and felt that this power would exalt his authority both in Borneo and along the coast, and he was not slow in magnifying the force of the Dido. The state in which Captain Keppel and his officers visited the Rajah all heightened the effect; and the marines and the band excited the admiration and the fears of the natives. I felt the Rajah's hand tremble at the first interview; and not all the well-known command of countenance, of which the natives are masters, could conceal his emotion."

Gentle reader, excuse my vanity if I continue a little further with my friend's journal, although it gets rather personal:

"I believe the first emotion was any thing but pleasurable; but Captain Keppel's conciliatory and kind manner soon removed any feeling of fear, and all along was of the greatest use to me in our subsequent doings. The first qualification, in dealing with a Malay, is a kind and gentle manner; for their habitual politeness is such that they are hurt by the ordinary *brusquerie* of the European.

"I shall not go over the chase of the three boats of the Balagnini pirates, or the attack made on the Dido's boats by the Sirhassan people, except to remark that, in the latter case, I am sure Lieutenant Horton acted rightly in sparing their lives and property; for, with these occasional pirates, a severe lesson, followed by that degree of conciliation and pardon which shall best ensure a correction of their vices, is far wiser and preferable to a course of undistinguishing severity."

I have now followed Mr. Brooke's journal up to the time of our first visit to Sarāwak, to which no remarks of mine could add the slightest interest.

No place could have suited us better for a refit. Within a few yards of the ship was a Chinese workshop. Our boats were hauled up to repair under sheds, and we drew our fresh water alongside; and while the Dido was at Sarāwak, Mr. Jago, the carpenter, built a very beautiful thirty-foot gig, having cut the plank up in the Chinaman's sawpit.

May 21st.—I received intimation that the Rajah had written a letter, and wished me to appoint a time and place, that it might be presented in due form. Accordingly, I attended in Mr. Brooke's hall of audience on the following day, where I found collected all the chiefs, and a crowd of natives, many of them having already been informed that the said letter was a requisition for me to assist in putting down the hordes of pirates who had so long infested the coast. I believe many of those present, especially the Borneons, to have been casually concerned, if not deeply implicated, in some of their transactions. After I had taken my seat with Mr. Brooke at the head of the table, the Rajah's sword-bearers entered, clearing the way for the huge yellow canopy, under the shade of which, on a large brass tray, and carefully sewn up in a yellow silk bag, was the letter, from which it was removed, and placed in my hands by the Pangeran Budrudeen. I opened the bag with my knife, and giving it to an interpreter, he read it aloud in the Malayan tongue. It was variously received by the audience, many of whose countenances were far from prepossessing.

The following is a copy of the letter, to which was affixed the Rajah's seal:

"This friendly epistle, having its source in a pure mind, comes from Rajah Muda Hassim, next in succession to the royal throne of the kingdom of Borneo, and who now holds his court at the trading city of Sarāwak, to our friend Henry Keppel, head captain of the war-frigate belonging to Her Britannic Majesty, renowned throughout all countries, —who is valiant and discreet, and endowed with a mild and gentle nature:

"This is to inform our friend that there are certain great pirates, of the people of Sarebus and Sakarran, in our neighbourhood, seizing goods and murdering people on the high seas. They have more than three hundred war-prahus, and extend their ravages even to Banjarmassim; they are not subject to the government of Bruni (Borneo); they take much plunder from vessels trading between Singapore and the good people of our country.

"It would be a great service, if our friend would adopt measures to put an end to these piratical outrages.

"We can present nothing better to our friend than a kris, such as it is.

"20th day of Rabial Akhir, 1257."

To which I sent the following reply:

"Captain Keppel begs to acknowledge the receipt of the Rajah Muda Hassim's letter, representing that the Dyaks of Sarebus and Sakarran are the pirates who infest the coast of Borneo, and do material damage to the trade of Singapore.

"Captain Keppel will take speedy measures to suppress these and all other pirates, and feels confident that Her Britannic Majesty will be glad to learn that the Rajah Muda Hassim is ready to cooperate in so laudable an undertaking."

Not being prepared for the oriental fashion of exchanging presents, I had nothing to offer to his Rajah-ship; but I found out afterwards that Mr. Brooke had (unknown to me) sent him a clock in my name. The royal kris was handsome, the handle of carved ivory, with a good deal of gold about it.

This information about the pirates gave me good ground to make a beginning; and having arranged with Mr. Brooke to obtain all necessary intelligence relative to their position, strength, and numbers,[1] I determined on attacking them in their

[1] Piratical habits are so interwoven with the character of these Sarebus people, that the capture at sea of a few prahus would have but small effect in curing the evil; whilst a harassing

strongholds, commencing with the Sarebus, who, from all accounts, were by far the most strongly fortified. Mr. Brooke accepted my invitation to accompany us, as well as to supply a native force of about three hundred men, who, should we succeed in the destruction of the pirate forts, would be useful in the jungle. Mr. Brooke's going to join personally in a war against (in the opinion of the Datus) such formidable opponents as the Sakarran and Sarebus pirates,—who had never yet been conquered, although repeatedly attacked by the united forces of the surrounding Rajahs,—was strongly opposed by the chiefs. On his informing them that he should go, but leaving it optional whether they would accompany him or not, their simple reply was, " What is the use of our remaining? If you die, we die; and if you live, we live; we will go with you." Preparations for the expedition were accordingly commenced.

While these were in progress, I accompanied Mr. Brooke up the river. The Royalist having been despatched to Singapore with our letters, we started on our pleasure-excursion. With the offi-

duty is encountered, the result is only to drive the pirates from one cruising-ground to another: but, on the contrary, a system which joins conciliation with severity, aiming at the correction of the native character as well as the suppression of piracy, and carrying punishment to the doors of the offenders, is the only one which can effectually eradicate an evil almost as disgraceful to those who permit it as to the native states engaged in it.

cers from the Dido and the chiefs, who always accompany the "Tuan Besar," we mustered about sixty persons; and with our guns, walking-sticks, cigars, and a well-supplied commissariat, determined to enjoy ourselves.

We were not long in making the acquaintances of the chiefs. Men who had formerly rebelled, who were conquered by Mr. Brooke, and had their (forfeited) lives saved, their families restored to them, and they themselves finally reinstated in the offices they had previously held—these men were very naturally and faithfully attached. Our young gentlemen found their Malayan names difficult to remember, so that the gallant old Patingi Ali was seldom called any other name than that of "Three-Fingered Jack," from his having lost part of his right hand; the Tumangong was spoken of as the "Father of Hopeful," from one of his children, a fine little fellow, to whom he was foolishly attached, and seldom seen without.

Der Macota, who had some time before received the appellation of "the Serpent," had, ever since he got his orders to quit, some six months before, been preparing his boats, but which were ready in an incredibly short time after the Dido's arrival; and thus Mr. Brooke got rid of the most intriguing and troublesome rascal; a person who had, from the commencement, been trying to supplant and ruin him. He it was that gave the Sakarran pirates permission to ascend the river for the purpose of attacking the comparatively defenceless mountain Dyaks; and he it was that persecuted the unfortunate young Illanun chief, " Si Tundo," even to his assassination. He was at last got rid of from Sarāwak, but only to join and plan mischief with that noted piratical chief, Seriff Sahib;—he, however, met his deserts.

We ascended the river in eight or ten boats. The scene to us was most novel, and particularly fresh and beautiful. We stopped at an empty house on a cleared spot on the left bank during the ebb-tide, to cook our dinner; in the cool of the afternoon we proceeded with the flood; and late in the evening brought up for the night in a snug little creek close to the Chinese settlement. We slept in native boats, which were nicely and comfortably fitted for the purpose. At an early hour Mr. Brooke was waited on by the chief of the Kunsi; and on visiting their settlement he was received with a salute of three guns. We found it kept in their usual neat and clean order, particularly their extensive vegetable-gardens; but being rather pressed for time, we did not visit the mines, but proceeded to the villages of different tribes of Dyaks living on the Sarambo mountain, numbers of whom had been down to welcome us, very gorgeously dressed in feathers and scarlet.

The foot of the mountain was about four miles from the landing-place; and a number of these kind savages voluntarily shouldered our provisions,

DIFFICULTY OF TRAVELLING.

beds, bags, and baggage, and we proceeded on our march. We did not expect to find quite a turnpike-road; but, at the same time, I, for one, was not prepared for the dance led us by our wild cat-like guides through thick jungle, and alternately over rocky hills, or up to our middles in the soft marshes we had to cross; our only means of doing which was by feeling on the surface of the mud (it being covered in most places about a foot deep with grass or discoloured water) for light spars thrown along lengthways and quite unconnected, the only support being an occasional stake at irregular distances, at which we used to rest, as the spars invariably sunk into the mud if we attempted to stop; and there being a long string, many a fall and flounder in the mud (gun and all) was the consequence.

The ascent of the hill, although as steep as the side of a house, was strikingly beautiful. Our resting-places, unluckily, were but few; but when we did reach one, the cool fresh breeze, and the increasing extent and variety of scene,—our view embracing, as it did, all the varieties of river, mountain, wood, and sea,—amply repaid us for the exertion of the lower walk; and, on either hand, we were sure to have a pure cool rivulet tumbling over the rocks. While going up, however, our whole care and attention was requisite to secure our own safety; for it is not only one continued climb up ladders, but such ladders! They are made of the single trunk of a tree in its rough and rounded state, with notches, not cut at the reasonable distance apart of the rattlins of our rigging, but requiring the knee to be brought up to the level of the chin before the feet are sufficiently parted to reach from one step to another; and that, when the muscles of the thigh begin to ache, and the wind is pumped out of the body, is distressing work.

We mounted, in this manner, some 500 feet; and it was up this steep that Mr. Brooke had ascended only a few months before, with two hundred followers, to attack the Singè Dyaks. He has already described the circular halls of these Dyaks, in one of which we were received, hung round, as the interior of it is, with hundreds of human heads, most of them dried with the skin and hair on; and to give them, if possible, a more ghastly appearance, small shells (the cowry) inserted where the eyes once were, and tufts of dried grass protrude from the ears. But my eye soon grew accustomed to the sight; and by the time dinner was ready (I think I may say *we*) thought no more about them than if they had been as many cocoa-nuts.

Of course the natives crowded round us; and I noticed that with these simple people it was much the same as with the more civilised, and that curiosity was strongest in the gentler sex; and again, that the young men came in more

WAR DANCE of the LUNDU DYAKS.

London Chapman & Hall, 180 Strand, Jan' 15th 1846.

gorgeously dressed—wearing feathers, necklaces, armlets, ear-rings, bracelets, besides jackets of various-coloured silks, and other vanities—than the older and wiser chiefs, who encumbered themselves with no more dress than what decency actually required, and were, moreover, treated with the greatest respect.

We strolled about from house to house without causing the slightest alarm: in all we were welcomed, and invited to squat ourselves on their mats with the family. The women, who were some of them very good-looking, did not run from us as the plain-headed Malays would have done; but laughed and chatted to us by signs in all the consciousness of innocence and virtue.

We were fortunate in visiting these Dyaks during one of their grand festivals (called Maugut); and in the evening, dancing, singing, and drinking were going on in various parts of the village. In one house there was a grand *fête*, in which the women danced with the men. The dress of the women was simple and curious—a light jacket open in front, and a short petticoat not coming below the knees, fitting close, was hung round with jingling bits of brass, which kept "making music" wherever they went. The movement was like all other native dances—graceful, but monotonous. There were four men, two of them bearing human skulls, and two the fresh heads of pigs; the women bore wax-lights, or yellow rice on brass dishes. They danced in line, moving backwards and forwards, and carrying the heads and dishes in both hands; the graceful part was the manner in which they half turned the body to the right and left, looking over their shoulders and holding the heads in the opposite direction, as if they were in momentary expectation of some one coming up behind to snatch the nasty relic from them. At times the women knelt down in a group, with the men leaning over them. After all, the music was not the only thing wanting to make one imagine oneself at the opera. The necklaces of the women were chiefly of teeth—bears' the most common—human the most prized.

In an interior house at one end were collected the relics of the tribe. These consisted of several round-looking stones, two deers' heads, and other inferior trumpery. The stones turn black if the tribe is to be beaten in war, and red if to be victorious: any one touching them would be sure to die; if lost, the tribe would be ruined.

The account of the deers' heads is still more curious: A young Dyak having dreamed the previous night that he should become a great warrior, observing two deer swimming across the river, he killed them; a storm came on with thunder and lightning, and darkness came over the face of the earth; he died immediately, but came to life again, and became a rumah guna (literally a *useful house*) and chief of his tribe; the two deer still live, and remain to watch over the affairs of the tribe. These heads have descended from their ancestors from the time when they first became a tribe and inhabited the mountain. Food is always kept placed before them, and renewed from time to time. While in the circular building, which our party named "the scullery," a young chief (Meta) seemed to take great pride in answering our interrogatories respecting different skulls which we took down from their hooks: two belonged to chiefs of a tribe who had made a desperate defence; and judging from the incisions on the heads, each of which must have been mortal, it must have been a desperate affair. Among other trophies was half a head, the skull separated from across between the eyes, in the same manner that you would divide that of a hare or rabbit to get at the brain—this was their division of the head of an old woman, which was taken when another (a friendly) tribe was present, who likewise claimed their half. I afterwards saw these tribes share a head. But the skulls, the account of which our informant appeared to dwell on with the greatest delight, were those which were taken while the owners were asleep—cunning with them being the perfection of warfare. We slept in their "scullery;" and my servant Ashford, who happened to be a sleep-walker, that night jumped out of the window, and unluckily on the steep side; and had not the ground been well turned up by the numerous pigs, and softened by rain, he must have been hurt.

May 25th.—Having returned to our boats, we moved up another branch of the river, for the purpose of deer-shooting, and landed under some large shady trees. The sportsmen divided into two small parties, and, under the guidance of the natives, went in search of game, leaving the remainder of the party to prepare dinner against our return.

The distance we had to walk to get to our ground was what our guides considered nothing— some five miles through jungle; and one of the most distressing parts in jungle-walking is the having to climb over the fallen trunks of immense trees.

A short time before sunset we came to a part of the jungle that opened on to a large swamp, with long rank grass about six feet high, across which was a sort of Dyak bridge. The guide having made signs for me to advance, I cautiously crept to the edge of the jungle; and after some little trouble, and watching the direction of his finger, I observed the heads of two deer, male and female, protruding just above the grass at about sixty yards distance. From the manner the doe was moving about her long ears, it had, to my view, all the appearance of a rabbit. Shooting for the pot, I selected her. As soon as I fired, some of my boat's crew made a dash into the grass; and in an instant three of them were nearly up to their chins in mud and water, and we had some difficulty in dragging them out. Our Malay guide more knowingly crossed the bridge; and, being acquainted with the locality, reached the deer from the opposite side, taking care to utter the prayer and cut the throat with the head in the direction of the Prophet's tomb at Mecca, without which ceremony no true follower of Islam could partake of the meat. The doe was struck just below the ear; and my native companion appeared much astonished at the distance and deadly effect with which my smooth-bored *Westley Richards* had conveyed the ball.

The buck had got off before the smoke had cleared sufficiently for me to see him. From what I had heard, I was disappointed at not seeing more game. The other party had not killed any thing, although they caught a little fawn, having frightened away the mother.

My time was so occupied during my stay in Borneo, that I am unable to give any account of the sports. Neither had Mr. Brooke seen much of it; unless an excursion or two he had made in search of new specimens of the ourang-outang, or mias, may be brought under that head. This excursion he performed not only with the permission and under the protection, but as the guest, of the piratical chief Seriff Sahib; little thinking that, in four years afterwards, he would himself, as a powerful Rajah, be the cause of destroying his town, and driving him from the country.

So much for sporting. The pleasure, I believe, increases in proportion to the risk. But, while on the subject, I may mention that of pig-shooting, which I found an amusement not to be despised, especially if you approach your game before life is extinct. The jaws are long, tusks also, and sharp as a razor; and when once wounded, the animals evince a strong inclination to return the compliment: they are active, cunning, and very fast. I shot several at different times. The natives also describe a very formidable beast, the size of a large bullock, found further to the northward, which they appear to hold in great dread. This I conceive to be a sort of bison; and if so, the sporting in Borneo altogether is not so bad.

The following day we went to other ground for deer; but the Dyaks had now enjoyed peace so long that the whole country was in a state of cultivation; and after scrambling over tracks of wild-looking country, in which Mr. Brooke, two years before, had seen the deer in hundreds, we returned to our boats, and down the river to Sarāwak.

We now began to prepare in earnest for work of another sort. The news of our intended attack on the Sarebus pirates had soon reached them, and spread all over the country; and we had daily accounts of the formidable resistance they intended to make. By the 4th July our preparations were complete; and the ship had dropped down to the mouth of the river. I forgot to mention, that all the adjoining Seriffs had, in the greatest consternation, sent me assurances of their future good intentions. Seriff Jaffer, who lived with an industrious but warlike race of Dyaks up the Linga river, a branch of the Batang Lupar, had never been known to commit piracy, and had been frequently at war with both the Sarebus and Sakarrans, offered to join our expedition. From Seriff Sahib, who lived up a river at Sadong adjoining the Sarebus territory, and to whom the "Serpent" Macota had gone—Mr. Brooke and myself had invitations to partake of a feast on our way to the Sarebus river. This was accompanied with a present of a couple of handsome spears and a porcupine; and also an offer to give up the women and children he had, with the assistance of the Sakarran pirates, captured from the poor Sow Dyaks up the Sarāwak.

Further to the eastward, and up the Batang Lupar, into which the Sakarran runs, lived another powerful Seriff, by the name of Muller, elder brother and coadjutor of Seriff Sahib. These all, however, through fear at the moment, sent in submissive messages; but their turn had not yet come, and we proceeded towards the Sarebus.

The island of Burong, off which the Dido was to remain at anchor, we made the first place of rendezvous. The force from the Dido consisted of her pinnace, two cutters, and a gig; besides which Mr. Brooke lent us his native-built boat, the Jolly Bachelor, carrying a long six-pounder brass gun, and thirty of our men; also a large Tope of thirty-five tons, which carried a well-supplied commissariat, as well as ammunition.

The native force was extensive; but I need only mention the names of those from Saràwak. The three chiefs (the Tumangong and two Patingis, Gapoor and Ali) had two large boats, each carrying about 180 men. Then there was the Rajah's large heavy boat, with the rascally Borneons, and about 40 men; and sundry other Saràwak boats: and besides, a Dyak force of about 400 men from the different tribes of Lundu, Sow, Singè, &c. Of course, it caused some trouble to collect this wild undisciplined armament, and two or three successive points of rendezvous were necessary; and it was the morning of the 8th before we entered the river. Lieutenant Wilmot Horton was to command the expedition; with him, in the pinnace, were Mr. W. L. Partridge, mate; Dr. Simpson, assistant-surgeon; Mr. Hallowes, midshipman; 14 seamen, and 5 marines. In the first cutter was Mr. D'Aeth, Mr. Douglas, from Saràwak, and Mr. Collins, the boatswain; in the second cutter, Mr. Elliott, the master, and Mr. Jenkins, midshipman. The Jolly Bachelor was commanded by Lieutenant Tottenham, and Mr. Comber, midshipman; with Mr. Brooke's medical friend, Dr. Treacher, and an amateur gentleman, Mr. Ruppel, from Sarāwak. The force from the Dido was about 80, officers and men. The command of the boats, when sent away from a man-of-war, is the perquisite of the first lieutenant. My curiosity, however, would not allow me to resist the temptation of attending the party in my gig; and I had my friend Mr. Brooke as a companion, who was likewise attended by a sampan and crew he had taken with him to Sarāwak from Singapore. His coxswain, Seboo, we shall all long remember: he was civil only to his master, and, I believe, brave while in his company. He was a stupid-looking and powerfully-built sort of savage, always praying, eating, smiling, or sleeping. When going into action, he always went down on his knees to pray, holding his loaded musket before him. He was, however, a curious character, and afforded us great amusement,—took good care of himself and his master, but cared for no one else.

In the second gig was Lieutenant E. Gunnell, whose troublesome duty it was to preserve order throughout this extensive musquito fleet, and to keep the natives from pressing too closely on the rear of our boats — an office which became less troublesome as we approached the scene of danger. The whole formed a novel, picturesque, and exciting scene; and it was curious to contemplate the different feelings that actuated the separate and distinct parties; the odd mixture of Europeans,

Malays, and Dyaks; the different religions; and the eager and anxious manner in which all pressed forward. The novelty of the thing was quite sufficient to excite our Jacks, after having been cooped up so long on board ship—to say nothing of the chance of a broken head.

Of the Malays and Dyaks who accompanied us, some came from curiosity, some from attachment to Mr. Brooke, and many for plunder, but I think the majority to gratify revenge; as there were but few of the inhabitants, on the north coast of Borneo, who had not suffered more or less from the atrocities of the Sarebus and Sakarran pirates —either their houses burnt, their relations murdered, or their wives and children captured and sold into slavery.

We did not get far up the river the first day, as the Tope was very slow, and carried that most essential part of all expeditions, the commissariat. Patingi Ali, who had been sent the day before to await the force in the mouth of the Sarebus, fell in with five or six native boats, probably on the look-out for us, to which he gave chase, and captured one, the rest retreating up the river.

On the 9th June, 1843, we had got some thirty miles in the same direction; every thing was in order; and, as we advanced, I pulled from one end of my little fleet to the other, and felt much the same sort of pride as Sir William Parker must have experienced when leading seventy-five sail of

British ships up the Yeang tse Keang river into the very heart of the Celestial Empire. It rained hard; but we were well supplied with kajans, a mat admirably adapted to keep out the wet; and securely covered in, my gig had all the appearance of a native boat, especially as I had substituted paddles for oars. In this manner I frequently went a little in advance of the force; and on the 9th I came on a couple of boats, hauled close in under the jungle, apparently perfectly unconscious of my approach. I concluded them to be part of the small fleet of boats that had been chased, the previous day, in the mouth of the river; and when abreast of them, and within range, I fired from my rifle. The crews of each boat immediately precipitated themselves into the water, and escaped into the jungle. They were so closely covered in, that I did not see any one at first; but I found that my ball had passed through both sides of an iron kettle, in which they were boiling some rice! How astonished the cook must have been! On coming up, our Dyak followers dashed into the jungle in pursuit of the fugitives, but without success.

We moved on leisurely with the flood-tide, anchoring always on the ebb, by which means we managed to collect our stragglers and keep the force together. Towards the evening, by the incessant sound of distant gongs, we were aware that our approach was known, and that preparations were making to repel us. These noises were kept up all night; and we occasionally heard the distant report of ordnance, which was fired, of course, to intimidate us. During the day, several deserted boats were taken from the banks of the river and destroyed, some of them containing spears, shields, and ammunition, with a few fire-arms.

The place we brought up at for the night was called Boling; but here the river presented a troublesome and dangerous obstacle in what is called the bore, caused by the tide coming in with a tremendous rush, as if an immense wave of the sea had suddenly rolled up the stream, and, finding itself confined on either side, extended across, like a high bank of water, curling and breaking as it went, and, from the frightful velocity with which it passes up, carrying all before it. There are, however, certain bends of the river where the bore does not break across: it was now our business to look out for and gain these spots between the times of its activity. The natives hold them in great dread.

From Boling the river becomes less deep, and not safe for large boats; so that here we were obliged to leave our Tope with the commissariat, and a sufficient force for her protection, as we had received information that thirteen piratical boats had been some time cruising outside, and were daily expected up the river on their return, when our unguarded Tope would have made them an acceptable prize. In addition to this, we were now fairly in the enemy's country: and for all we knew, hundreds of canoes might have been hid in the jungle, ready to launch. Just below Boling, the river branches off to the right and left; that to the left leading to another nest of pirates at Pakoo, who are (by land) in communication with those of Paddi, the place it was our intention to attack first.

Having provisioned our boats for six days, and providing a strong guard to remain with the Tope, —an arrangement which gave but little satisfaction to those left, our men not liking to exchange an expedition where a fight was certain, for a position in which, although one of danger, being open to attack from three different parts of the river, it was doubtful,—and the native force not feeling themselves safe separated from the main body; — we started, a smaller and more select party than before, but, in my opinion, equally formidable, leaving about 150 men. Our party now consisted of the Dido's boats, the three Datus from Sarāwak, and some Sow Dyaks, eager for heads and plunder. We arrived at our first resting-place early in the afternoon, and took up a position in as good order as the small space would admit.

I secured my gig close to the bank, under the shade of a large tree, at some little distance from the fleet of boats; and, by myself, contemplated my novel position—in command of a mixed force of 500 men, some seventy miles up a river in the interior of Borneo; on the morrow about to carry all the horrors of war amongst a race of savage pirates, whose country no force had ever yet dared to invade, and who had been inflicting with impunity every sort of cruelty on all whom they encountered, for more than a century.

As the sun went down, the scene was beautiful —the variety and picturesque appearance of the native prahus, and the praying of the Mussulman, with his head in the direction of the Prophet's tomb, bowing his head to the deck of his boat, and from whose devotions nothing would draw his attention. For a time—it being that for preparing the evening meal—no noise was made : it was a perfect calm; and the rich foliage was reflected in the water as in a mirror, while a small cloud of smoke ascended from each boat, to say nothing of that from my cigar, which added much to the charm I then experienced.

Late in the evening, when the song and joke was passed from boat to boat, and the lights from the different fires were reflected in the water, the scenery was equally pleasing; but later still, when the lights were out, there being no moon, and the banks overhung with trees, it was so dark that no one could see beyond his own boat.

A little after midnight, a small boat was heard passing up the river, and was regularly hailed by us in succession; to which they replied, "We belong to your party." And it was not until the yell of triumph, given by six or eight voices, after they had (with a strong flood-tide in their favour) shot past the last of our boats, that we found how we had been imposed on.

CHAPTER III.

Ascent of the river to Paddi. Town taken and burnt. Narrow escape of a reinforcement of friendly Dyaks. Night-attack by the pirates. Conference: they submit. Proceed against Pakoo. Dyak treatment of dead enemies. Destruction of Pakoo, and submission of the pirates. Advance upon Rembas. The town destroyed: the inhabitants yield. Satisfactory effects of the expedition. Death of Dr. Simpson. Triumphant return to Sarāwak.

June 11*th*.—We moved on immediately after the passing up of the bore, the dangers of which appeared to have been greatly exaggerated. The beating of gongs and discharge of cannon had been going on the whole of the previous night.

The scenery improved in beauty every yard that we advanced; but our attention was drawn from it by the increase of yelling as we approached the scene of action. Although as yet we had only heard our enemies, our rapid advance, with a strong tide, must have been seen by them from the jungle on the various hills which now rose to our view.

Being in my gig, somewhat ahead of the boats, I had the advantage of observing all that occurred. The scene was the most exciting I ever experienced. We had no time for delay or consideration:

the tide was sweeping us rapidly up; and had we been inclined to retreat then, we should have found it difficult. A sudden turn in the river brought us (Mr. Brooke was by my side) in front of a steep hill which rose from the bank. It had been cleared of jungle, and long grass grew in its place. As we hove in sight, several hundred savages rose up, and gave one of their war-yells: it was the first I had heard. No report from musketry or ordnance could ever make a man's heart feel so *small* as mine did at that horrid yell: but I had no leisure to think. I had only time for a shot at them with my double-barrel, as they rushed down the steep, whilst I was carried past. I soon after heard the report of our large boat's heavy gun, which must have convinced them that we likewise were prepared.

On the roof of a long building, on the summit of the hill, were several warriors performing a war-dance, which it would be difficult to imitate on such a stage. As these were not the forts we were in search of, we did not delay longer than to exchange a few shots in sweeping along.

Our next obstacle was more troublesome, being a strong barrier right across the river, formed of two rows of trees placed firmly in the mud, with their tops crossed and secured together by rattans; and along the fork, formed by the crossing of the tops of these stakes, were other trees firmly secured. Rapidly approaching this barrier, I observed a small opening that might probably admit a canoe; and gathering good way, and putting my gig's head straight at it, I squeezed through. On reaching it the scene again changed, and I opened on three formidable-looking forts, which lost not a moment in opening a discharge of cannon on my unfortunate gig. Luckily their guns were properly elevated for the range of the barrier; and, with the exception of a few straggling grape-shot that splashed the water round us, the whole went over our heads. For a moment I found myself cut off from my companions, and drifting fast upon the enemy. The banks of the river were covered with warriors, yelling and rushing down to secure—what I suppose they considered me—their prize. I had some difficulty in getting my long gig round, and paddling up against the stream; but while my friend Brooke steered the boat, my coxswain and myself kept up a fire, with tolerable aim, on the embrasures, to prevent, if possible, their reloading before the pinnace, our leading boat, could bring her twelve-pound carronade to bear. I was too late to prevent the pinnace falling athwart the barrier, in which position she had three men wounded. With the assistance of some of our native followers, the rattan-lashings which secured the heads of the stakes were soon cut through; and I was not sorry when I found the Dido's first cutter on the same side with myself. The other boats soon followed; and while the pinnace kept

THE ATTACK on PADDI by the BOATS of H.M.S. DIDO.

London Chapman & Hall, 180 Strand, Jan: 15th 1846.

up a destructive fire on the fort, Mr. D'Aeth, who was the first to land, jumped on shore, with his crew, at the foot of the hill on the top of which the nearest fort stood, and at once rushed for the summit. This mode of warfare—this dashing at once in the very face of their fort—was so novel and incomprehensible to our enemies, that they fled, panic-struck, into the jungle; and it was with the greatest difficulty that our leading men could get even a snap-shot at the rascals as they went.

That evening the country was illuminated for miles by the burning of the capital, Paddi, and adjacent villages; at which work, and plundering, our native followers were most expert.

At Paddi the river branches off to the right and left; and it was on the tongue of land formed by them that the forts were very cleverly placed. We took all their guns, and burnt the stockades level with the ground.

The banks of the river were here so confined, that a man might with ease throw a spear across; and as the jungle was close, it was necessary to keep pretty well on the alert. For the greater part of the night the burning of the houses made it as bright as day. In the evening, the Drs. Simpson and Treacher amputated a poor fellow's arm close to the shoulder, which, in the cramped space of a boat, was no easy operation. He was one of our best men, and captain of the forecastle on board the Dido.

Early on the following morning (12th) our boats, with the exception of the Jolly Bachelor, now become the hospital, proceeded up the two branches of the river; almost all the native force remaining to complete the work of destruction.

An accident had nearly occurred at this period. A report had reached us that several large boats—supposed to be a fleet of Sarebus pirates returning from a cruise—were in the river; and knowing that they could not well attack and pass our force at Boling without our hearing of it, I took no further notice of the rumour, intending to go down in my gig afterwards, and have a look at them. While we were at breakfast in the Jolly Bachelor, a loud chattering of many voices was heard, attended by a great beating of tom-toms; and suddenly a large prahu, crowded with savages, came sweeping round the bend of the river, rapidly nearing us with a strong flood-tide. As she advanced, others hove in sight. In a moment pots and spoons were thrown down, arms seized, and the brass six-pounder, loaded with grape and canister, was on the point of being fired, when Williamson, the only person who understood their character, made us aware that they were a friendly tribe of Dyaks, from the river Linga, coming to our assistance, or, more likely, coming to seek for plunder and the heads of their enemies, with whom they had for many years been at war. Those in the leading boat had, however, a narrow escape. I had already given the order to fire; but luckily the priming had been blown off from the six-pounder. Had it not been so, fifty at least out of the first hundred would have been sent to their long homes. They were between eight and nine hundred strong. The scene to me was indeed curious and exciting: for the wild appearance of these fellows exceeded any thing I had yet witnessed. Their war-dresses —each decorating himself according to his own peculiar fancy, in a costume the most likely at once to adorn the wearer and strike terror into the enemy—made a remarkable show. Each had a shield and a handful of spears; about one in ten was furnished with some sort of fire-arm, which was of more danger to himself or his neighbour than to any one else. They wore short padded jackets, capable of resisting the point of a wooden spear.

The first thing necessary was to supply each with a strip of white calico, to be worn in the head-dress as a distinguishing mark, to prevent our people knocking them over if met by accident while prowling about the jungle. We also established a watchword, 'Datu,' which many of them, who had great dread of the white men, never ceased to call out. Seriff Jaffer, in command of their force, had promised to join us from the beginning; but as they did not make their appearance off the mouth of the river, we thought no more of them. It was necessary to despatch messengers up the rivers to inform our boats of this reinforcement, as in all probability an attack would have been made immediately on appearing in sight of so formidable a force.

At 10 A.M. our boats returned, having gone up the right-hand branch as far as it was practicable. That to the left having been obstructed by trees felled across the stream, was considered, from the trouble taken to prevent our progress, to be the branch up which the enemy had retreated; and not being provisioned for more than the day, they came back, and started again in the afternoon with the first of the flood-tide. Of this party Lieutenant Horton took charge, accompanied by Mr. Brooke. It was a small but an effective and determined and well-appointed little body, not likely to be deterred by difficulties. A small native force of about forty men accompanied them, making, with our own, between eighty and ninety people. The forts having been destroyed, no further obstacles were expected to our advance beyond the felling of trees and the vast odds as to numbers in case of attack, the pirates being reckoned at about 6000 Dyaks and 500 Malays.

The evening set in with rain and hazy weather. Our native skirmishing parties were returning to their boats and evening meals; our advancing party had been absent about an hour and a half; and I had just commenced a supper in the Jolly Bachelor on ham and poached eggs, when the sound of the pinnace's twelve-pounder carronade broke through the stillness of the night. This was responded to by one of those simultaneous war-yells apparently from every part of the country. My immediate idea was that our friends had been surrounded. It was impossible to move so large a boat as the Jolly Bachelor up to their assistance; nor would it be right to leave our wounded without a sufficient force for their protection. I immediately jumped into my gig, taking with me a bugler, whom I placed in the bow; and seeing our arms in as perfect readiness as the rain would allow us to keep them, I proceeded to join the combatants.

Daylight had disappeared, as it does in tropical climates, immediately after the setting of the sun. The tide had just turned against me; and as I advanced up the river, the trees hung over many parts, nearly meeting across; at the same time the occasional firing that was kept up assured me that the enemy were on the alert, and with all the advantages of local knowledge and darkness on their side. From the winding of the stream, too, the yells appeared to come from every direction, sometimes ahead and sometimes astern. I had pulled, feeling my way, for nearly two hours, when a sudden and quick discharge of musketry, well on my left hand, intimated to me that I was approaching the scene of action; and, at the same time, passing several large canoes hauled up on the bank, I felt convinced that my anticipation was right, that our party were surrounded, and that we should have to fight our way to each other. My plan was to make it appear as if I was bringing up a strong reinforcement; and the moment the firing ceased, I made the bugler strike up 'Rory O'More,' which was immediately responded to by three British cheers; and then followed a death-like stillness—if any thing, more unpleasant than the war-yell; and I could not help feeling certain that the enemy lay between us.

The stream now ran rapidly over loose stones. Against the sky, where the jungle had been cleared, I could distinctly see the outlines of human beings. I laid my double-barrel across my knees, and we pulled on. When within shot-range I hailed, to make certain; and receiving no answer, after a second time, I fired, keeping the muskets of the gig's crew ready to repel the first attack in case the enemy did not decamp. My fire was answered by Lieutenant Horton: "We are here, sir." At first I was much distressed, from the fear that I might have hurt any one. They had not heard me hail, owing, I suppose, to the noise of the water rushing over the stones; and they had not hailed me, thinking that I must of course know that it was them; and the enemy being in the jungle all round, they did not like to attract attention to where they were. I found they had taken up a very clever position. The running stream had washed the ground away on the right bank, leaving a sort of little deep bay, just big enough to hold the boats, from which the bank rose quite perpendicularly. On the top of this bank the jungle had been cleared for about thirty yards; and on this Lieutenant Gunnell, with seven royal marines, was posted as a rear-guard. This was an important position, and one of danger, as the jungle itself was alive with the enemy; and although the spears were hurled from it continually during the night, no shot was thrown away unless the figure of the pirate could be distinctly seen.

It continued to rain : the men wore their greatcoats for the purpose of keeping their pieces dry; and several times, during that long night, I observed the muskets of these steady and good men brought to the shoulder and again lowered without firing, as that part of the jungle whence a spear had been hurled to within a few feet of where they stood did not shew a distinct form of any thing living. The hours were little less interesting for those who, in the boats below, stood facing the opposite bank of the river with their arms in their hands. It appears that the enemy had come down in great force to attack the boats from that side; and as the river was there very shallow, and the bottom hard, they could, by wading not more than knee-deep, have approached to within five or six yards of them: but in the first attack they had lost a great many men; and it is supposed that their repeated advances throughout the night were more to recover their dead and wounded than to make any fresh attack on our compact little force, whose deadly aim and rapid firing must have astonished them, and who certainly were, one and all, prepared to sell their lives as dearly as possible.

To the left of our position, and about 200 yards up the river, large trees were being felled during the night; and by the torch-lights shewing the spot, the officer of the boat, Mr. Partridge, kept up a very fair ball-practice with the pinnace's gun. Towards morning a shot fell apparently just where they were at work; and that being accompanied by what we afterwards ascertained caused more horror and consternation among the enemy than any thing else, a common signal sky-rocket, made them resign the ground entirely to us. The last shot, too, that was fired from the pinnace had killed three men.

As daylight broke I found the greater part of our party had squatted down with their guns between their knees; and, completely exhausted, had, in spite of the rain, fallen asleep. Few will ever forget that night. There were two natives and one marine only of our party badly wounded: the latter was struck by a rifle-shot, which entered his chest and lodged in the shoulder; and this poor fellow, a gallant young officer named Jenkins, already distinguished in the Chinese war, volunteered to convey in the second gig, with four boys only, down to the Jolly Bachelor. He performed this duty, and was again up with the party before daylight.

At daylight we found the pirates collecting in some force above us; and several shots were fired, as if to try the range of their rifles; but they took good care not to come within reach of our muskets. Shortly after, the tide beginning to rise, we made preparations for ascending further up the river. This was more than they bargained for, as we were close to where they had removed their families, with such little valuables as they could collect, when we so unexpectedly carried their forts and took possession of their town; and we were not sorry on observing, at that moment, a flag of truce advancing from their party down the stream, and halt half-way to our position. We immediately sent an unarmed Malay to meet them; and after a little talk, they came to our boats. The message was, that they were ready to abide by any terms we might dictate. I promised that hostilities should cease for two hours; but that we could treat only with the chiefs, whose persons should be protected, and invited them to a conference at 1 P.M.

In the mean while, having first sent notice by the messengers, I took advantage of the time, and ascended in my gig, without any great difficulty, above the obstruction they had been so busy throwing across the river during the night. The news that hostilities were to cease was not long in being communicated; and, by the time I had got up, the greatest confidence appeared to be established. Having pulled up into shoal-water, and where the river widened, the banks were soon covered with natives; and some seventy or eighty immediately laid aside their spears and walked off to my boat, the whole of which, together with its crew, they examined with the greatest curiosity.

In the heat of the day we indulged in a most refreshing bathe under the shade of overhanging trees, the bottom of the river being fine sand and pebbles worn smooth by the running stream.

At the appointed hour the chiefs made their appearance, dressed in their best, but looking haggard and dejected. Mr. Brooke, the "Tuan Besar," or great man, officiated as spokesman.

He fully explained that our invasion of their country, and destruction of their forts and town, was not for the purposes of pillage or gain to ourselves, but as a punishment for their repeated and aggravated acts of piracy; that they had been fully warned, for two years before, that the British nation would no longer allow the native trade between the adjacent islands and Singapore to be cut off and plundered, and the crews of the vessels cruelly put to death, as they had been.

SUBMISSION OF THE PIRATES. 63

They were very humble and submissive; admitted that their lives were forfeited; and if we said they were to die, they were prepared, although, they explained, they were equally willing to live. They promised to refrain for ever from piracy, and offered hostages for their good behaviour.

Mr. Brooke then explained how much more advantageous trade would be than piracy, and invited them to a further conference at Sarāwak, where they might witness all the blessings resulting from the line of conduct he had advised them to follow. If, on the other hand, we heard of a single act of piracy being committed by them, their country should be again invaded and occupied; and their enemies, the whole tribe of Linga Dyaks, let loose upon them, until they were rooted out and utterly destroyed.

To other questions they replied, that although the chief held communication and was in the habit of cruising with the people of the other settlements of Pakoo and Rembas, still they could not hold themselves responsible for their good conduct; and as both held strongly fortified positions (of course supposed by themselves to be impregnable), they did not think that they would abstain altogether from piracy unless we visited and inflicted a similar chastisement to that they themselves had suffered. They also stated that, although they never would again submit to the orders of the great and powerful chiefs, Seriffs Sahib and Muller, still they could not join in any expedition against them or their old allies, the bloodthirsty and formidable neighbours in the Sakarran river.

On our return to the still-smoking ruins of the once picturesque town of Paddi, we found that Seriff Jaffer, with his 800 warriors, had not been idle. The country round had been laid waste. All had been desolated, together with their extensive winter-stores of rice. It was a melancholy sight; and, for a moment, I forgot the horrid acts of piracy and cruel murders of these people, and my heart relented at what I had done—it was but for a few minutes.

Collecting our forces, we dropped leisurely down the river, but not without a parting yell of triumph from our Dyak force—a yell that must have made the hearts of those quail whose wives and children lay concealed in the jungle near to where we had held our conference.

We arrived at Boling soon after midnight, where we found the Tope, with our provision, quite safe. Several shots had been fired at her the night before; and large parties had repeatedly come down to the banks, and endeavoured to throw spears on board.

At daylight (Wednesday, 14th) we lost no time in completing to four days' provisions, and starting, with the flood-tide, for Pakoo. It took us until late in the evening before we appeared in sight of two newly built stockades, from which the pirates fled, panic-struck, without firing a shot, on our first discharge. We had evidently come on them before they were prepared, as some of the guns, in the forts, we found with the slings still on by which they had been carried.

The positions of the forts here, as at Paddi, were selected with great judgment; and had their guns been properly served, it would have been sharp work for boats. The same work of destruction was carried on; but the town was larger than at Paddi, and night setting in, the conflagration had a grand effect.

Although the greater part of their valuables had been removed, the place was alive with goats and poultry, the catching of which afforded great sport for our men. Some of the Singè Dyaks succeeded in taking the heads of a few pirates, who probably were killed or wounded in the forts on our first discharge. I saw one body, afterwards, without its head, in which each passing Dyak had thought proper to stick a spear, so that it had all the appearance of a huge porcupine.

The operation of extracting the brains from the lower part of the skull, with a bit of bamboo shaped like a spoon, preparatory to preserving, is not a pleasing one. The head is then dried, with the flesh and hair on it, suspended over a slow fire, during which the chiefs and elders of the tribe perform a sort of war-dance.

Soon after daylight the following morning (Thursday, 15th), the chiefs of the tribe came down with a flag of truce, when much the same sort of conference took place as at Paddi. They were equally submissive, offering their own lives, but begging those of their wives and children might be spared. After promising to accede to all we desired, they agreed to attend the conference about to assemble at Sarāwak, where the only terms on which they could expect lasting peace and mutual good understanding would be fully explained and discussed.

Like their friends at Paddi, they were of opinion that their neighbours at Rembas would not abstain from piracy until they had received convincing proof that there was strength, and that the power existed, which was capable of, and determined to, put down piracy. All these misguided people appeared not only to listen to reason, but to be open to conviction; and I am far from imputing to them that treachery so commonly attributed to all classes of Malays. The higher grades, I admit, are cunning and deceitful; but subsequent events during the last two years have proved the truth and honesty of the intentions of these people. They have strictly adhered to their promises; and have since, although surrounded by piratical tribes, been carrying on a friendly trade with Sarāwak.

Our next point of attack was Rembas. Although there was a nearer overland communication between those places, the distance by water was upwards of sixty miles; but the strong tides were of great assistance, as we could always rest when they were against us. High water was the only time, however, that suited us for landing, as the fall of tide left a considerable space of soft mud to wade through before reaching *terra firma*, which to our men was sufficiently unpleasant, without the additional trouble of having to load and fire when in that position,—besides, when stuck fast in the mud, you become a much easier object to be fired at. At Rembas the tide was not up until just before daylight; and having no moon to light us, a night attack was not considered advisable; so that we brought up about a quarter-tide below the town on the evening of the 16th. As Rembas contained a larger proportion of Malays (who are always well supplied with fire-arms) than the other settlements, though we had not experienced any opposition at Pakoo, we fully expected they would here make a better stand.

We advanced early in the morning, and soon came up with a succession of formidable barriers, more troublesome to cut through than any we had before encountered. About a mile below the town we landed 700 of the Linga Dyaks on the left bank of the river, who were to separate into two divisions,—commanded by Seriff Jaffer and his son, a remarkably fine and spirited youth,—

and creep stealthily through the jungle, for which the country was well adapted, so as to get to the rear of the town and forts, and make a simultaneous attack on the first shot being fired from our boats. The last barrier (and there were four of them) was placed just within point-blank range; the gig being a light boat, I managed to haul her over, close to the bank, and advanced so as to be both out of sight and out of range; and just as our first boat came up with the barrier, I pushed out from under the bank and opened a fire of musketry on the stockade, which was full of men. This, with the war-yell that followed from their rear (both unexpected), together with their fears having been already worked upon by the destruction of Paddi and defeat of Pakoo, threw them into the greatest confusion. They fled in all directions, without provoking us by firing a shot, although we found the guns loaded. Seriff Jaffer and his Dyaks were gratified by having all the fighting to themselves, and by some very pretty hand-to-hand encounters. We were much amused afterwards by their own account of the heroic deeds they had performed. Lives were lost on both sides, and heads taken. This Rembas was by far the largest and strongest place we had assaulted. We found some very large war-boats, both fitted and building; one measured ninety-two feet in length, with fourteen beam; and in addition to the usual good supply of fruit, goats, and poultry, our men were gratified by finding several bullocks. The plunder was great; and although, with the exception of the guns, of no value to us, it was very much so to our native followers.

After we had destroyed every thing, we received a flag of truce, when similar explanations and promises were made as at Paddi and Pakoo; and here ended, for the present, the warlike part of our expedition. The punishment we had inflicted was severe, but not more than the crime of their horrid piracies deserved. A few heads were brought away by our Dyak followers as trophies; but there was no unnecessary sacrifice of life, and I do not believe there was a woman or child hurt. The destruction of these places astonished the whole country beyond description. In addition to the distance and difficulty of access to their strongly-fortified positions, they looked for protection from the bore that usually ran up the Sarebus, and which they imagined none but their own boats could manage. As the different Malay chiefs heard that in ten days a handful of white men had totally destroyed their strongholds, they shook their heads, and exclaimed, " God is great!" and the Dyaks declared that the Tuan Besar (Mr. Brooke) had charmed the river to quiet the bore,[1] and that the whites were invul-

[1] It had never been known so quiet as during the days we were up their river.

nerable. Although this expedition would have a great moral effect on all the more respectable and thinking natives, inasmuch as the places destroyed were looked upon, from the large proportion of Malays, as more civilised than their formidable and savage neighbours, the Dyaks inhabiting the Sakarran river; still it was not to be supposed, when the settlements of Paddi, Pakoo, and Rembas, could not be responsible for the good behaviour of one another, that it was probable the severe lesson taught them would have any great effect on the Sakarrans: so that after a few days' recruiting on board the Dido, it was my intention to have paid them a visit also; but on reaching Sarāwak, I found orders for my return to China.

On regaining the Tope at Boling, we found our assistant-surgeon, Dr. Simpson, who had been left in charge of the sick, laid up with fever and ague. For conveniency's sake, the wounded men had been removed to a large native boat; and while the doctor was passing along the edge of the boat, his foot slipped, he fell overboard, and not being much of a swimmer, and a strong tide running, he was a good while in the water before a native went after him. He had for some time past been in bad health; but the cold he then caught brought on inflammation in the lungs, under the effects of which he sunk soon after our return to Singapore. Poor Simpson! he was not only clever in his profession, but endeared to us all by his kind and gentle manner, so grateful to the sick. There were few of us while in China who had not come under his hands, and experienced his tender, soothing, and unremitting attention.

We now gave our native followers permission to depart to their respective homes, which they did loaded with *plunder*, usually in India called *loot;* ourselves getting under weigh to rejoin the Dido off the island of Burong, and from thence we proceeded to the mouth of the Morotaba, where, leaving the ship, Mr. Brooke and I went in my boat, with two others in attendance, to take leave of the Rajah, prior to my return to Singapore and China. Although the greater part of the native boats attached to the expedition had already arrived at Sarāwak, the Rajah had sent them back, some miles down the river, with as many others as he could collect, gorgeously dressed out with flags, to meet Mr. Brooke and myself, the heroes of the grandest expedition that had ever been known in the annals of Malayan history. Our approach to the grand city was, to them, most triumphant, although to us a nuisance. From the moment we entered the last reach, the saluting from every gun in the capital that could be fired without bursting was incessant; and as we neared the royal residence, the yells, meant for cheers, and the beating of gongs, intended to be a sort of "See, the conquering hero comes," were quite deafening. The most minute particulars of our deeds, of course greatly exaggerated, had been detailed, long before our arrival, by the native chiefs, who were eye-witnesses; and when seated in the Rajah's presence, the royal countenance relaxed into a smile of real pleasure as he turned his wondering eyes from Mr. Brooke to myself and back again. I suppose he thought a great deal of us, as he said little or nothing; and as we were rather hungry after our pull, we were glad to get away once more to Brooke's hospitable board, to which we did ample justice.

As the tide would not suit for my return to the Dido until two o'clock the following morning, we sat up until that hour, when, with mutual regret, we parted. I had just seen enough of Borneo and my enterprising friend Mr. Brooke, to feel the deepest interest in both. No description of mine can in any way give my readers a proper idea of the character of the man I had just then left; and however interesting his journal may appear in the reading, it is only by being in his company, and by hearing him advocate the cause of the persecuted inland natives, and listening to his vivid and fair description of the beautiful country that he has adopted, that one can be made to enter fully into and feel what I would now describe.

We parted; and I did not then expect to be able so soon to return to finish what I had intended, viz. the complete destruction of the strongholds of the worst of the hordes of pirates, so long the terror of the coast, either by the capture of the piratical Seriffs Sahib and Muller, by whose evil influence they had been chiefly kept up, or by driving them from the country. From all that I had seen, the whole country appeared to be a large garden, with a rich and varied soil, capable of producing any thing. The natives, especially the mountain Dyaks, are industrious, willing, inoffensive, although a persecuted race; and the only things wanted to make it the most productive and happiest country in the world were, the suppression of piracy, good government, and opening a trade with the interior, which could not fail of success. All these I saw partially begun; and which Mr. Brooke, with the assistance of a vessel of war, and the countenance only of the government, would, although slowly yet surely, bring about.

CHAPTER IV.

Captain Keppel sails for China. Calcutta. The Dido ordered to Borneo again. Arrival at Sarāwak. Great improvements visible. Atrocities of the Sakarran pirates. Mr. Brooke's letter. Captain Sir E. Belcher's previous visit to Sarāwak in the Samarang. Coal found. Second letter from the Rajah Muda Hassim. Expedition against the Sakarran pirates. Patusen destroyed. Macota remembered, and his retreat burnt. Further fighting, and advance. Ludicrous midnight alarm.

June 24*th.*—I reached the Dido at 8 o'clock, and immediately got under weigh. After remaining twenty-four hours to water at Singapore, I sailed for Hong Kong. My time, during the year that I was absent from Borneo, if not quite so usefully, was not unpleasantly passed. We lay a few months in the Canton river. In addition to having good opportunities of seeing the natives of China in their domestic state, I witnessed one of those most curious and extraordinary sights that occasionally occur during the winter months in the city of Canton, namely, a fire. The one I witnessed was about the most extensive that had ever been experienced; and the Dido's crew had the gratification of being of some assistance in the protection of British property. From China the Dido accompanied the commander-in-chief, in the Cornwallis, to the Spanish colony at Manilla, which is a place that few forget; and a short description of our visit there has been given in an interesting little work, written by Captain Cunynghame. On my return to Hong Kong, I had the gratification of receiving on board the Dido, Major-General Lord Saltoun and his staff, consisting of two old and esteemed friends of mine, Captain, now Major Arthur Cunynghame, his lordship's aide-de-camp, and Major Grant, of the 9th Lancers, who had been adjutant-general to the forces. A more agreeable cruise at sea I never experienced. We called at the island of Pinang, in the Malacca Straits, on our way, where we again fell in with the admiral; and I was most agreeably surprised at meeting my friend Mr. Brooke, who had come on to Singapore to meet Sir William Parker, and had followed him up in the Wanderer, commanded by my friend Captain Henry Seymour,—the Wanderer, in company with the Harlequin, Captain the Hon. George Hastings, and the H.C. steamer Diana, having just returned from an expedition to Acheen, whither they had been despatched by the commander-in-chief, to inquire into and demand redress for an act of piracy committed on an English merchant-vessel. An account of the expedition has already been published. The pirates had made a desperate resistance, and several lives were lost, and many severely wounded on our side; among the latter was my friend Mr. Brooke in the head and arm, for which I took the liberty of giving him a lecture for his rashness, he having quite sufficient ground for fighting over in his newly-adopted country. He was much pleased at the admiral's having promised that the Dido should return again to the Straits station as soon as she had completed her voyage to Calcutta.

On the 11th March, 1844, we anchored off the grand City of Palaces, and well does it merit the name. We could not have timed our visit better. The Governor-General was being *fêted* on his return from the frontiers, which *fêtes* were continued on the arrival, a few days after ourselves, of the Cornwallis at Kedgeree, when the flag of Sir William Parker was shifted to the Dido. The admiral experienced the same style of hospitable entertainment that had previously been given to General Sir Hugh Gough on his return from the Chinese expedition. At Calcutta I was kindly invited by the "Tent Club," and introduced to that noble and most exciting of all field-sports, "Hog-hunting in India;" but with which the pleasures of the day did not cease. Few who have witnessed it can ever forget the convivial board afterwards. Although under a tent pitched by the edge of the jungle, thirty miles from the city, none of the comforts of the house were wanting; there were the punkah and the hookah, those luxuries of the East, to say nothing of heaps of ice from the far West, which aided considerably the consumption of champagne and claret; and the joke, the song, good story or good humour, never for a moment flagged.

A few days before my departure from Calcutta, the Governor-General, finding it necessary to send treasure to China, the admiral desired me to receive it on board. Although a welcome cargo, it delayed for a couple of months my return to Borneo. I found Mr. Brooke awaiting my arrival at Singapore; but as I could not then receive him on board, Captain Hastings took him over to Sarāwak in the Harlequin.

On arriving at Hong Kong, Rear-Admiral Sir T. Cochrane appointed Mr. Frederick Wade as first lieutenant, Lieutenant Wilmot Horton having been promoted to the rank of commander for his gallant defence when the Dido's boats were attacked by the very superior force of pirates off the island of Sirhassan.

Having landed the treasure at Hong Kong, and completed stores and provisions, I sailed from Macao on 21st June, and working down against the monsoon, arrived at Singapore on the 18th July. I here found letters from Mr. Brooke, stating that the Sakarrans had been out in great force; and although he was not aware of any danger to himself or settlement, still, by coming over quickly, I might have a fair chance of catching and crushing them in the very act of piracy. I lost no time in preparing for another expedition. The government at Calcutta had become fully sensible of the necessity of protecting the native trade to Singapore, and had sent down the Phlegethon steamer, of light draught of water, and better adapted to service in the straits or rivers than any of her Majesty's larger vessels. She was, moreover, fitted in every way for the peculiar service on which she was to be employed, with a zealous, experienced, and active Commander, F. Scott,[1] as well as a fine enterprising set of young officers. I lost no time in making application for her to the resident councillor, Mr. Church (in the absence of Colonel Butterworth, the Governor of the Straits), who immediately placed her at my disposal; and with such means, I was anxious to commence operations as speedily as possible, leaving the Vixen and Wolverine to perform the other duties of the station.

Thursday, 25th July.—Sailed from Singapore, having despatched the Phlegethon the previous night, with orders to rendezvous at the entrance to the Morotaba, which we entered in the evening of the 29th; and anchoring the ship inside the river, I went on in the steamer to within four miles of Sarāwak, when I pulled up in my gig, not without some fear of a shot from the forts, as I knew that before Mr. Brooke's return they had been put in a state of defence, and regular watch kept, by self-appointed officers, sleeping on

[1] I have lately heard, with much regret, of the death of this valuable officer.

their arms. I, however, got up without accident, in time to receive a hearty welcome, about daylight.

I found the place much altered for the better, and the population considerably increased. Mr. Brooke had established himself in a new house, built on a beautiful and elevated mound, from which the intriguing Macota had just been ejected on my first visit. Neat and pretty-looking little Swiss cottages had sprung up on all the most picturesque spots, which gave it quite a European look. He had also made an agreeable addition to his English society; and a magazine of English merchandise had been opened to trade with the natives, together with many other improvements.

On the other hand, Seriff Sahib, undeterred, as I anticipated he would be, by the example I made of his neighbours in the Sarebus, and who had been living in a comparatively unguarded state in the adjoining river of Sadong, had, during the last nine months, been making busy preparations for fortifying himself at a place called Patusen, up the Batang Lupar; and having lately got things in a forward state, he had called out a large fleet of Sakarrans as an escort; and being puffed up with his own power and importance, had thought proper to extend the time for the performance of his voyage, of about 100 miles, from his residence in Sadong to his fortified position at Patusen, for three weeks or a month, during which time he had despatched small parties of his fleet, which consisted of upwards of 150 war-prahus, on piratical excursions. These robbers had, in addition to their piracies on the high seas, scoured the coast in all directions, and committed the greatest atrocities, attended with some of the most cruel murders. One sample will be sufficient to shew their brutal character :—A detachment of three of their boats, having obtained information that a poor Dyak family, belonging to a tribe in Mr. Brooke's territory, had come down from their mountain to cultivate a small portion of land nearer the coast, and, for their better security, had made their dwelling in the upper branches of a large tree on the outskirts of the forest, determined to destroy them. Their little children were playing in the jungle when the pirates were seen approaching the tree with their diabolical war-yells. As the poor man did not descend immediately on being summoned, he was shot; when other ruffians, to save their ammunition, mounted the tree and cut his head off, with which they returned in triumph to their boats. The children, who had witnessed this from their hiding-places, succeeded in getting to Sarāwak.

Taking advantage of Mr. Brooke's unusually long absence, Sarāwak itself was threatened, and open defiance hurled at any European force that should dare approach Patusen. Reports, too, had been industriously spread that Mr. Brooke never intended to return; and when he did get back to his home, he found the town guarded and watched like a besieged city. With his usual nerve and decision he withdrew his men from the forts, and sent to Seriff Sahib to inform him that he should suffer for his temerity.

Of these events a letter I received from him is so characteristic, and gives so lively a description, that I am tempted to print it:

"Sarāwak, 26th May, 1844.

"MY DEAR KEPPEL,—It is useless applying a spur to a willing horse; so I will only tell you that there is plenty to do here, and the sooner you can come the better for all of us, especially your poor friends the Dyaks. Bring with you as much force as you can to attack Sakarran.

"The case stands thus:—Seriff Sahib, quite frightened at Sadong since last year, enraged likewise at his loss of power and his incapability of doing mischief, collected all the Sakarran Dyaks, and was joined by many of the Dyaks of Sarebus and some Balows. He likewise had a good many Malays, and bullied every one in his vicinity. This force met at the entrance of the Sadong Delta, and committed depredations. They were not less than 200 Dyak boats and some 15 or 20 armed Malay prahus, besides others. Just as they were collected, the Harlequin appeared off the coast, and we might have *had them all;* but the opportunity will never again occur, and how I wished that I had come over in the Dido! Seriff Sahib, with this force, has started to-day for Sakarran, and I was not strong enough with my eight native boats to attack him. It is really greatly to be lamented, because we should most completely have crushed the head of the snake. We must, however, make the best of it. It is his intention, on his arrival at Sakarran, to fortify and wait for our attack, and in the mean time to send out his Dyaks along the coast and inland to such places as they dare venture to attack.

"Come, then, my dear Keppel, for there is plenty to do for all hands. I have ordered a gunboat from Mr. Goldie to make our force stronger; and had I possessed such a one the day before yesterday, I would have pulled away for the Sadong to-day.

"My regards to all. I still propose Pepper-Pot Hall for your residence. I only wish I felt *quite sure* that Fortune had it in store that you would be here on your return from China. That dame, however, seems to delight in playing me slippery tricks just at present; and never was the time and tide so missed before, which would have led to fortune, as the other day. All the Queen's ships and all the Queen's men could not bring such a chance together again.—Ever, my dear Keppel, your sincere friend, J. BROOKE.

"Captain the Hon. Henry Keppel."

No one could have been more disappointed or have regretted more than my gallant friend Captain Hastings, that his orders did not admit of any delay, or of his attacking that redoubtable pirate Seriff Sahib, especially as he had a small score to settle with these kind of gentry, having had his first lieutenant, H. Chads, severely wounded in two places, and several men killed, in the affair at Acheen Head. It was, however, all for the best, as the few boats that the Harlequin could have sent would have stood but a poor chance against upwards of 200 war-prahus, all fitted and prepared for fight.

On the 1st of August, with the Dido and Phlegethon at anchor off Sarāwak, the warlike preparations were going on rapidly. I had saluted and paid my visit to Muda Hassim; he was delighted to see me again, and we went through the form of holding several conferences of war in his divan. He appears to be a good well-meaning man, well inclined towards the English, moderately honest, and, if roused, I daresay, not without animal courage; and altogether, with the assistance of his clever younger brother, Budrudeen, a very fit person to govern that part of Borneo of which he is Rajah.

During my absence, Sarāwak had been visited by H.M.S. Samarang, Captain Sir Edward Belcher, who had received directions to call on and communicate with Mr. Brooke. In dropping down the river the Samarang grounded on a long shelf of rocks, at the top of high water, and with the ebb-tide rolled over, filling with the succeeding flood. She was nearly a fortnight in this position, but was ultimately saved by the skill and almost unparallelled perseverance (aided by such assistance of men and spars as Mr. Brooke could afford) of her captain, officers, and crew—a feat that must have given the natives a good idea of what British seamen are capable of. This accident delayed for a short time a visit that was afterwards made by Sir Edward Belcher, accompanied by Mr. Brooke, to Borneo Proper. A hurried inspection of the capabilities of that part of the coast took place; and the fact of there being coal on the island was ascertained.

I received a second letter from Muda Hassim, of which the following is a translation:

> "This comes from Pangeran Muda Hassim, Rajah of Borneo, to our friend Captain Keppel, in command of Her Britannic Majesty's ship.

(After the usual compliments):

"We beg to let our friend Captain Keppel know, that the pirates of Sakarran, whom we mentioned last year, still continue their piracies by sea and land; and that many Malays, under Seriff Sahib, who have been accustomed to send or to accompany the pirates and to share in their spoils, have gone to the Sakarran river, with a resolve of defending themselves rather than accede to our wishes that they should abandon piracy.

"Last year Captain Belcher told the Sultan and myself, that it would be pleasing to the Queen of England that we should repress piracy; and we signed an agreement, at his request, in which we promised to do so; and we tell our friend of the piracies and evil actions of the Sakarran people, who have, for many years past, done much mischief to trade, and make it dangerous for boats to sail along the coast; and this year many prahus, which wanted to sail to Singapore, have been afraid. We inform our friend Captain Keppel of this, as we desire to end all the piracy, and to perform our agreement with the Queen of England."

Monday, 5th August, 1844, being the morning fixed for the departure of our expedition against the Sakarran pirates, the Phlegethon steamer weighed at 8 o'clock, and proceeded down the river to await at the mouth the collection of our force. Among those who accompanied us from Sarāwak was the Pangeran Budrudeen, the intelligent brother of the Rajah already noticed. This was a great and unusual event in the royal family; and the departure from the Rajah's wharf, which I viewed from Mr. Brooke's house, on the opposite bank of the river, was intended to be very imposing. The barge of state was decked out with banners and canopies; all the chiefs attended, with the Arab priest Mudlana at their head, and the barge pushed off amidst the firing of cannon, and a general screech, invoking the blessing of Mahomet.

Having seen the last boat off, Mr. Brooke and myself took our departure in the gig, when another and last farewell salute was fired from the Rajah's wharf.

Three hours brought us to the steamer, anchored off the fishing-huts at the mouth of the river. Here we heard that a small boat from the enemy's country had, under the pretence of trading, just been in to spy into our force, but decamped again on the appearance of the steamer. We now all got fairly away together, the smaller boats keeping near the shoals in shore, while the steamer was obliged to make an offing some miles from the coast. From the masthead we distinctly made out the small boat that had left the mouth of the river before, both pulling and sailing in the direction of the Batang Lupar, up which the Sakarran country lies; and it being desirable that the pirates should not get information of our approach, at dusk, being well in advance, and our auxiliary force following, I despatched Mr. Brooke's Singapore sampan and one of the Dido's cutters in chase. At half-past nine we anchored in the stream within the entrance.

We were fortunate at Sarāwak in picking up

two excellent and intelligent pilots, who had long known the whole river, and had themselves been several times forced to serve in the boats while on their piratical excursions.

Tuesday, 6th.—With the flood-tide arrived all the well-appointed and imposing little fleet, and with them the cutter and sampan with two out of the three men belonging to the boat of which they had been in chase; the third having been speared by Seboo, on shewing a strong inclination to run a-muck in his own boat, *i.e.* to sell his life as dearly as he could. From these men we obtained information that Seriff Sahib was fully prepared for defence—that his harem had been removed—and that he would fight to the last. We also learned that Macota, better known among us by the name of the " Serpent," and often mentioned in Mr. Brooke's journal, was the principal adviser, in whose house the councils of war were generally held.

We anchored, in the afternoon, off the mouth of the river Linga; and while there we despatched a messenger to Seriff Jaffer to caution him against giving any countenance or support to either Seriffs Sahib or Muller, on whose punishment and destruction we were determined.

The Batang Lupar, as far as this, is a magnificent river, from three to four miles wide, and, in most parts, from five to seven fathoms water.

Wednesday, 7th.—We weighed at daylight, but

were obliged to anchor again before appearing in sight of Patusen, for the tide to rise sufficiently to enable us to pass a long flat shoal, over which, during the spring-tides, a bore rushes with frightful velocity.

We now collected our boats, and made our arrangements as well as we could, for attacking a place we had not yet seen. We had now a little more difficulty in keeping our native force back, as many of those who had accompanied the expedition last year had gained so much confidence that the desire of plunder exceeded the feeling of fear.

After weighing at 11, with a strong tide sweeping us up, we were not many minutes in coming in sight of the fortifications of Patusen; and indeed they were not to be despised. There were five of them, two not quite finished. Getting suddenly into six-feet water, we anchored the steamer; although well within musket-range, not so formidable a berth as we might have taken up had I been aware of the increasing depth of water nearer the town; but we approached so rapidly there was no time to wait the interpretation of the pilot's information.

The Dido and Phlegethon's boats were not long in forming alongside. They were directed to pull in shore, and then attack the forts in succession; but my gallant first-lieutenant, Wade, who had the command, was the first to break the line, and pull directly in the face of the largest fort. His example was followed by the others; and dividing, each boat pulled for that which appeared to the officer in command to be the one most likely to make a good fight. The forts were the first to open fire on both steamer and boats, which was quickly and smartly returned. It is impossible to imagine a prettier sight than it was from the top of the Phlegethon's paddle-box. It was my intention to have fired on the enemy from the steamer, so as to draw their attention off the boats; but owing to the defective state of the detonating priming-tubes, the guns from the vessel did not go off, and the boats had all the glory to themselves.

They never once checked in their advance; but the moment they touched the shore the crews rushed up, entering the forts at the embrasures, while the pirates fled by the rear.

In this sharp and short affair we had but one man killed, poor John Ellis, a fine young man, and captain of the main-top in the Dido. He was cut in two by a cannon-shot while in the act of ramming home a cartridge in the bow-gun of the Jolly Bachelor. This, and two others badly wounded, were the only accidents on our side.

Our native allies were not long in following our men on shore. The killed and wounded on the part of the pirates must have been considerable. Our followers got several heads. There were no less than sixty-four brass guns of different sizes, besides many iron, found in and about the forts: the latter we spiked and threw into the river. The town was very extensive; and after being well looted, made a glorious blaze.

Our Sarāwak followers, both Malays and Dyaks, behaved with the greatest gallantry, and dashed in under the fire of the forts. In fact, like their country, any thing might be made of them under a good government; and such is their confidence in the judgment of, and their attachment to, Mr. Brooke, that he might safely defy in his own stronghold the attacks of any foreign power.

After our men had dined, and had a short rest during the heat of the day, we landed our whole force in two divisions—and a strange but formidable-looking force they made—to attack a town situated about two miles up, on the left bank of a small river called the Grahan, the entrance to which had been guarded by the forts; and immediately after their capture the tide had fallen too low for our boats to get up. Facing the stream, too, was a long stockade; so that we determined on attacking the place in the rear, which, had the pirates only waited to receive us, would have caused a very interesting skirmish. They, however, decamped, leaving every thing behind them. In this town we found Seriff Sahib's residence, and, among other things, all his curious and extensive wardrobe. It was ridiculous to see our

Dyaks dressed out in all the finery and plunder of this noted pirate, whose very name, a few days previous, would have made them tremble. Goats and poultry there were in abundance. We likewise found a magazine in the rear of the Seriff's house, containing about two tons of gunpowder; also a number of small barrels of fine powder, branded 'Dartford,' in exactly the same state as it had left the manufactory in England. It being too troublesome and heavy to convey on board the steamer, and each of our native followers staggering up to his knees in mud, under a heavy load of plunder, I had it thrown into the river. It was evident how determined the chief had been to defend himself, as, besides the defences already completed, eight others, in different states of forwardness, were in the course of erection; and had the attack been delayed a few weeks, Patusen would not have been carried by boats without considerable loss of life. It was the key to this extensive river; the resort of the worst of pirates; and each chief had contributed his share of guns and ammunition towards its fortification and defence.

We returned to our boats and evening meal rather fatigued, but much pleased with our day's work, after ascending near seventy miles from the mouth of the river. The habitations of 5000 pirates had been burnt to the ground; four strong forts destroyed, together with several hundred boats; upwards of sixty brass cannons captured, and about a fourth that number of iron spiked and thrown into the river, besides vast quantities of other arms and ammunition; and the powerful Seriff Sahib, the great pirate-patron for the last twenty years, ruined past recovery, and driven to hide his diminished head in the jungle.

The 8th and 9th were passed in burning and destroying the rest of the straggling town, and a variety of smaller boats, which were very numerous. I had also an account to settle with that cunning rascal Macota, for his aiding and abetting Seriff Sahib in his piracies. He had located himself very pleasantly near a bend in the river, about a mile above Seriff Sahib's settlement, and was in the act of building extensive fortifications, when I had the satisfaction of returning the visit and some of the compliments he would have conferred on my friend Mr. Brooke at Sarāwak. Budrudeen, the Rajah's brother, had likewise been duped by this fellow, and was exceedingly anxious to insert the blade of a very sharp and beautiful kris into the body of his late friend. Mr. Brooke, however, was anxious to save his life, which he afterwards had the satisfaction of doing. I shall never forget the tiger-like look of the young Pangeran when we landed together in the hopes of surprising the "Serpent" in his den; but he was too quick for us, having decamped with his followers, and in so great a hurry as to leave all his valuables behind,

—among them a Turkish pipe, some chairs once belonging to the Royalist, and other presents from Mr. Brooke. Every thing belonging to him was burnt or destroyed save some handsome brass guns. There was one of about 12 cwt. that had been lent by the Sultan when Macota was in favour, and which I returned to Budrudeen for his brother.

We were here joined by a large number of the Linga Dyaks, the same force that had joined us the year previous while up the Sarebus, but unaccompanied by Seriff Jaffer, of whom it was not quite clear that he had not been secretly aiding the pirates. I sent them back with assurances to their chiefs that they should not be molested unless they gave shelter or protection to either Seriff Sahib or Muller. Seriff Sahib, with a considerable body of followers, escaped inland in the direction of the mountains, from the other side of which he would be able to communicate with the river Linga. Macota was obliged to fly up the river towards the Undop, on which the village and residence of Seriff Sahib's brother, Seriff Muller, was situated.

Having destroyed every boat and sampan, as well as house or hut, on the 10th, as soon as the tide had risen sufficiently to take us over the shoals, we weighed, in the steamer, for the country of the Sakarran Dyaks, having sent the boats on before with the first of the flood.

About fifteen miles above Patusen is the

branch of the river called the Undop : up this river I despatched Lieutenant Turnour, with Mr. Comber, in the Jolly Bachelor and a division of our native boats, while we proceeded to where the river again branches off to the right and left, as on the tongue of land so formed we understood we should find a strong fort; besides, it was the highest point to which we could attempt to take the steamer. The branch to the left is called the Sakarran; that to the right retains the name of Lupar, inhabited chiefly by Sakarrans. We found the place deserted and the houses empty. Knowing that these people depended almost entirely for protection on the strongly fortified position at Patusen, I did not expect any similar opposition from either Seriff Muller or the desperate bloodthirsty Sakarrans, and consequently divided my force into three divisions — the one, already mentioned, under Lieutenant Turnour, up the Undop; another, under Mr. D'Aeth, up the Lupar; while Lieutenant Wade, accompanied by Mr. Brooke, ascended the Sakarran. I had not calculated on the disturbed and excited state in which I found the country; and two wounded men having been sent back from the Undop branch with accounts of the pirates, chiefly Malays, collected in great numbers, both before and in the rear of our small force; and an attempt having been made to cut off the bearer of this information, Nakodah Bahar, who had had a very narrow escape, and had no idea of being the bearer of an answer unless attended by a European force,— I had some difficulty in mustering another crew from the steamer, leaving my friend Captain Scott, with only the idlers, rather critically situated.

I deemed it advisable to re-collect my whole force; and before proceeding to the punishment of the Sakarrans, to destroy the power and influence of Seriff Muller, whose town was situated about twenty miles up, and was said to contain a population of 1500 Malays, independent of the surrounding Dyak tribes. Having despatched boats with directions to Lieutenant Wade and Mr. D'Aeth to join us in the Undop, I proceeded in my gig to the scene of action, leaving the steamer to maintain as strict a blockade of the Sakarran and Lupar branches as, with their reduced force, they were capable of. On my joining Lieutenant Turnour, I found him just returned from a very spirited attack which he had made, assisted by Mr. Comber, on a stockade situated on the summit of a steep hill; Mr. Allen, the master, being still absent, on a similar service, on the opposite side of the river. The gallant old chief Patingi Ali was likewise absent, in pursuit of the enemy that had been driven from the stockades, with whom he had had a hand-to-hand fight, the whole of which —being on the rising ground—was witnessed by our boats' crews, who could not resist hailing his return from his gallant achievement with three hearty British cheers. This had the effect of giving such an impulse to his courage, that, in a subsequent affair, it unhappily caused a serious loss among this active and useful branch of our force.

We had now to unite in cutting our way through a barrier across the river similar to that described in the attack on the Sarebus, which, having passed, we brought up for the night close to a still more serious obstacle, in a number of huge trees felled, the branches of which meeting midway in the river, formed apparently an insurmountable obstacle to our progress. But "patience and perseverance overcome all difficulties;" and by night only three of the trees remained to be cleared away. We were now within a short distance of their town, so that we could distinctly hear the noise and confusion which our advance had occasioned. On the right bank, and about fifty yards in advance of the barrier, stood a farmhouse, which we considered it prudent to occupy for the night as our advanced post. Having collected about fifty volunteers, consisting of Messrs. Steward, Williamson, and Comber; a corporal and four marines; my gig's crew; and the remainder composed of a medley of picked men from our Dyak and Malay followers, not forgetting my usual and trusty attendant John Eager with his bugle, the sounding of which was to be the signal for the whole force to come to the rescue, in the event of surprise, not at all improbable from the nature of our warfare and our proximity to the enemy's town.

And here a most ludicrous scene occurred during the night. Having placed our sentries and look-out men, and given "Tiga" as the watchword, we were, shortly after midnight, suddenly aroused from sound sleep by a Dyak war-yell, which was immediately responded to by the whole force. It was pitch dark: the interior of our farmhouse, the partitions of which had been removed for the convenience of stowage, was crowded to excess. In a moment every man was on his legs: swords, spears, and krisses dimly glittered over our heads. It is impossible to describe the excitement and confusion of the succeeding ten minutes: one and all believed that we had been surrounded by the enemy, and cut off from our main party. I had already thrust the muzzle of my pistol close to the heads of several natives, whom, in the confusion, I had mistaken for Sakarrans; and as each in his turn called out "Tiga," I withdrew my weapon to apply to somebody else; until, at last, we found that we were all "Tigas." I had prevented Eager, more than once, from sounding the alarm, which, from the first, he had not ceased to press me for permission to do. The Dyak yell had, however, succeeded in throwing the whole force afloat into a similar confusion, who, not hearing the signal, concluded that they, and not we, were the party attacked. The real cause we afterwards ascertained to have arisen from the alarm of a Dyak, who dreamt, or imagined, he felt a spear thrust upwards through the bamboo-flooring of our building, and immediately gave his diabolical yell. The confusion was ten times as much as it would have been had the enemy really been there. So ended the adventures of the night in the wild jungle of Borneo.

CHAPTER V.

Seriff Muller's town sacked. Ascend the river in pursuit of the enemy. Gallant exploit of Lieutenant Wade. His death and funeral. Interesting anecdote of him. Ascend the Sakarran branch. Native boats hemmed in by pirates, and their crews slaughtered to a man. Karangan destroyed. Captain Sir E. Belcher arrives in the Samarang's boats. Return to Saräwak. New expedition against Seriffs Sahib and Jaffer. Macota captured. Flight of Seriff Sahib. Conferences. Seriff Jaffer deposed. Mr. Brooke's speech in the native tongue. End of the expedition, and return to Saräwak. The Dido sails for England.

AT daylight we were joined by Lieutenant Wade and Mr. Brooke — their division making a very acceptable increase to our force — and by 8 o'clock the last barrier was cut through between us and Seriff Muller's devoted town. With the exception of his own house, from which some eight or nine Malays were endeavouring to move his effects, the whole place was deserted. They made no fight; and an hour afterwards the town had been plundered and burnt. The only lives lost were a few unfortunates, who happened to come within range of our musketry in their exertions to save some of their master's property. A handsome large boat, belonging to that chief, was the only thing saved; and this I presented to Budrudeen. After a short delay in catching our usual supply of goats and poultry, with which the place abounded, we proceeded up the river in chase of the chief and his people; and here again we had to encounter the same obstacle presented by the felled trees thrown across the river—if possible of increased difficulty, owing to their greater size and the narrow breadth of the stream: but although delayed, we were not to be beaten. We ascertained that the pirates had retreated to a Dyak village, situated on the summit of a hill, some twenty-five miles higher up the Undop, five or six miles only of which we had succeeded in ascending, as a most dreary and rainy night closed in, during which we were joined by Mr. D'Aeth and his division from the Lupar river.

The following morning, the 13th of August, at daybreak, we again commenced our toilsome work. With the gig and the lighter boats we succeeded better; and I should have despaired of the heavier boats ever getting up, had they not been assisted by an opportune and sudden rise of the tide, to the extent of twelve or fourteen feet, though with this we had to contend against a considerably increased strength of current. It was on this day that my ever-active and zealous first lieutenant, Charles Wade, jealous of the advanced position of our light boats, obtained a place in my gig. That evening the

Phlegethon's first and second cutters, the Dido's two cutters, and their gigs, were fortunate enough to pass a barrier composed of trees evidently but recently felled; from which we concluded ourselves to be so near the enemy that, by pushing forward as long as we could possibly see, we might prevent further impediments from being thrown in our way. This we did; but at 9 P.M. arriving at a broad expanse of the river, and being utterly unable to trace our course, we anchored our advanced force for the night.

On Wednesday, 14th, we again pushed on at daylight. We had gained information of two landing-places leading to the Dyak village on the hill, round three-fourths at the foot of which the Undop flowed. The first landing-place we had no trouble in discovering, from the number of deserted boats collected near it. Leaving these to be looted by our followers, we proceeded in search of the second, which we understood was situated more immediately under the village, and which, having advanced without our guides, we had much difficulty in finding. The circuit of the base of the hill was above five miles. In traversing this distance, we had repeated skirmishing with straggling boats of the enemy, upon whom we came unexpectedly. During this warfare, Patingi Ali, who, with his usual zeal, had here come up, bringing a considerable native force of both Malays and Dyaks, was particularly on the alert; and while we in the gig attacked the large war-prahu of Seriff Muller himself—the resistance of whose followers was only the discharge of their muskets, after which they threw themselves into the river, part only effecting their escape—the Patingi nearly succeeded in capturing that chief in person. He had escaped from his prahu into a remarkably beautiful and fast-pulling sampan, in which he was chased by old Ali, and afterwards only saved his life by throwing himself into the water, and swimming to the jungle; and it was with no small pride that the gallant old chief appropriated the boat to his own use. In the prahu were captured two large brass guns, two smaller ones, a variety of small arms, ammunition, provisions, colours, and personal property, amongst which were also two pair of handsome jars of English manufacture. After this, having proceeded some considerable distance without finding the second landing-place, we put in close to a clear green spot, with the intention of getting our breakfasts, and of waiting the arrival of the other boat with the guides.

While our crew were busily employed cooking, Lieutenant Wade and myself fancied we heard the suppressed voices of many people not far distant, and taking up our guns we crept into the jungle. We had not penetrated many yards before I came in sight of a mass of boats concealed in a snug little inlet, the entrance to which had escaped our notice. These were filled with the piratical

Dyaks and Malays, and on shore at various points were placed armed sentinels. My first impulse was to conceal ourselves until the arrival of our force; but my rash, though gallant friend deemed otherwise; and without noticing the caution of my upheld hand, dashed in advance, discharging his gun, and calling upon our men to follow. It is impossible to conceive the consternation and confusion this our sudden sally occasioned among the pirates. The confused noise and scrambling from their boats I can only liken to that of a suddenly-roused flock of wild ducks. Our attack from the point whence it came was evidently unexpected; and it is my opinion that they calculated on our attacking the hill, if we did so at all, from the nearest landing-place, without pulling round the other five miles, as the whole attention of their scouts appeared to be directed towards that quarter. A short distance above them was a small encampment, probably erected for the convenience of their chiefs, as in it we found writing materials, two or three desks of English manufacture, on the brass plate of one of which, I afterwards noticed, was engraved the name of "*Mr. Willson.*" To return to the pirates: with our force, such as it was—nine in number—we pursued, headed by Lieutenant Wade, our terrified enemy. They foolishly themselves had not the courage to rally in their judiciously selected and naturally protected encampment, but continued their retreat (firing on us from the jungle) towards the Dyak village on the summit of the hill.

We here collected our force, reloaded our fire-arms; and Lieutenant Wade, seeing from this spot the arrival at the landing-place of the other boats, again rushed on in pursuit. Before arriving at the foot of the steep ascent on the summit of which the before-mentioned Dyak village stood, we had to cross a small open space of about sixty yards, exposed to the fire from the village as well as the surrounding jungle. It was before crossing this plain that I again cautioned my gallant friend to await the arrival of his men, of whom he was far in advance; and almost immediately afterwards he fell mortally wounded at my feet, having been struck by two rifle-shots, and died instantaneously. I remained with the body until our men came up, and giving it in charge, we carried the place on the height without a check or further accident. The Dyak village we now occupied I would have spared, as on no occasion had we noticed any of the tribe fighting against us; but it was by shot fired from it that poor Wade was killed, and the work of destruction commenced simultaneously with the arrival of our men. It was most gratifying to me throughout the expedition to observe the friendly rivalry and emulation between the crews of the Phlegethon and Dido's boats; and on this occasion the former had the glory of first gaining the height; and one of their officers, Mr. Simpson, wounded, with a pistol-shot, a man with a rifle, supposed to have been the person who had slain our first-lieutenant.

I may here narrate a circumstance, from which one may judge of the natural kind-heartedness of my lamented friend. During the heat of the pursuit, although too anxious to advance to await the arrival of his men, he nevertheless found time to conceal in a place of security a poor terrified Malay girl whom he overtook, and who, by an imploring look, touched his heart. The village and the piratical boats destroyed, and the excitement over, we had time to reflect on the loss we had sustained of one so generally beloved as the leader of the expedition had been among us all.[1] Having laid the body in a canoe, with the British union-jack for a pall, we commenced our descent of the river with very different spirits from those with which we had ascended only a few hours before. In the evening, with our whole force assembled, we performed the last sad ceremony of committing the body to the deep, with all the honours that time and circumstance would allow. I read that beautiful, impressive service from a Prayer-book, the only one, by the by, in the expedition, which he himself had brought, as he said, "in case of accident."

Before we again got under weigh, several

[1] See Appendix.

FUNERAL of LIEUTENANT WADE.

London Chapman & Hall, 180 Strand, Jan'y 15th 1846.

G. Hawkins, lith.

Day & Haghe Lith'rs to the Queen.

Malay families, no longer in dread of their piratical chief, Seriff Muller, who had fled nobody knew where, gave themselves up to us as prisoners, trusting to the mercy of a white man; the first instance of any of them having done so. We heard, also, that Macota had retreated with the Seriff; and on examination we found the papers captured in the encampment belonged to them, exposing several deep intrigues and false statements addressed to the Sultan, the purport of which was to impress his mind with a hostile intention on the part of the British government towards his country. We brought-up for the night off the still-burning ruins of Seriff Muller's town.

On Thursday the 15th we again reached the steamer. We found her prepared for action, having been much annoyed during the night by the continued Dyak war-yells—sounds, to uninitiated ears, as unpleasant as those of musketry. Having driven away and destroyed the strongholds of the two principal instigators and abettors of all the piracies committed along the coast of Borneo and elsewhere, it now remained for us to punish, as far as in our power lay, the pirates themselves. The Sakarran Dyaks being the only ones now remaining who had not received convincing proofs that their brutal and inhuman trade would no longer be allowed, the 15th and 16th were passed in the steamer, to rest the men after the severe fatigue encountered up the Undop, and in making preparations for an advance up the Sakarran. During the night of the 16th several of our native followers were wounded. Their boats not being furnished with anchors, and the river being deep, they were obliged to make fast to the bank, which in the dark afforded great facility for the enemy to creep down through the jungle unperceived, so close as to fire a shot and even thrust their spears through the thin mat covering of the boats. One poor fellow received a shot in his lungs, from which he died the following day; a Dyak likewise died from a spear-wound; and in the morning we witnessed the pile forming for burning the Dyak, and the coffin making for the conveying the body of the Malay to Sarāwak, his native place; both parties having an equal horror of their dead falling into the hands of the enemy, although differing in their mode of disposing of them.

On Saturday the 17th, the expedition, consisting of the Dido's pinnace, her two cutters and gig, the Jolly Bachelor, and the Phlegethon's first and second cutters and gig, started up the Sakarran. A small division of light native boats, under the command of the brave old Patingi Ali, were selected to keep as a reconnoitring party with our leading boats, while the remaining native force, of above thirty boats, followed as a reserve. We advanced the first day some twenty miles without so much as seeing a native, although our progress was considerably delayed by stopping to burn farmhouses, and a number of war-prahus found concealed in the jungle or long grass on either side of the river. We brought up early in the afternoon, for the purpose of strongly fortifying ourselves, both ashore and afloat, against surprise before the night set in, by which time it would have taken a well-disciplined and powerful force to have dislodged us.

This evening we had unusually fine weather; and we squatted down to our meal of curry and rice with better appetites and higher spirits than we had done for some days. We advanced the following day: and although we reached several villages, the grain had been removed from them all; which, in all probability, was done immediately upon their hearing of the fall of their supposed impregnable Patusen. In the evening we took the same precautions as on the preceding night, considering that our enemies were not to be despised. Owing to heavy rains which fell during the night, and caused a strong current, our progress was considerably retarded. The scenery was beautiful—more so than in any of the rivers we had yet visited. We likewise now repeatedly fell in with small detachments of the enemy, and spears were thrown from the banks, which added considerably to our excitement and amusement. On every point we found the remains of the preceding night's watch-fires, so that news of our approach would have been conveyed rapidly along. While leading in the gig with a select few of our followers, we came suddenly on a boat full of warriors, all gorgeously dressed, apparently perfectly unconscious of our approach. The discharge of our muskets and the capsizing of their war-boat was the work of an instant, most of the crew of which saved their lives by escaping into the jungle.

This evening, Sunday, the 18th, we experienced some difficulty in finding a suitable place for our bivouac. While examining the most eligible-looking spot on the bank of the river, the crew of one of the Phlegethon's boats, having crept up the opposite bank, came suddenly on a party of Dyaks, who saluted them with a war-yell and a shower of spears; and it was absurd to see the way in which they precipitated themselves into the water again to escape from this unexpected danger. The Dyaks, too, appear to have been equally surprised. The place we selected for the night was a large house about forty yards from the edge of the river; and for a musket-range around which we had not much difficulty in clearing the ground. Here we all united our different messes, and passed a jovial evening. The night, however, set in with a most fearful thunder-storm, accompanied by the most vivid flashes of lightning I ever witnessed. The rain continued to fall in torrents: it cleared up at daylight, when we proceeded. As yet the banks of the river had been a continued garden, with sugar-cane plantations and banana-trees in abundance. As we advanced, the scenery assumed a wilder and still more beautiful appearance, presenting high steep points, with large over-hanging trees, and occasionally forming into pretty picturesque bays, with sloping banks. At other times we approached narrow gorges, looking so dark that, until past, you almost doubted there being a passage through. We were in hopes that this morning we should have reached their capital, a place called Karangan, supposed to be about ten miles further on. At 9 o'clock Mr. Brooke, who was with me in the gig, stopped to breakfast with young Jenkins in the second cutter. Not expecting to meet with any opposition for some miles, I gave permission to Patingi Ali to advance cautiously with his light division, and with positive orders to fall back upon the first appearance of any natives. As the stream was running down very strong, we held on to the bank, waiting for the arrival of the second cutter. Our pinnace and second gig having passed up, we had remained about a quarter of an hour, when the report of a few musket-shots told us that the pirates had been fallen in with. We immediately pushed on; and as we advanced, the increased firing from our boats, and the war-yells of some thousand Dyaks, let us know that an engagement had really commenced. It would be difficult to describe the scene as I found it. About twenty boats were jammed together, forming one confused mass; some bottom up; the bows or sterns of others only visible; mixed up, pellmell, with huge rafts; and amongst which were nearly all our advanced little division. Headless trunks, as well as heads without bodies, were lying about in all directions; parties were engaged hand to hand, spearing and krissing each other; others were striving to swim for their lives; entangled in the common *mêlée* were our advanced boats; while on both banks thousands of Dyaks were rushing down to join in the slaughter, hurling their spears and stones on the boats below. For a moment I was at a loss what steps to take for rescuing our people from the embarrassed position in which they were, as the whole mass (through which there was no passage) were floating down the stream, and the addition of fresh boats arriving only increased the confusion. Fortunately, at this critical moment one of the rafts, catching the stump of a tree, broke this floating bridge, making a passage, through which (my gig being propelled by paddles instead of oars) I was enabled to pass.

It occurred to Mr. Brooke and myself simultaneously, that, by advancing in the gig, we should draw the attention of the pirates towards us, so as to give time for the other boats to clear themselves. This had the desired effect. The whole force on shore turned, as if to secure—what they rashly conceived to be—their prize.

We now advanced mid-channel: spears and stones assailed us from both banks. My friend Brooke's gun would not go off; so giving him the yoke-lines, he steered the boat, while I, with my never-failing rifles—having my coxswain to load—had time to select the leaders from amongst this savage mass, on which I kept up a rapid fire. Mr. Allen, in the second gig, quickly coming up, opened upon them, from a congreve-rocket tube, such a destructive fire as caused them to retire panic-struck behind the temporary barriers where they had concealed themselves previous to the attack on Patingi Ali, and from whence they continued, for some twenty minutes, to hurl their spears and other missiles—among which may be mentioned short lengths of bamboo, one end of which was heavily loaded with stone, and thrown with great force and precision; the few fire-arms of which they were possessed being of but little use to them after the first discharge, the operation of loading, in their inexperienced hands, requiring a longer time than the hurling of some twenty spears. The sumpitan was likewise freely employed by these pirates; and although several of our men belonging to the pinnace were struck, no fatal results ensued, from the dexterous and expeditious manner in which the wounded parts were excised by Mr. Beith, the assistant-surgeon;

and afterwards any poison that might remain being sucked out by one of the comrades of the wounded men. From this position, however, they retreated as our force increased, and could not again muster courage to rally. Their loss must have been considerable; ours might have been light, had poor old Patingi Ali attended to orders.

It appears that the Patingi (over-confident, and probably urged on by Mr. Steward, who, unknown to me, was concealed in Ali's boat when application was made to me by that chief for permission to proceed in advance for the purpose of reconnoitring), instead of falling back, as particularly directed by me on the first appearance of any of the enemy, made a dash, followed by his little division of boats, through the narrow pass above described; having entered which, large rafts of bamboo were launched across the river, so as to cut off his retreat. Six large war-prahus, probably carrying 100 men each, then bore down—three on either side—on his devoted followers; and one only of a crew of seventeen that manned his boat escaped to tell the tale. When last seen by our advanced boats, Mr. Steward and Patingi Ali were in the act (their own boats sinking) of boarding the enemy. They were doubtless overpowered and killed, with twenty-nine others, who lost their lives on this occasion. Our wounded in all amounted to fifty-six.

A few miles higher up was the town and capital of Karangan, which place it was their business to defend, and mine to destroy, which I succeeded in effecting without further opposition. We ascended a short distance above this, but found the river impracticable for the further progress of the boats; but our object having been achieved, the expedition may be said to have closed, as no more resistance was offered; and we dropped leisurely down the river, and that evening reached our resting-place of the previous night: though, having burnt the house in the morning, we were obliged to sleep in our boats, with a strong guard on shore.

Attempts were made to molest the native boats by hurling spears into them from the jungle under cover of the night; but after a few discharges of musketry the enemy retired, leaving us to enjoy another stormy and rainy night as we best could.

On the 20th we reached the steamer, where we remained quiet all the next day, attending to the wounded, and ascertaining the exact extent of our loss. On the 22d we again reached Patusen. We found every thing in the same wretched state as when we left; and a pile of firewood, previously cut for the use of the steamer, had not been removed. After dark a storm of thunder, lightning, and heavy rain, came on as usual, and with it a few mishaps. A boat belonging to the old Tumangong had been capsized by the bore, by which his plunder, including a large brass gun, was lost, and the crew with difficulty saved their lives. At eight we heard the report of a gun, which was again repeated much nearer at nine; and before a signal-rocket could be fired, or a light shewn, we were astonished by being hailed by the boats of a British man-of-war; and the next moment Captain Sir E. Belcher, having been assisted by a rapid tide, came alongside the steamer with the welcome news of having brought our May letters from England. It appears that, on the arrival of the Samarang off the ·Morotaba, Sir Edward heard of the loss we had sustained; and, with his usual zeal and activity, came at once to our assistance, having brought his boats no less than 120 miles in about thirty hours. At the moment of his joining us our second mishap occurred. The night, as previously mentioned, was pitch dark, and a rapid current running, when the cry of a man overboard caused a sensation difficult to describe. All available boats were immediately despatched in search; and soon afterwards we were cheered by the sound of "all right." It appears that the news of the arrival of the mail was not long in spreading throughout our little fleet; when Mr. D'Aeth, leaving the first cutter in a small sampan, capsized in coming alongside the steamer; the man in the bow (who composed the crew) saved himself by catching hold of the nearest boat: Mr. D'Aeth would have been drowned had he not been an excellent swimmer. This was not the last of our mishaps; for we had no sooner arranged ourselves and newly-arrived visitors from the Samarang comfortably on board the steamer from the pelting rain, than the accustomed and quick ear of Mr Brooke heard the cry of natives in distress; and jumping into his Singapore sampan, pushed off to their assistance—returning immediately afterwards, having picked up three, half-drowned, of our Dyak followers, whom he had found clinging to the floating trunk of a tree. They too had been capsized by the bore; when, out of eleven composing the crew, only these three were saved— although invariably expert swimmers.

On the 23d, after waiting to obtain meridian observations, we moved down as far as the mouth of the river Linga; and then despatched one of our Malay chiefs to the town of Bunting to summon Seriff Jaffer to a conference. This, however, he declined on a plea of ill health, sending assurance, at the same time, of his good-will and inclination to assist us in our endeavours to suppress piracy.

On the night of the 24th we once again reached Sarāwak. Here the rejoicings of the previous year, when we returned from a successful expedition, were repeated; and I received information that Seriff Sahib had taken refuge in the Linga river, where, assisted by Seriff Jaffer, he was again collecting his followers. No time was to be lost; and on the 28th, with the addition of the Samarang's boats, we once more started, to crush, if possible, this persevering and desperate pirate; and, in the middle of the night, came to an anchor inside the Linga river.

When our expedition had been watched safely outside the Batang Lupar, on its return to Sarāwak, all those unfortunate families that had concealed themselves in the jungle, after the destruction of the different towns of Patusen and Undop, had emerged from their hiding-places, and, embarking on rafts, half-ruined boats, or, in short, any thing that would float, were in the act of tiding and working their passage towards the extensive and flourishing town of Bunting—and their dismay can well be imagined, when, at daylight on the morning of the 29th, they found themselves carried by the tide close alongside the long black terror-spreading steamer, and in the midst of our augmented fleet. Escape to them was next to hopeless; nor did the softer sex seem much to mind the change—probably thinking that to be swallowed up by the white man was not much worse than dying in the jungle of starvation. I need not say that, instead of being molested, they were supplied with such provisions and assistance as our means would permit us to afford, and allowed to pass quietly on; in addition to which we despatched several of our native followers into the Batang Lupar to inform the poor fugitives that our business was with the chiefs and instigators of piracy, and not to molest the misguided natives.

With the ebb-tide a large number of boats came down from the town—the news of our arrival having reached them during the night—containing the principal chiefs, with assurances of their pacific intentions, and welcoming us with presents of poultry, goats, fruit, &c., which we accepted, paying them, either in barter or hard dollars, the fair market-price. They assured us that Seriff Sahib should not be received among them; but that they had heard of his having arrived at Pontranini, on a small tributary stream, some fifty miles above their town. We immediately decided on proceeding in pursuit before he could have time to establish himself in any force. It was also evident that the Balow Dyaks, who inhabit this part of the country, were decidedly in favour of our operations against Seriff Sahib, although afraid—on account of Seriff Jaffer and his Malays—to express their opinions openly. We also ascertained that Macota, with a remnant of his followers, was hourly expected in the mouth of the river, from the jungle, into which he had been driven during the fight on the Undop heights. Knowing that it would fare badly with this treacherous and cunning, although now harmless chief, should he fall into the hands of any of our native followers, I despatched two boats to look out for and bring him to us alive. This they succeeded in doing, securing him in a deep muddy jungle, into which he had thrown himself upon perceiving the approach of our men. Leaving him a prisoner on board the Phlégethon, we, with the flood-tide, pushed forward in pursuit of Seriff Sahib.

For two days we persevered in dragging our boats, for the distance of twenty miles, up a small jungly creek, which, to all appearance, was impassable for any thing but canoes. But it had the desired effect, proving to the natives what determination could achieve in accomplishing our object, even beyond the hopes of our sanguine Balow Dyak guides. The consequence was, that Seriff Sahib made a final and precipitate retreat, across the mountains, in the direction of the Pontiana river. So close were we on his rear—harassed as he was by the Balow Dyaks, who had refused him common means of subsistence — that he threw away his sword, and left behind him a child whom he had hitherto carried in the jungle; and this once-dreaded chief was now driven, single and unattended, out of the reach of doing any further mischief.

The boats returned, and took up a formidable position off the town of Bunting, where we summoned Seriff Jaffer to a conference. To this he was obliged to attend, as the natives had learnt that we were not to be trifled with, and would have forced him on board rather than have permitted their village to have been destroyed. With Pangeran Budrudeen as the representative of the Sultan, Seriff Jaffer was obliged to resign all pretensions to the government of the province over which he had hitherto held sway, since it was considered, from his being a Malay and from his relationship to Seriff Sahib, that he was an unsafe person to be entrusted with so important a post.

A second conference on shore took place, at which the chiefs of all the surrounding country attended, when the above sentence was confirmed. On this occasion I had the satisfaction of witnessing what must have been—from the effect I observed it to have produced on the hearers—a splendid piece of oratory, delivered by Mr. Brooke in the native tongue, with a degree of fluency I had never witnessed before, even in a Malay. The purport of it, as I understood, was, to point out emphatically the horrors of piracy on the one hand, which it was the determination of the British government to suppress, and on the other hand, the blessings arising from peace and trade, which it was equally our wish to cultivate; and it concluded by fully explaining, that the measures lately adopted by us against piracy were for the protection of all the peaceful communities along the coast. So great was the attention bestowed during the delivery of this speech that the dropping of a pin might have been heard.

From these people many assurances were received of their anxiety and willingness to co-operate with us in our laudable undertaking; and one and all were alike urgent that the government of their river should be transferred to the English.

On the 4th September, the force again reached Sarāwak; and thus terminated a most successful expedition against the worst pirates on the coast of Borneo.

Another conference with Muda Hassim took place, and I subsequently quitted Sarāwak for Singapore, intending to re-provision the Dido at that port, and then return to Sarāwak, in order to convey the Rajah and his suite to Borneo Proper. At Singapore, however, I found orders for England, and sailed accordingly; but the service alluded to was readily performed by Sir Edward Belcher, in H. M. S. Samarang, accompanied by the H. C.'s steamer Phlegethon.

On my return to England I had the gratification to learn that Mr. Brooke had been appointed agent for the British government in Borneo, and that Captain Bethune, R.N., C.B., had been despatched on special service to that island: events I cannot but consider of great importance to the best interests of humanity, and to the extension of British commerce throughout the Malayan Archipelago.

CHAPTER VI.

Later portion of Mr. Brooke's Journal. Departure of Capt. Keppel, and arrival of Sir E. Belcher. Mr. Brooke proceeds with Muda Hassim, in the Samarang, to Borneo. Labuan examined. Returns to Sarāwak. Visit of Lingire, a Sarebus chief. The Dyaks of Tumma and Bandar Cassim. Meets an assembly of Malays and Dyaks. Arrival of Lingi, as a deputation from the Sakarran chiefs. The Malay character. Excursion up the country. Miserable effects of excess in opium-smoking. Picturesque situation of the Sow village of Ra-at. Nawang. Feast at Ra-at. Returns home. Conferences with Dyak chiefs.

THE return to England of Captain Bethune, C.B., bringing with him a further portion of Mr. Brooke's Journal to my charge, enables me to afford my readers some interesting details relative to the important events that have occurred in Borneo subsequent to my departure from Sarāwak.

"*January*, 1845.—The departure of the Dido left me sad and lonely, for Captain Keppel had been really my companion and friend; and he so thoroughly entered into my views for the suppression of piracy, and made them his own, that I may not expect any successor to act with the same vigour and the same decision. Gallant Didos! I would ask no further aid or protection than I received from you. Sir Edward Belcher, with the Phlegethon in company, arrived not long after the Dido's departure, and conveyed the Rajah Muda Hassim and his train to Borneo Proper. H.M.S. Samarang and Phlegethon visited and examined Labuan, and proceeded thence to Ambun. Ambun is a miserable village ; and it at once gave the lie to the report of a European female being there in captivity, for no *poor Orang Kaya* could retain such a prize. The inhabitants of Ambun are Badjows, and the country people or Dyaks of the interior are called Dusuns, or villagers. I saw many of them, and they appeared a gentle mild race, and far less warlike by account than our Dyaks. They are not tattooed, and the sumpitan is unknown amongst them. Leaving Ambun, which is situated in a pretty bay, we proceeded to Tampasuk, a considerable town, inhabited by Illanuns and Badjows. This is a piratical town; and I was informed by an Arab in captivity there that scarcely a week passes without strife and contention amongst themselves. There likewise I received information respecting the Balagnini, the great pirates of these seas. They are represented as inhabiting numerous small islands in the vicinity of Sooloo: their origin is Badjow. I apprehend there would be little difficulty in breaking their power, and curing their propensity to piracy.

"This cruise being over, I established myself quietly at Sarāwak. The country is peaceable; trade flourishes; the Dyaks are content; the Malays greatly increased in number—in short, all goes well. I received a visit from Lingire, a Dyak chief of Sarebus. At first he was shy and somewhat suspicious; but a little attention soon put him at his ease. He is an intelligent man; and I hail with pleasure his advent to Sarāwak, as the dawn of a friendship with the two pirate tribes. It is not alone for the benefit of these tribes that I desire to cultivate their friendship, but for the greater object of penetrating the interior through their means. There are no Malays there to impede our progress by their lies and their intrigues; and, God willing, these rivers shall be the great arteries by which civilisation shall be circulated to the heart of Borneo.

"14*th*.—The Dyaks of Tumma, a runaway tribe from Sadong, came down last night, as Bandar Cassim of Sadong wishes still to extract property from them. Bandar Cassim I believe to be a weak man, swayed by stronger-headed and worse rascals; but, now that Seriff Sahib and Muda Hassim are no longer in the country, he retains no excuse for oppressing the poor Dyaks. Si Nankan and Tumma have already flown, and most of the other tribes are ready to follow their example, and take refuge in Sarāwak. I have fully explained to the Bandar that he will lose all his

Dyaks if he continues his system of oppression, and more especially if he continues to resort to that most hateful system of seizing the women and children.

"I had a large assembly of natives, Malay and Dyaks, and held forth many good maxims to them. At present, in Sarāwak, we have Balows and Sarebus, mortal enemies; Lenaar, our extreme tribe, and our new Sadong tribe of Tumma. Lately we had Kantoss, from near Sarambow, in the interior of Pontiana; Undops, from that river; and Badjows, from near Lantang—tribes which had never thought of Sarāwak before, and perhaps never heard the name. Oh, for power to pursue the course pointed out!

"16th.—The Julia arrived, much to my relief; and Mr. Low, a botanist and naturalist, arrived in her. He will be a great acquisition to our society, if devoted to these pursuits. The same day that the Julia entered, the Ariel left the river. I dismissed the Tumma Dyaks; re-warned Bandar Cassim of the consequences of his oppression; and had a parting interview with Lingire. I had another long talk with Lingire, and did him honour by presenting him with a spear and flag, for I believe he is true, and will be useful; and this Orang Kaya Pa-muncha, the most powerful of these Dyaks, must be mine. Lingire described to me a great fight he once had with the Kayans, on which occasion he got ninety-one heads, and forced a large body of them to retire with inferior numbers. I asked him whether the Kayans used the sumpitan? he answered, 'Yes.' 'Did many of your men die from the wounds?' 'No; we can cure them.' This is one more proof in favour of Mr. Crawfurd's opinion that this poison is not sufficiently virulent to destroy life when the arrow is (as it mostly is) plucked instantly from the wound.

"26th.—Lingi, a Sakarran chief, arrived, deputed (as he asserted, and I believe truly) by the other chiefs of Sakarran to assure me of their submission and desire for peace. He likewise stated, that false rumours spread by the Malays agitated the Dyaks; and the principal rumour was, that they would be shortly attacked again by the white men. These rumours are spread by the Sariki people, to induce the Sakarrans to quit their river and take refuge in the interior of the Rejong; and once there, the Sakarrans would be in a very great measure at the mercy of the Sariki people. This is a perfect instance of Malay dealing with the Dyaks; but in this case it has failed, as the Sakarrans are too much attached to their country to quit it. I am inclined to believe their professions; and at any rate it is convenient to do so and to give them a fair trial.

"28th.—How is it to be accounted for, that the Malays have so bad a character with the public, and yet that the few who have had opportunities of knowing them well speak of them as a simple and not unamiable people? With the vulgar, the idea of a Malay—and by the Malay he means the entire Polynesian race, with the exception of the Javanese—is that of a treacherous bloodthirsty villain; and I believe the reason to be, that from our first intercourse to the traders of the present time, it is the Pangerans or Rajahs of the country, with their followers, who are made the standard of Malay character. These Rajahs, born in the purple, bred amid slaves and fighting-cocks, inheriting an undisputed power over their subjects, and under all circumstances, whether of riches or poverty, receiving the abject submission of those around their persons, are naturally the slaves of their passions—haughty, rapacious, vindictive, weak, and tenacious unto death of the paltry punctilio of their court. The followers of such Rajahs it is needless to describe;— they are the tools of the Rajah's will, and more readily disposed for evil than for good; unscrupulous, cunning, intriguing, they are prepared for any act of violence. We must next contrast these with a burly independent trader, eager after gain, probably not over-scrupulous about the means of obtaining it, ignorant of native character, and heedless of native customs and native etiquette. The result of such a combination of ingredients causes an explosion on the slightest occasion. The European is loud, contemptuous, and abusive; the Malay cool and vindictive. The regal dignity has been insulted; the Rajah has received "shame" before his court; evil counsellors are at hand to whisper the facility of revenge, and the advantages to be derived from it. The consequence too frequently follows — the captain and crew are krissed, and their vessel seized and appropriated. The repeated tragedy shocks the European mind; and the Malay received, and continues to this day to receive, a character for treachery and bloodthirstiness. Even in these common cases an allowance must be made for the insults received, which doubtless on numerous occasions were very gross, and such flagrant violations of native customs as to merit death in native eyes; and we must bear in mind, that we never hear but one side of the tale, or only judge upon a bloody fact. It is from such samples of Malays that the general character is given by those who have only the limited means of trade for forming a judgment; but those who have known the people of the interior and lived amongst them, far removed from the influence of their Rajahs, have given a very different character of the people. Simple in their habits, they are neither treacherous nor bloodthirsty; cheerful, polite, hospitable, gentle in their manners, they live in communities with fewer crimes and fewer punishments than most other people of the globe. They are passionately fond of their children, and indulgent even to a fault; and the ties of family relationship and good feeling continue in force for several generations. The feeling of the Malay, fostered by education, is acute, and his passions are roused if shame be put upon him; indeed, this dread of shame amounts to a disease; and the evil is, that it has taken a wrong direction, the dread of shame being more of exposure or abuse, than shame or contrition for any offence.

"I have always found them good-tempered and obliging, wonderfully amenable to authority, and quite as sensible of benefits conferred, and as grateful, as other people of more favoured countries. Of course there is a reverse to this picture. The worst feature of Malay character is the want of all candour or openness, and the restless spirit of cunning intrigue which animates them, from the highest to the lowest. Like other Asiatics, truth is a rare quality amongst them. They are superstitious, somewhat inclined to deceit in the ordinary concerns of life, and they have neither principle nor conscience when they have the means of oppressing an infidel, and a Dyak who is their inferior in civilisation and intellect.

"If this character of the Malay be summed up, it will be anything but a bad one on the whole; it will present a striking contrast to the conduct and character of their Rajahs and followers, and I think will convince any impartial inquirer that it is easily susceptible of improvement. One of the most fertile sources of confusion is, classing at one time all the various nations of the Archipelago under the general name of Malay, and at another restricting the same term to one people, not more ancient, not the fountain-head of the others, who issued from the centre of Sumatra, and spread themselves in a few parts of the Archipelago.

"The French, the German, the English, Scotch, and Irish, are not more different in national character than the Malay, the Javanese, the Bugis, the Illanun, and the Dyak; and yet all these are ungeneralisingly called Malay, and a common character bestowed upon them. It would be as wise and as sensible to speak of an European character.

" 31st.—Started on a short excursion up the country, and slept at Siniawan. Here I found a young Pangeran (who came from Sambas with Mr. Hupé, a German missionary) enchained in the delights of opium. He left Sarāwak for Sambas two months since, proceeded five hours' journey, and has since been smoking the drug and sleeping alternately. His life passes thus: between four and five he wakes, yawns, and smokes a pipe or two, which fits him for the labours of taking his guitar and playing for an hour. Then follows a slightly tasted meal, a pipe or two succeeds, and content and merriment for another hour or two. About eight o'clock the gentleman reclines, and pipe succeeds pipe till, towards daylight, he sinks intoxicated and stupid on his pillow, to wake up again in due course to play again the same part.

Poor wretch! two months of this life of dissipation have reduced him to a shadow—two more months will consign him to his grave.

"*Feb.* 1*st.*—Started after breakfast and paddled against a strong current past Tundong, and, some distance above, left the main stream and entered the branch to the right, which is narrower, and rendered difficult of navigation by the number of fallen trees which block up the bed, and sometimes obliged us to quit our boat, and remove all the kajang covers, so as to enable us to haul the boat under the huge trunks. The main stream was rapid and turbid, swollen by a fresh, and its increase of waters blocked up the waters of the tributary, so as to render the current inconsiderable. The Dyaks have thrown several bridges across the rivers, which they effect with great ingenuity; but I was surprised on one of these bridges to observe the traces of the severe flood which we had about a fortnight since. The water on that occasion must have risen twenty feet perpendicularly, and many of the trees evidently but recently fallen, are the effects of its might. The walk to Rāt, or Ra-at, is about two miles along a decent path. Nothing can be more picturesque than the hill and the village. The former is a huge lump (I think of granite), almost inaccessible, with bold bare sides rising out of a rich vegetation at the base, and crowned with trees. The height is about 500 feet; and about a hundred feet lower is a shoulder of the hill on which stands the eagle-nest-like village of Ra-at, the ascent to which is like climbing by a ladder up the side of a house. This is one of the dwelling-places of the Sow Dyaks, a numerous but dispersed tribe. Their chief, or Orang Kaya, is an imbecile old man, and the virtual headship is in the hands of Nimok, of whom more hereafter. Our friends seemed pleased to see us, and Nimok apologised for so few of his people being present, as the harvest was approaching; but being anxious to give a feast on the occasion of my first visit to their tribe, it was arranged that to-morrow I should shoot deer, and the day following return to the mountain. The views on either side from the village are beautiful—one view enchanting from its variety and depth, more especially when lighted up by the gleam of a showery sunshine, as I first saw it. Soon, however, after our arrival, the prospect was shut out by clouds, and a soaking rain descended, which lasted for the greater part of the night.

" 2d.—Started after breakfast, and after a quiet walk of about three hours through a pleasant country of alternate hill and valley, we saw the valley of Nawang below us. Nawang is the property of the Singè Dyaks, and is cultivated by poor families, at the head of which is Niarak. The house contained three families, and our party was distributed amongst them, ourselves, *i. e.* Low,

Crookshank, and myself, occupying one small apartment with a man, his wife, and daughter. The valley presented one of the most charming scenes to be imagined—a clearing amid hills of moderate elevation, with the distant mountains in the background; a small stream ran through it, which, being dammed in several places, enables the cultivator to flood his padi-fields. The padi looked beautifully green. A few palms and plantains fringed the farm at intervals, whilst the surrounding hills were clothed in their native jungle. Here and there a few workmen in the fields heightened the effect; and the scene, as evening closed, was one of calm repose, and, I may say, of peace. The cocoa-nut, the betel, the sago, and the gno or gomati, are the four favourite palms of the Dyaks. In their simple mode of life, these four trees supply them many necessaries and luxuries. The sago furnishes food; and, after the pith has been extracted, the outer part forms a rough covering for the rougher floor, on which the farmer sleeps. The leaf of the sago is preferable for the roofing of houses to the nibong. The gomati, or gno, gives the black fibre which enables the owner to manufacture rope or cord for his own use; and over and above, the toddy of this palm is a luxury daily enjoyed. When we entered, this toddy was produced in large bamboos, both for our use and that of our attendant Dyaks; I thought it, however, very bad. In the evening we were out looking for deer, and passed many a pleasant spot which once was a farm, and which will become a farm again. These the Dyaks called rapack, and these are the favourite feeding-grounds of the deer. To our disappointment we did not get a deer, which we had reckoned on as an improvement to our ordinary dinner-fare. A sound sleep soon descended on our party, and the night passed in quiet; but it is remarkable how vigilant their mode of life renders the Dyak. Their sleep is short and interrupted; they constantly rise, blow up the fire, and look out on the night: it is rarely that some or other of them are not on the move.

" Yearly the Dyaks take new ground for their farm; yearly they fence it in, and undergo the labour of reclaiming new land; for seven years the land lies fallow, and then may be used again. What a waste of labour! more especially in these rich and watered valleys, which, in the hands of the Chinese, might produce two crops yearly.

"3d.—Took leave of this pleasant valley, and by another and shorter road than we came reached Ra-at. We arrived in good time on the hill, and found every thing prepared for a feast. There was nothing new in this feast. A fowl was killed with the usual ceremony; afterwards a hog. The hog is paid for by the company at a price commensurate with its size: a split bamboo is passed round the largest part of the body, and knots tied on it at given distances; and according to the number of these knots are the number of pasus of padi for the price.

" Our host of Nawang, Niarak, arrived to this feast with a plentiful supply of toddy; and before the dance commenced, we were requested to take our seats. The circumstances of the tribe, and the ability of Nimok, rendered this ceremony interesting to me. The Sow tribe has long been split into four parties, residing at different places. Gunong Sow, the original locality, was attacked by the Sakarran Dyaks, and thence Nimok and his party retired to Ra-at. A second smaller party subsequently located at or near Bow, as being preferable; whilst the older divisions of Jaguen and Ahuss lived at the places so named. Nimok's great desire was to gather together his scattered tribe, and to become *de facto* its head. My presence and the Datus' was a good opportunity for gathering the tribe; and Nimok hoped to give them the impression that we countenanced his proposition. The dances over, Nimok pronounced an oration: he dwelt on the advantages of union; how desirous he was to benefit his tribe; how constantly it was his custom to visit Sarāwak in order to watch over the interests of the tribe—the trouble was his, the advantage theirs; but how, without union, could they hope to gain any advantage—whether the return of their remaining captive women, or any other? He proposed this union; and that, after the padi was ripe, they should all live at Ra-at, where, as a body, they were always ready to obey the commands of the Tuan Besar or the Datu.

"This was the substance of Nimok's speech. But the effect of his oratory was not great; for the Bow, and other portions of the tribe, heard coldly his proposition, though they only opposed it in a few words. It was evident they had no orator at all a match for Nimok: a few words from Niana drew forth a second oration. He glanced at their former state; he spoke with animation of their enemies, and dwelt on their great misfortune at Sow; he attacked the Singè as the cause of these misfortunes; and spoke long and eloquently of things past, of things present, and things to come. He was seated the whole time; his voice varied with his subject, and was sweet and expressive; his action was always moderate, principally laying down the law with his finger on the mats. Niarak, our Singè friend, attempted a defence of his tribe; but he had drunk too freely of his own arrack; and his speech was received with much laughter, in which he joined. At this juncture I retired, after saying a few words; but the talk was kept up for several hours after, amid feasting and drinking.

"4th.—After breakfast, walked to our boats, and at six P. M. reached home, just in time; weather very rainy.

"*10th.*—Nothing to remark in these days, except the ordinary course of business and of life.

"*13th.*—The Tumangong returned from Sadong, and brought me a far better account of that place than I had hoped for. It appears that they really are desirous to govern well, and to protect the Dyaks; and fully impressed with the caution I gave them, that unless they protect and foster their tribes, they will soon lose them from their removal to Sarāwak.

"One large tribe, the Maluku, a branch of the Sibnowans, are, it appears, very desirous of being under my protection. It is a tempting offer, and I should like to have them; but I must not deprive the rulers of Sadong of the means of living comfortably, and the power of paying revenue. Protect them I both can and will. There are great numbers of Sarāwak people at Sadong, all looking out for birds-nests; new caves have been explored; mountains ascended for the first time in the search. It shews the progress of good government and security, and, at the same time, is characteristic of the Malay character. They will endure fatigue, and run risks, on the chance of finding this valuable commodity; but they will not labour steadily, or engage in pursuits which would lead to fortune by a slow progress.

"*15th.*—Panglima Laksa, the chief of the Undop tribe, arrived, to request, as the Badjows and Sakarrans had recently killed his people, that I would permit him to retort. At the same time came Abong Kapi, the Sakarran Malay, with eight Sakarran chiefs, named Si Miow, one of the heads, and the rest Tadong, Lengang, Barunda, Badendang, Si Bùnie, Si Ludum, and Kuno, the representatives of other heads. Nothing could be more satisfactory than the interview, just over. They denied any knowledge or connexion with the Badjows, who had killed some Dyaks at Undop, and said all that I could desire. They promised to obey me, and look upon me as their chief; they desired to trade, and would guarantee any Sarāwak people who came to their river; but they could not answer for all the Dyaks in the Batang Lupar. It is well known, however, that the Batang Lupar Dyaks are more peaceable than those of Sakarran, and will be easily managed; and as for the breaking out of these old feuds, it is comparatively of slight importance, compared to the grand settlement; for as our influence increases we can easily put down the separate sticks of the bundle. There is a noble chance, if properly used! It may be remarked that many of their names are from some peculiarity of person, or from some quality. Tadong is a poisonous snake; but, on inquiry, I found the young chief so named had got the name from being black. They are certainly a fine-looking race.

"17*th*.—Plenty of conferences with the Sakarran chiefs; and, as far as I can judge, they are sincere in the main, though some reserves there may be. Treachery I do not apprehend from them; but, of course, it will be impossible, over a very numerous, powerful, and warlike tribe, to gain such an ascendancy of a sudden as at once to correct their evil habits."

Here again Mr. Brooke appears to have been placed on the horns of a dilemma by his ignorance of the views of the British Government. Had his position in Borneo been certain—had he either been supported or deserted—his path of policy would have been clear; whereas he evidently did not know what the morrow would bring forth; whether it would find him with an English force at his back, or abandoned to his own resources.

CHAPTER VII.

Arrival of Captain Bethune and Mr. Wise. Mr. Brooke appointed her Majesty's Agent in Borneo. Sails for Borneo Proper. Muda Hassim's measures for the suppression of piracy. Defied by Seriff Houseman. Audience of the Sultan, Muda Hassim, and the Pangerans. Visit to Labuan. Comparative eligibility of Labuan and Balambangan for settlement. Coal discovered in Labuan. Mr. Brooke goes to Singapore and visits Admiral Sir T. Cochrane. The upas-tree. Proceeds with the Admiral to Borneo Proper. Punishment of Pangeran Usop. The battle of Malludu. Seriff Houseman obliged to fly. Visit to Balambangan. Mr. Brooke parts with the Admiral, and goes to Borneo Proper. An attempt of Pangeran Usop defeated. His flight, and pursuit by Pangeran Budrudeen. Triumphant reception of Mr. Brooke in Borneo. Returns to Saráwak.

" *February 25th.*—Borneo River, H. M. S. Driver. Scarcely, on the 17th, had I finished writing, when a boat from her Majesty's steamer Driver, bringing Captain Bethune and my friend Wise, arrived. How strange, the same day and almost the same hour I was penning my doubts and difficulties, when a letter arrives from Lord Aberdeen appointing me confidential Agent in Borneo to her Majesty, and directing me to proceed to the capital, with a letter addressed to the Sultan and the Rajah Muda Hassim, in reply to the documents requesting the assistance of the British government to effect the suppression of piracy!

"My friend Wise I was glad to see; and a few hours' conversation convinced me how greatly I have been indebted to his exertions for success and my present position. His knowledge of trade, his cheerfulness regarding our pecuniary future, all impart confidence. Thus I may say, without much self-flattery, that the first wedge has been driven which may rive Borneo open to commerce and civilisation, which may bestow happiness on its inhabitants. Captain Bethune is commissioned to report on the best locality for a settlement or station on the N.W. coast. I will only say here, that no other person's appointment would have pleased me so well: he is intelligent, educated, and liberal, and in concert with him I am too happy to work.

"On the 18th February the Driver arrived; on the 21st left Sarāwak, and at noon of the 24th arrived at the anchorage in Borneo river, having towed the gun-boat against the N.E. monsoon. Mr. Williamson was despatched to Borneo, and found all right. They were delighted with our coming and our mission, and the Sultan himself has laid aside his fears. A few presents have been sent, which will delight the natives; and all will prosper.

"*26th.*—Budrudeen arrived, and from him I learned the politics of Borneo since my last visit, when Muda Hassim was reinstated in authority.

"As my mission refers more especially to piracy, I may here notice Muda Hassim's measures relative to that subject. Shortly after his arrival he addressed a letter to the Illanuns of Tampasuk, informing them of the engagement with the English to discourage and suppress piracy, advising them to desist, and ordering them not to visit Borneo until he (Muda Hassim) was convinced they were pirates no longer. This is good and candid. Muda Hassim at the same time requested Seriff Schaik to address a communication to Seriff Houseman of Malludu, acquainting him with his engagements, and the resolve of the Europeans to suppress piracy; adding that he was friends with the English, and no man could be friends with the English who encouraged piracy. The answer to this letter of Seriff Schaik, as far as I have yet learned, is a positive defiance. Three months since, I am informed, a brig or schooner was wrecked at a place called Mangsi, and she has been completely plundered and burned by Seriff Houseman: her cargo consisted of red woollens, fine white cloths, Turkey red cotton handkerchiefs, tin, pepper, Malacca canes, rattans, &c. &c. This evidently is a vessel bound to China, whether English or not is doubtful: the crew have not been heard of or seen here, and it is to be hoped may have reached Manilla.

"*28th.*—Borneo, or Bruni city. Left the Driver at 9 A.M. in the gun-boat, with the pinnace and cutter in company: a fine breeze carried us to Pulo Chermin, and nearly the whole way to Pulo Combong, where we met with the state-boat bearing the letter. We entered the town straggling, and *the letter* having been received with firing of guns, banners displayed, and all the respect due to a royal communication, we were dragged in haste to the audience; the Sultan on his throne, Muda Hassim and every principal Pangeran waiting for us—Pangeran Usop to boot. The letter was read; twenty-one guns fired. I told them in all civility that I was deputed by her Majesty the Queen to express her feelings of good will, and to offer every assistance in repressing piracy in these seas. The Sultan stared. Muda Hassim said, "We are greatly indebted; it is good, very good." Then heated, and sunburnt, and tired, we took our leave, and retired to the house prepared for us.

"*March* 1*st*.—A long conference with Budrudeen, when, I believe, we exhausted all the important topics of Borneo politics: subsequently we visited Muda Hassim and the Sultan. The latter was profuse in his kind expressions, and inquired of the interpreter when the English would come to Labuan; adding, "I want to have the Europeans near me." On this head, however, he gained no information. The presents were given to the Sultan and Rajah.

"5*th*.—In the evening visited Muda Hassim, and heard news from Malludu, which, divested of exaggerations, amounted to this: that Seriff Houseman was ready to receive us; was fortified, and had collected a fleet of boats; and that if the English did not come and attack him, he would come and attack Borneo, because they were in treaty with Europeans. After leaving Muda Hassim, paid the Sultan a visit.

"10th.—I have nothing to say of our departure. Budrudeen accompanied us to the Mooarra, and thence, on Friday evening, we crossed to the anchorage of Labuan.

"12th.—Labuan. An island of about fifty feet high; twenty-five miles in circumference; woody; timber good; water from wells and a few small streams, which, after a drought, are dry; natives say, water never fails. Anchorage good for the climate; well protected from the N.E.; not extensive; situation of contemplated town low; climate healthy, *i. e.* the same as Borneo; soil, as far as seen, sandy or light sandy loam. Coal found near the extreme N.E. point: by native reports it is likewise to be found in many other places; traces of coal are frequent in the sandstone strata. Anchorage not difficult of defence against an European enemy; entrance sufficiently broad and deep between two islands, with a shoal: vide chart. The island of Labuan, for the purposes of refuge for shipwrecked vessels, of a windward post relative to China, for the suppression of piracy, and the extension of our trade, is well suited; it is no paradise; and any other island, with good climate, wood, and water, would suit as well. Its powerful recommendation is its being in the neighbourhood of an unwarlike and friendly people. There is no other island on the N.W. coast; and the abandoned Balambangan, to the northward of Borneo, is the only other place which could by possibility answer. The comparison between Balambangan and Labuan may be stated as follows. Balambangan, as a windward post relative to China, is superior; and it commands in time of war the inner passage to Manilla, and the eastern passages to China by the Straits of Makassar. Of its capabilities of defence we know nothing. It was surprised by the Sooloos. Its climate was not well spoken of. The island is larger than that of Labuan, and, as far as we know, has no coal. The great, and to me conclusive consideration against Balambangan is, that it is in the very nest of pirates, and surrounded by warlike and hostile people; and that to render it secure and effective, at least double the force would be necessary there than at Labuan. If Labuan succeeds and pays its own expenses, we might then take Balambangan; for the next best thing to a location on the main is to influence the people thereon by a succession of insular establishments. Yesterday we made an agreeable excursion to the N.E. point of Labuan; near the point it is picturesque, the cliffs are bold and cave-worn; the trees hang over the cliffs, or encroach on the intermediate sands, till they kiss the wave. Near a small cavern we discovered a seam of coal, which afforded us employment whilst Captain Bethune and Mr. Wise walked to obtain a view of the southern coast of the island.

"*Bruni, 21st May,* 1845.—After a longer time passed in Singapore than I wished, we at length started in the Phlegethon steamer for this city. At Singapore I had several interviews with Sir Thomas Cochrane.

"*22d.*—On the authority of Sulerman, an intelligent Meri man, I am told that the tree below the town is the real upas, called by the Meri men *tajim*—the Borneons call it *upas*. *Bina* (the name we formerly got from a Borneon for upas) is, by Sulerman's statement, a thin creeper, the root or stem of which, being steeped in water, is added to the upas to increase the poisonous quality—it is not, however, poisonous itself. There is another creeper likewise called bina, the leaves of which are steeped and mixed with the upas, instead of the stem of the first sort. This information may be relied on (in the absence of personal knowledge), as the man is of a tribe which uses the sumpitan, and is constantly in the habit of preparing the poison.

"*August* 8*th.*—Off Ujong Sapo, at the entrance of Borneo river. The time since I last added to my most desultory journal is easily accounted for. I have been at Singapore and Malacca, and am now anchored off Borneo Proper, with seven vessels, and an eighth is hourly expected. It is difficult with such a force to be moderate; and with Sir Thomas Cochrane's other duties and engagements, it is probably impossible to devote any length of time on this coast; yet moderation and time are the key-stones of our policy. I have settled all the ceremonial for a meeting between the Sultan and the Admiral.

"The Pangeran Budrudeen came on board H. M. S. Agincourt, with every circumstance of state and ceremony, and met the Admiral, I acting as interpreter. It was pleasing to witness his demeanour and bearing, which proved that in minds of a certain quality the power of command, though over savages, gives ease and freedom. The ship, the band, the marines, the guns, all excited Budrudeen's attention. On the 9th it is arranged that the Admiral shall meet the Sultan and the Rajah.

"*9th.*—In the course of the day, after the audience had terminated, the Admiral made his demand of reparation on the Sultan and Muda Hassim for the detention and confinement of two British subjects subsequent to their agreement with the British government. Of course the Sultan and the Rajah replied that they were not in fault, that the act was Pangeran Usop's, and that he was too powerful for them to enforce. If Sir Thomas Cochrane would punish him, they should be much obliged, as they desired to keep the treaty inviolate.

"10th.—Pangeran Usop had to be summoned; come he would not, and yet I was in hopes that, when he saw the overwhelming force opposed to him, his pride would yield to necessity. About 2 P.M. the steamers took up their positions; the marines were landed, every thing was prepared—yet no symptom of obedience. At length a single shot was fired from the Vixen by the Admiral's order through the roof of Usop's house, which was instantly returned, thus proving the folly and the temper of the man. In a few minutes his house was tenantless, having been overwhelmed with shot. Usop was a fugitive; the amount of mischief done inconsiderable, and no damage except to the guilty party. Twenty captured guns the Admiral presented to the Sultan and the Rajah; two he kept, from which to remunerate the two detained men. So far nothing could be more satisfactory. Usop has been punished severely, the treaty strictly enforced, and our supremacy maintained. No evil has been done except to the guilty; his house and his property alone have suffered, and the immediate flight has prevented the shedding of blood.

"11th.—At mid-day the Admiral with the Vixen and Nemesis went down the river, leaving the Pluto to me to follow in next day.

"12th.—This morning I visited the Sultan in

company with Muda Hassim. By twelve at night the Pluto was anchored in the creek at Labuan, and on the 13th I once more took up my quarters aboard the flag-ship.

"14th.—Wooding.

"16th.—Last evening anchored within the point called in the chart Sampormangio, or properly Sampang Mengayu, which, being translated, signifies piratical or cruising waiting-place. The weather was thick and squally, and it was late before the Dædalus and Vestal arrived with their tows the Nemesis and Pluto, the former frigate having carried away her mizen topmast.

"17th.—Squadron under weigh pretty early, getting into Malludu bay. After breakfast had a very heavy squall. Agincourt heeled to it, and sails of various sorts and sizes were blowing about in ribbons aboard some of the ships: afterwards brought up nearly off the Melow river.

"18th.—Vixen, Nemesis, Pluto, and boats, proceeded up the bay, and anchored as near as possible to the entrance of the Marudu, or Malludu river. The character of Malludu bay, generally, may be described as clear of danger, with high wooded banks on either side, till in the bight, when the land gets flat and mangrovy, and the water shallow, and where the mouths of several small rivers are seen, one of which is Malludu.

"19th.—On the 19th August was fought the celebrated battle of Malludu. The boats, 24 in number, and containing 550 marines and blue-jackets, having left the previous afternoon. As I was not present, I can say only what I heard from others, and from what I know from subsequently viewing the position. A narrow river with two forts mounting 11 or 12 heavy guns (and defended by from 500 to 1000 fighting men), protected by a strong and well-contrived boom, was the position of the enemy. Our boats took the bull by the horns, and indeed had little other choice; cut away part of the boom under a heavy fire; advanced, and carried the place in a fight protracted for fifty minutes. The enemy fought well and stood manfully to their guns; and a loss of six killed, two mortally and fifteen severely wounded, on our side, was repaid by a very heavy loss of killed and wounded on theirs. Gallant Gibbard[1] of the Wolverine fell mortally wounded whilst working at the boom, axe in hand. In short, the engagement was severe and trying to our men from the fire they were exposed to. At two minutes to nine, aboard Vixen, we heard the report of the first heavy gun, and it was a time of anxiety and uneasiness till the first column of black smoke proclaimed that the village was fired.

---

[1] Leonard Gibbard made his first trip to sea under my charge in 1834, when I commanded the Childers in the Mediterranean, and at that early age promised what he afterwards proved himself to be—a gallant officer and thorough seaman. Poor fellow! he was always a general favourite wherever he went.—H. K.

"I may here mention, that before the fight commenced, a flag of truce came from the enemy, and asked for me. Captain Talbot (in command) offered to meet Seriff Houseman either within or without the boom, provided his whole force was with him. Seriff Houseman declined; but offered (kind man!) to admit two gigs to be hauled over the boom. No sooner was this offer declined, and the flag returned the second time with a young Seriff, son of Seriff Layak of Bruni, than the enemy opened fire, which was promptly returned. Had Captain Talbot entered as proposed, I deem it certain he would never have quitted the place alive; for the Seriff and his followers had made themselves up to fight, and nothing but fight. Many chiefs were killed; two or three Seriffs in their large turbans and flowing robes; many Illanuns in their gay dresses and golden charms; many Badjows; many slaves — amongst them a captive Chinaman; many were wounded; many carried away; and many left on the ground dead or dying.

"*20th.* — On the evening of the 19th, a detachment of ten boats, with fresh men and officers, quitted the Vixen, and arrived at the forts shortly after daylight. I accompanied this party; and the work of destruction, well begun yesterday, was this day completed. Numerous proofs of the piracies of this Seriff came to light. The boom was ingeniously fastened with the chain-cable of a vessel of

300 or 400 tons; other chains were found in the town; a ship's long-boat; two ship's bells, one ornamented with grapes and vine-leaves, and marked 'Wilhelm Ludwig, Bremen;' and every other description of ship's furniture. Some half-piratical boats, Illanun and Balagnini, were burned; twenty-four or twenty-five brass guns captured; the iron guns, likewise stated to have been got out of a ship, were spiked and otherwise destroyed. Thus has Malludu ceased to exist; and Seriff Houseman's power received a fall from which it will never recover.

"Amid this scene of war and devastation was one episode which moved even harder hearts than mine. Twenty-four hours after the action, a poor woman, with her child of two years of age, was discovered in a small canoe; her arm was shattered at the elbow by a grape-shot; and the poor creature lay dying for want of water in an agony of pain, with her child playing around her and endeavouring to derive the sustenance which the mother could no longer give. This poor woman was taken on board the Vixen, and in the evening her arm was amputated. To have left her would have been certain death; so I was strongly for the measure of taking her to Saráwak, where she can be protected. To all my inquiries she answered, 'If you please to take me, I shall go. I am a woman, and not a man; I am a slave, and not a free woman: do as you like.' She stated too, positively, that she herself had seen Seriff Houseman wounded in the neck, and carried off; and her testimony is corroborated by two Manilla men, who, amongst others, ran away on the occasion, and sought protection from us, who likewise say that they saw the Seriff stretched out in the jungle, but they cannot say whether dead or wounded. The proof how great a number must have been killed and wounded on their part is, that on the following day ten dead men were counted lying where they fell; amongst them was Seriff Mahomed, the bearer of the flag of truce, who, though offered our protection, fought to the last, and in the agonies of death threw a spear at his advancing foes.

" The remnant of the enemy retired to Bungun; and it will be some time before we learn their real loss and position. It is needless here to say any thing on the political effects to be expected from the establishment of a government in Bruni, and the destruction of this worst of piratical communities. When I return to Bruni, and see how measures advance, I may mention the subject again; but I will venture here to re-urge, that mere military force, however necessary, cannot do what it is desirable should be done. Supervision and conciliation must go hand in hand with punishment; and we must watch that the snake does not again rear his head through our neglect. The key-stone is wanting as yet, and must be supplied if possible; we must, to back the gallant deeds of the Admiral and fleet, continue to pursue a steady course of measures. In the evening returned to the Vixen.

"21st.—The morning quiet. After breakfast under weigh, proceeded off the river Bankoka, where we found the Cruiser at anchor. As there was nothing to detain us, crossed over to the squadron—remained an hour aboard Agincourt; then rejoined Sir Thomas Cochrane aboard Vixen, and before dinner-time were at anchor in the north-east harbour of Balambangan. Our woman prisoner doing well, and pleased with the attention paid her.

"23d.—South-western harbour of Balambangan. Yesterday examined the N.E. harbour; a dreary-looking place, sandy and mangrovy, and the harbour itself filled with coral patches; here the remains of our former settlement were found—it is a melancholy and ineligible spot. The s.w. harbour is very narrow and cramped, with no fitting site for a town, on account of the rugged and unequal nature of the ground; and if the town were crammed in between two eminences, it would be deprived of all free circulation of air. Water is, I hear, in sufficient quantity, and good. On the whole, I am wretchedly disappointed with this island; it has one, and only one, recommendation, viz. that it is well situated in the Straits for trading and political purposes; in every other requisite, it is inferior to Labuan. Balambangan is commercially and politically well placed. Labuan, though inferior, is not greatly inferior in these points; the harbour, the aspect, the soil, are superior: it may probably be added, that the climate is superior likewise; and we must remember that those who had an opportunity of trying both places give the preference to Labuan.

"Then, on other points, Labuan has a clear advantage. It commands the coal; it is in the vicinity of a friendly people, and settlement may be formed with certainty at a moderate expense, and with small establishments. Can this be done at Balambangan? I own I doubt it; the people in the vicinity we know nothing of, but we shall find them in all probability hostile. The Sooloos we are already too well acquainted with. The Illanuns are in the vicinity. In the case of Labuan, the details of the first establishment (no small step) can be clearly seen and arranged; but I do not see my way regarding Balambangan. The matter is of secondary importance, but a languishing settlement at first is to be dreaded; food will be scarce, and houses difficult to build; whilst at Labuan the population of Bruni are at our disposal, and the government our own. I leave others to judge whether a superior (but somewhat similar) position, commercially and politically, will outweigh the other disadvantages mentioned, and repay us for the extra expenses of the establishment;

but, for myself, I can give a clear verdict in favour of Labuan.

"*24th.*—Buried poor Mr. East, of the Agincourt, on Balambangan. Gibbard, poor gallant fellow! was consigned to the deep a day or two before.

"*25th.*—A day of disaster and parting: the morning blowy, with an unpleasant sea. Vestal ran ashore on a coral-patch, but soon swung off. I was very sorry to part with the Agincourt. Farewell, gallant Agincourts! farewell, kind Admiral! farewell, the pride, pomp, and panoply of a flag-ship liner! My occupation's over for the present, and I retire with content to solitude and the jungle of Sarāwak. I step down the huge side, wave a parting adieu, jump on the Cruiser's deck—the anchor is weighed, and away we fly.

"*30th.*—Coming down in her Majesty's ship Cruiser, and now off Ujong Sapo. On our passage we had some good views of Kina Balow; and from various points, judging the distance by the chart, the angle of elevation gives the mountain not less than 12,000 feet and up to 14,000; the latter result agreeing with the computation of the Master of the Dædalus.

"*31st.*—Started for Bruni, and half-way met a boat with Pangeran Illudeen, bringing the news of the place. Two days after the Admiral and his steamers left, Pangeran Usop seized the hill behind his late house with 300 Kadiens, and commenced an attack on the town. Pangeran Budrudeen on this mustered about the like number and mounted the hill, and by a fire of musketry dislodged the enemy, who retired—stood again—were again defeated—and finally dispersed. This victory raised the courage of the Brunions, and a counter-attack was planned, when the arrival of her Majesty's ship Espiegle delayed them. As the officers of the Espiegle and the Rajah could not speak a word of each other's language, the boat only stayed a few hours, and went away in ignorance of the condition of the town. After her departure, Budrudeen gathered about a thousand men of all arms, with some hundred muskets; and leaving Bruni at three o'clock in the morning, reached the landing-place at 6 A.M., and at eight marched for Barŭkas, where they arrived at one o'clock. On the way the Kadiens humbled themselves, and begged their houses might be spared, which were spared accordingly. On reaching Barŭkas, they found Pangeran Usop had been deserted by the Kadiens, and was in no way expecting their coming. The few persons who remained fled ignominiously, Pangeran Usop shewing them the example; and his women, children, gold, and other property, fell into the hands of his victors. The same evening Budrudeen and his army returned to the city in triumph; and there can be no doubt these vigorous measures have not only settled them in power, but have likewise raised the spirits of their adherents, and awed the few who remain adverse. 'Never,' the Brunions exclaim, 'was such a war in Bruni. Pangeran Budrudeen fights like an European; the very spirit of the Englishman is in him; he has learned this at Sarāwak.' Fortune favoured Usop's escape. He fled to the sea-shore near Pulo Badukan, and there met a boat of his entering from Kimanis: he took possession and put out to sea, and returned with her to that place.

"Budrudeen we found in active preparation for pursuit. A dozen war-prahus were nearly ready for sea, and this force starts directly we depart.

"Budrudeen's vigour has given a stimulus to this unwarlike people, and he has gained so great a character—victory sits so lightly on his plume —that his authority will now be obeyed; whilst Usop, in consequence of his cowardly flight (for so they deem it), from the want of energy he has displayed, has lost character as well as wealth, and would scarce find ten men in Bruni to follow him. Unluckily for himself he was a great boaster in the days of his prosperity; and now the contrast of his past boasting with his present cowardice is drawn with a sneer. 'His mouth was brave,' they exclaim, 'but his heart timid.' 'He should have died as other great men have died, and not have received such shame; he should have amoked,[1] or

---

[1] *Anglice*, run-a-muck.

else given himself up for execution.' This seems to be the general impression in the city.

"My mind is now at rest about the fate of my friends; but I still consider a man-of-war brig coming here every month or two as of great importance; for it will be necessary for the next six months to consolidate the power of Muda Hassim and Budrudeen; and if, with the new order of things, they constantly see white faces, and find that they are quiet and inoffensive, the ignorant terror which now prevails will abate. Besides this, we might find the opportunity a favourable one for becoming acquainted with the Kadiens and the Marats, and giving them just impressions of ourselves; for I have no doubt that on the late occasion the Kadiens were worked upon by all kinds of false reports of the pale faces taking their lands, burning their houses, &c. &c. &c. We only see the effects; we do not see (until we become very well acquainted with them) the strings which move the passions of these people. The Kadiens are, however, an unwarlike and gentle race, and have now given in their submission to Muda Hassim. I do not mention the Sultan, because, as I before said, he is so imbecile that, as regards public affairs, he is a cipher: he will some day cease to be Sultan, and give place to a better man.

"Our interview with the Rajah, with Budrudeen, and all the other host of our acquaintance, was quite a triumph—they hot with their success, and we bringing the account of Malludu's sanguinary fight. Happy faces and wreathed smiles supplied the place of the anxious and doubtful expression which I had left them wearing. All vied in their attentions; fruit enough to fill a room— the luscious durian, the delicate mangosteen and lousch, the grateful rombusteen, the baluna, pitabu, mowha, plantain, &c. &c. were showered upon us from all quarters. The Rajah daily sent a dinner; all was rejoicing, and few or no clouds lowered in the distance. I was proud and happy; for I felt and feel that much of this has been owing to my exertions. I will not stop to say how or why; but I first taught them to respect and to confide in Englishmen, and no one else has yet untaught them this lesson.

"*September 3d.*—After parting interviews we quitted the city at two, and arrived aboard her Majesty's ship Cruiser at eight P.M. To-morrow morning we sail for Sarāwak, where, at any rate, I hope for rest for a month or two.

"*19th.*—Sarāwak. Thus concludes a large volume. Captain Bethune and myself, with Commander Fanshawe and a party of Cruisers, returned from a five days' excursion amongst the Dyaks, having visited the Suntah, Stang, Sigo, and Sanpro tribes. It was a progress; at each tribe there was dancing, and a number of ceremonies. White fowls waved, as I have before described, slaughtered, and the blood mixed with kuny-ĭt, a yellow root, &c. &c., which delightful mixture was freely scattered over them and their goods by me, holding in my hand a dozen or two women's necklaces. Captain Bethune has seen and can appreciate the Dyaks: to-morrow he leaves me, and most sorry shall I be to lose him. A better man or a better public servant is not to be found.

" Amongst my Dyak inquiries, I found out that the name of their god is Tuppa, and not Jovata, which they before gave me, and which they use but do not acknowledge. Tuppa is the great god; eight other gods were in heaven; one fell or descended into Java,—seven remained above; one of these is named Sakarra, who, with his companions and followers, is (or is in) the constellation of a cluster of stars, doubtless the Pleiades; and by the position of this constellation the Dyaks can judge good and bad fortune. If this cluster of stars be high in the heavens, success will attend the Dyak; when it sinks below the horizon, ill luck follows; fruit and crops will not ripen; war and famine are dreaded. Probably originally this was but a simple and natural division of the seasons, which has now become a gross superstition.

" The progress is ended; to-morrow I shall be left in the solitude and the quiet of the jungle: but, after witnessing the happiness, the plenty, the growing prosperity of the Dyak tribes, I can scarcely believe that I could devote my life to better purpose, and I dread that a removal might destroy what I have already done.

"We must now wait the decision of government with patience. Captain Bethune, in making his report, will have the advantage of real substantial personal knowledge. I esteem him highly; and regard him as a man of the most upright principles, who is not and will not be swayed in his duty by any considerations whatever. I am glad we are to stand the ordeal of such a man's inquiry."

CHAPTER VIII.

Borneo, its geographical bounds and leading divisions. British settlements in 1775. The province of Sarāwak formally ceded by the Sultan in perpetuity to Mr. Brooke its present ruler. General view of the Dyaks, the aborigines of Borneo. The Dyaks of Sarāwak, and adjoining tribes; their past oppression and present position.

I WILL now endeavour to make the reader better acquainted with the nature of a country and people so imperfectly known, by offering that general view of past events and present condition which will make the information respecting them more intelligible, as well as applicable to new circumstances and future measures.

By looking at the map, it will be seen that the island of Borneo extends over 11 degrees of latitude and the same of longitude, from 4^0 N. to 7^0 S., and 108^0 to 119^0 E. The N. W. coast is but thinly populated; and the natives who inhabit the banks of some of the beautiful rivers differ, as has been already stated, from each other in manners and customs, and have but little communication among themselves. The S., E., and N. E. coasts of Borneo are also but thinly inhabited, and very little known. There are various divisions of Malays, as well as different tribes of Dyaks, who live in an unsettled state, and occasionally make war on one another: their principal occupation, however, is piracy. The north part of the island was once in the possession of the East India Company, who had a settlement and factory on the island of Balambangan, which was attacked in 1775, when in a weak and unguarded state, by a powerful piratical tribe of Sooloos, who surprised the fort, put the sentries to death, and turned the guns on the troops, who were chiefly Buguese (or Bugis) Malays. Those who escaped got on board the vessels in the harbour, and reached the island of Labuan, near the mouth of the Borneo river; whilst the booty obtained by the pirates was estimated at 375,000*l.* From that time to this these atrocious pirates have never been punished, and still continue their depredations.

The remainder of the coast on the N.W. is now called Borneo Proper, to distinguish it from the name that custom has given to the whole island, the original name of which was Kalamantan, and Bruni that of the town now called Borneo, and which was probably the first part of the coast ever visited by Europeans, who extended the appellation throughout. The town of Borneo, situated on the river of that name, was, until the last few years, a port of some wealth, and carrying on an extensive trade, which has been ruined entirely by the rapacity of the Malay chiefs, who have now but little control over that part of Borneo Proper which lies to the northward of the river. The province of Sarāwak is situated at the s.w. end of Borneo Proper, and was formally ceded in perpetuity by the Sultan to Mr. Brooke in 1843, although he had possessed the almost entire management of the district for the two previous years. " It extends from Tanjong Datu (I quote from Mr. Brooke's description of his territory) to the entrance of the Samarahan river, a distance along the coast of about sixty miles in an E.S.E. direction, with an average breadth of fifty miles. It is bounded to the westward by the Sambas territory, to the southward by a range of mountains which separate it from the Pontiana river, and to the eastward by the Borneon territory of Sadong. Within this space there are several rivers and islands, which it is needless here to describe at length, as the account of the river of Sarāwak will answer alike for the rest. There are two navigable entrances to this river, and numerous smaller branches for boats, both to the westward and eastward; the two principal entrances combine at about twelve miles from the sea, and the river flows for twenty miles into the interior in a southerly and westerly direction, when it again forms two branches—one running to the right, the other to the left hand, as far as the mountain range.

Besides these facilities for water-communication, there exist three other branches from the easternmost entrance, called Morotaba, one of which joins the Samarahan river, and the two others flow from different points of the mountain range already mentioned. The country is diversified by detached mountains, and the mountain range has an elevation of about three thousand feet. The aspect of the country may be generally described as low and woody at the entrance of the rivers, except a few high mountains; but in the interior undulating in parts, and part presenting fine level plains. The climate may be pronounced healthy and cool, though for the six months from September to March a great quantity of rain falls. During my three visits to this place, which have been prolonged to eight months, and since residing here, we have been clear of sickness, and during the entire period not one of three deaths could be attributed to the effects of climate. The more serious maladies of tropical climates are very infrequent; from fever and dysentery we have been quite free, and the only complaints have been rheumatism, colds, and ague; the latter, however, attacked us in the interior, and no one has yet had it at Sarāwak, which is situated about twenty-five miles from the mouth of the river.

"The soil and productions of this country are of the richest description, and it is not too much to say, that, within the same given space, there are

VEGETABLE PRODUCTS. 167

not to be found the same mineral and vegetable riches in any land in the world. I propose to give a brief detail of them, beginning with the soil of the plains, which is moist and rich, and calculated for the growth of rice, for which purpose it was formerly cleared and used, until the distractions of the country commenced. From the known industry of the Dyaks, and their partiality to rice-cultivation, there can be little doubt that it would become an article of extensive export, provided security be given to the cultivator and a proper remuneration for his produce. The lower grounds, besides rice, are well adapted for the growth of sago, and produce canes, rattans, and forest-timber of the finest description for ship-building and other useful purposes. The Chinese export considerable quantities of timber from Sambas and Pontiana, particularly of the kind called Balean by the natives, or the lion-wood of the Europeans; and at this place it is to be had in far greater quantity and nearer the place of sale. The undulating ground differs in soil, some portions of it being a yellowish clay, whilst the rest is a rich mould; these grounds generally speaking, as well as the slopes of the higher mountains, are admirably calculated for the growth of nutmegs, coffee, pepper, or any of the more valuable vegetable productions of the tropics. Besides the above mentioned articles, there are birds-nests, bees-wax, and several kinds of scented wood, in demand at

Singapore, which are all collected by the Dyaks, and would be collected in far greater quantity provided the Dyak was allowed to sell them.

"Turning from the vegetable to the mineral riches of the country, we have diamonds, gold, tin, iron, and antimony-ore certain; I have lately sent what I believe to be a specimen of lead-ore to Calcutta; and copper is reported. It must be remembered, in reading this list, that the country is as yet unexplored by a scientific person, and that the inquiries of a geologist and a mineralogist would throw further light on the minerals of the mountains, and the spots where they are to be found in the greatest plenty. The diamonds are stated to be found in considerable numbers, and of a good water; and I judge the statement to be correct from the fact that the diamond-workers from Sandak come here and work secretly, and the people from Banjamassim, who are likewise clever at this trade, are most desirous to be allowed to work for the precious stone. Gold of a good quality certainly is to be found in large quantities. The eagerness and perseverance of the Chinese to establish themselves is a convincing proof of the fact; and ten years since a body of about 3000 of them had great success in procuring gold by their ordinary mode of trenching the ground.

"The quantity of gold yearly procured at Sambas is moderately stated at 130,000 bunkals, which reckoned at the low rate of 20 Spanish dollars a bunkal, gives 2,600,000 Spanish dollars, or upwards of half a million sterling. The most intelligent Chinese are of opinion, that the quantity here exceeds the quantity at Sambas; and there is no good reason to suppose it would fall short of it were once a sufficient Chinese population settled in the country.

"Antimony-ore is a staple commodity, which is to be procured in any quantity. Tin is said to be plentiful, and the Chinese propose working it; but I have had no opportunity of visiting the spot where it is found. The copper, though reported, has not been brought; and the iron-ore I have examined is of inferior quality. The specimen of what I supposed to be lead-ore has been forwarded to Calcutta, and it remains to be seen what its value may be. And besides these above-mentioned minerals, there can be little doubt of many others being discovered, if the mountain range was properly explored by any man of science. Many other articles of minor importance might be mentioned; but it is needless to add to a list which contains articles of such value, and which would prove the country equal in vegetable and mineral productions to any in the world.

"From the productions (continues Mr. Brooke) I turn to the inhabitants, and I feel sure that in describing their sufferings and miseries I shall command the interest and sympathy of every person of humanity, and that the claims of the virtuous and most unhappy Dyaks will meet with the same attention as those of the African. And these claims have the advantage, that much good may be done without the vast expenditure of lives and money which the exertions on the African coast yearly demand, and that the people would readily appreciate the good that was conferred upon them, and rapidly rise in the scale of civilisation."

The inhabitants may be divided into three different classes, viz. the Malays, the Chinese, and the Dyaks; of the two former little need be said, as they are so well known.

The Dyaks (or more properly Dyak) of Borneo offer to our view a primitive state of society; and their near resemblance to the Tarajahs of Celebes,[1] to the inland people of Sumatra, and probably to the Arafuras of Papua,[2] in customs, manners, and language, affords reason for the conclusion that these are the aboriginal race of the Eastern Archipelago, nearly stationary in their original condition. Whilst successive waves of civilisation have swept onward the rest of the

[1] See Prichard's Researches, 1826, which, meagre as they must have been from the want of data, tell us in two or three pages nearly all we know on the subject. That able investigator states that the Dyaks of Borneo resemble the Taraj of the Celebes.

[2] With regard to the Arafuras, or Haraforas, it is stated that they are termed in some districts Idaan, in others Murut, and in others Dayaks. See Raffles' Java. And Leyden assures us that all these varieties were originally called Idaan.

inhabitants, whilst tribes as wild have arisen to power, flourished, and decayed, the Dyak in his native jungles still retains the feelings of earlier times, and shews the features of society as it existed before the influx of foreign races either improved or corrupted the native character.

The name 'Dyak' has been indiscriminately applied to all the wild people on the island of Borneo; but as the term is never so used by themselves, and as they differ greatly, not only in name, but in their customs and manners, we will briefly, in the first instance, mention the various distinct nations, the general locality of each, and some of their distinguishing peculiarities.

1st. The Dusun, or villagers of the northern extremity of the island, are a race of which Mr. Brooke knows nothing personally; but the name implies that they are an agricultural people: they are represented as not being tattooed, as using the sumpitan, and as having a peculiar dialect.[1]

2d. The Murut. The Murut inhabits the interior of Borneo Proper. They are not tattooed, always use the sumpitan, and have a peculiar dialect. In the same locality, and resembling the Murut, are some tribes called the Basaya.

3d. The Kadians (or Idaans of voyagers) use

[1] A singular contrast to preceding accounts, which represent the north and north-eastern population not only as pirates, called Tiran or Zedong, but even as cannibals. Near them there appear to be the piratical nests of Magindano, Sooloo, &c.

the sumpitan, and have likewise a peculiar dialect; but in other respects they nowise differ from the Borneons, either in religion, dress, or mode of life. They are, however, an industrious, peaceful people, who cultivate the ground in the vicinity of Borneo Proper, and nearly as far as Tanjong Barram. The wretched capital is greatly dependent upon them, and, from their numbers and industry, they form a valuable population. In the interior, and on the Balyet river, which discharges itself near Tanjong Barram, is a race likewise called Kadian, not converted to Islam, and which still retains the practice of "taking heads."

4th. The Kayan. The Kayans are the most numerous, the most powerful, and the most warlike people in Borneo. They are an inland race, and their locality extends from about sixty miles up the country from Tanjong Barram to the same extent farther into the interior, in latitude 3° 30′ N., and thence across the island to probably a similar distance from the eastern shore. Their customs, manners, and dress are peculiar, and present most of the characteristic features of a wild and independent people. The Malays of the N. W. coast fear the Kayans, and rarely enter their country; but the Millanows are familiar with them, and there has thence been obtained many particulars respecting them. They are represented as extremely hospitable, generous and kind to strangers when with them, strictly faithful to their word, and honest in their dealings; but on the other hand, they are fierce and bloodthirsty, and when on an expedition, slaughter without sparing. The Kayans are partially tattooed, use the sumpitan, have many dialects, and are remarkable for the strange and apparently mutilating custom adopted by the males, and mentioned by Sir Stamford Raffles.

5th. To the southward and westward of Barram are the Millanows,[1] who inhabit the rivers not far from the sea. They are, generally speaking, an intelligent, industrious, and active race, the principal cultivators of sago, and gatherers of the famous camphor barus. Their locality extends from Tanjong Barram to Tanjong Sirak. In person they are stout and well made, of middling height, round good-tempered countenances, and fairer than the Malays. They have several dialects amongst them, use the sumpitan, and are not tattooed. They retain the practice of taking heads, but they seldom seek them, and have little of the ferocity of the Kayan.

6th. In the vicinity of the Kayans and Millanows are some wild tribes, called the Tatows,

[1] There are several rivers, Meri, Bentulu, &c., the inhabitants of which, says Mr. Brooke, I class under the general term Millanow, as their dialects shew a very close connexion, and their habits are the same. Evidently from language they are civilised tribes of Kayans.

Balanian, Kanowit, &c. They are probably only a branch of Kayans, though differing from them in being elaborately tattooed over the entire body. They have peculiar dialects, use the sumpitan, and are a wild and fierce people.

7th. The Dyaks. The Dyaks are divided into Dyak Darrat and Dyak Laut, or land and sea Dyaks. The Dyak Lauts, as their name implies, frequent the sea; and it is needless to say much of them, as their difference from the Dyak Darrat is a difference of circumstances only. The tribes of Sarebus and Sakarran, whose rivers are situated in the deep bay between Tanjong Sipang and Tanjong Sirak, are powerful communities, and dreadful pirates, who ravage the coasts in large fleets, and murder and rob indiscriminately; but this is by no means to be esteemed a standard of Dyak character. In these expeditions the Malays often join them, and they are likewise made the instruments for oppressing the Laut tribes. The Sarebus and Sakarran are fine men, fairer than the Malays, with sharp keen eyes, thin lips, and handsome countenances, though frequently marked by an expression of cunning. The Balows and Sibnowans are amiable tribes, decidedly warlike, but not predatory; and the latter combines the virtues of the Dyak character with much of the civilisation of the Malays. The Dyak Laut do not tattoo, nor do they use the sumpitan; their language assimilates closely to the Malay, and was doubtless originally identical with that of the inland tribes. The name of God amongst them is Battara (the Avatara of the Hindoos). They bury their dead, and in the graves deposit a large portion of the property of the deceased, often to a considerable value in gold ornaments, brass guns, jars, and arms. Their marriage-ceremony consists in two fowls being killed, and the forehead and breast of the young couple being touched with the blood; after which the chief, or an old man, knocks their heads together several times, and the ceremony is completed with mirth and feasting. In these two instances they differ from the Dyak Darrat.

It must be observed that the Dyak also differs from the Kayan in not being tattooed; and from the Kayan Millanows, &c., in not using the *national* weapon—the sumpitan. The Kayan and the Dyak, as general distinctions, though they differ in dialect, in dress, in weapons, and probably in religion, agree in their belief of similar omens, and, above all, in their practice of taking the heads of their enemies; but with the Kayan this practice assumes the aspect of an indiscriminate desire of slaughter, whilst with the Dyak it is but the trophy acquired in legitimate warfare. The Kadians form the only exception to this rule, in consequence of their conversion to Islam; and it is but reasonable to suppose, that with a slight exertion in favour of Christianity, others might be induced to lay aside this barbarous custom.

With respect to the dialects, though the difference is considerable, they are evidently derived from a common source; but it is remarkable that some words in the Millanow and Kayan are similar to the Bugis and Badjow language. This intermixture of dialects, which can be linked together, appears to be more conclusive of the common origin of the wild tribes and civilised nations of the Archipelago than most other arguments; and if Marsden's position be correct (which there can be little or no reason to doubt), that the Polynesian is an original race with an original language,[1] it must likewise be conceded that the wild tribes represent the primitive state of society in these islands.

We know little of the wild tribes of Celebes beyond their general resemblance to the Kayans of the east coast of Borneo; and it is probable that the Kayans are the people of Celebes, who, crossing the Strait of Makassar, have in time by their superior prowess possessed themselves of the country of the Dyaks. Mr. Brooke (from whom I am copying this sketch) is led to entertain this opinion from a slight resemblance in their dialects with those used in Celebes, from the difference in

[1] Leyden concluded that the language was allied to the Batta and Tagala, and the whole derived from and varieties of the primitive tongue of the Philippine Islands.

so many of their customs from those of the Dyaks, and from the Kayans of the *north-west coast of Borneo* having one custom in common with the wild tribe of Minkoka in the Bay of Boni. Both the Kayans and Minkokas on the death of a relative seek for a head; and on the death of their chief many human heads must be procured: which practice is unknown to the Dyak. It may further be remarked, that their probable immigration from Celebes is supported by the statement of the Millanows, that the Murut and Dyak give place to the Kayan whenever they come in contact, and that the latter people have depopulated large tracts in the interior, which were once occupied by the former.

Having thus briefly noticed the different wild people of the island, I proceed with the more particular task of describing the Dyak Darrats.

The locality of these Dyaks may be marked as follows:—The Pontiana river, from its mouth, is traced into the interior towards the northward and westward, until it approaches at the furthest within 100 miles of the north-west coast; a line drawn in latitude 3° N. till it intersects the course of the Pontiana river will point out the limit of the country inhabited by the Dyak. Within this inconsiderable portion of the island, which includes Sambas, Landak, Pontiana, Sangow, Sarāwak, &c., are numerous tribes, all of which agree in their leading customs, and make use of nearly the same dialect.

Personally (writes our sole authority for any intelligence respecting them), I am acquainted only with the tribes of Sarāwak and some tribes further in the interior beyond the government of the Malays, who inhabit the country between Sarāwak and Landak; and the description of one tribe will serve as a description of all, so little do they vary.

Before, however, I say any thing of the character of the Dyaks, or their temper, it will be necessary to describe briefly the government under which they live, and the influence it has upon them; and if afterwards in the recital there appear some unamiable points in their character, an allowance will be made for their failings, which those who rule them would not deserve.

The Dyaks have from time immemorial been looked upon as the bondsmen of the Malays, and the Rajahs consider them much in the same light as they would a drove of oxen—*i. e.* as personal and disposable property. They were governed in Sarāwak by three local officers, called the Patingi, the Bandar, and the Tumangong. To the Patingi they paid a small yearly revenue of rice, but this deficiency of revenue was made up by sending a quantity of goods—chiefly salt, Dyak cloths, and iron—and demanding a price for them six or eight times more than their value. The produce collected by the Dyaks was also monopolised, and the edible birds-nests, bees-wax, &c. &c., were taken at a price fixed by the Patingi, who moreover claimed mats, fowls, fruit, and every other necessary at his pleasure, and could likewise make the Dyaks work for him for merely a nominal remuneration. This system, not badly devised, had it been limited within the bounds of moderation, would have left the Dyaks plenty for all their wants; or had the local officers known their own interest, they would have protected those upon whom they depended for revenue, and under the worst oppression of one man the Dyaks would have deemed themselves happy. Such unfortunately was not the case; for the love of immediate gain overcame every other consideration, and by degrees old-established customs were thrown aside, and new ones substituted in their place. When the Patingi had received all he thought proper to extort, his relatives first claimed the right of arbitrary trade, and gradually it was extended as the privilege of every respectable person in the country to serra[1] the Dyaks. The poor Dyak, thus at the mercy of half the Malay population, was never allowed to refuse compliance with these demands; he could plead neither poverty, inability, nor even hunger, as an excuse, for the answer was ever ready: "Give me your wife or one of your children;" and in case he could not supply what was required, the wife or the child was taken, and became a slave. Many modes of extortion were resorted to;

[1] Probably a Dyak phrase for levying exactions on the oppressed people. It is not Malay.

a favourite one was convicting the Dyak of a fault and imposing a fine upon him. Some ingenuity and much trickery were shewn in this game, and new offences were invented as soon as the old pleas would serve no longer: for instance, if a Malay met a Dyak in a boat which pleased him, he notched it, as a token that it was his property; in one day, if the boat was a new one, perhaps three or more would place their marks on it; and as only one could get it, the Dyak to whom the boat really belonged had to pay the others *for his fault.* This, however, was only "a fault;" whereas, for a Dyak to injure a Malay, directly or indirectly, purposely or otherwise, was a *high offence*, and punished by a proportionate fine. If a Dyak's house was in bad repair, and a Malay fell in consequence and was hurt, or pretended to be hurt, a fine was imposed; if a Malay in the jungle was wounded by the springs set for a wild boar, or by the wooden spikes which the Dyaks for protection put about their village, or scratched himself and said he was injured, the penalty was heavy; if the Malay was *really hurt*, ever so accidentally, it was the ruin of the Dyak. And these numerous and uninvited guests came and went at pleasure, lived in free quarters, made their requisitions, and then forced the Dyak to carry away for them the very property of which he had been robbed.

This is a fair picture of the governments under which the Dyaks live; and although they were often roused to resistance, it was always fruitless, and only involved them in deeper troubles; for the Malays could readily gather a large force of sea Dyaks from Sakarran, who were readily attracted by hope of plunder, and who, supported by the fire-arms of their allies, were certain to overcome any single tribe that held out. The misfortunes of the Dyaks of Sarāwak did not stop here. Antimony-ore was discovered; the cupidity of the Borneons was roused; then Pangerans struggled for the prize; intrigues and dissensions ensued; and the inhabitants of Sarāwak in turn felt the very evil they had inflicted on the Dyaks; whilst the Dyaks were compelled, amidst their other wrongs, to labour at the ore without any recompense, and to the neglect of their rice-cultivation. Many died in consequence of this compulsory labour, so contrary to their habits and inclinations; and more would doubtless have fallen victims, had not civil war rescued them from this evil, to inflict upon them others a thousand times worse.

Extortion had before been carried on by individuals, but now it was systematised; and Pangerans of rank, for the sake of plunder, sent bodies of Malays and Sakarran Dyaks to attack the different tribes. The men were slaughtered, the women and children carried off into slavery, the villages burned, the fruit-trees cut down,[1] and all their property destroyed or seized.

[1] The utter destruction of a village or town is nothing to the

182   THE DYAK TRIBES.

The Dyaks could no longer live in tribes, but sought refuge in the mountains or the jungle, a few together; and as one of them pathetically described it—"We do not live," he said, "like men; we are like monkeys; we are hunted from place to place; we have no houses; and when we light a fire, we fear the smoke will draw our enemies upon us."

In the course of ten years, under the circumstances detailed—from enforced labour, from famine, from slavery, from sickness, from the sword,—one half of the Dyak population[1] disappeared;

infliction of cutting down the fruit-trees. The former can be rebuilt, with its rude and ready materials, in a few weeks; but the latter, from which the principal subsistence of the natives is gathered, cannot be suddenly restored, and thus they are reduced to starvation.

[1] The grounds for this opinion are an estimate personally made amongst the tribes, compared with the estimate kept by the local officers before the disturbance arose; and the result is, that only two out of twenty tribes have not suffered, whilst some tribes have been reduced from 330 families to 50; about ten tribes have lost more than half their number; one tribe of 100 families has lost all, its women and children made slaves; and one tribe, more wretched, has been reduced from 120 families to 2, that is, 16 persons; whilst two tribes have entirely disappeared. The list of the tribes and their numbers formerly and now are as follows:—Suntah, 330—50; Sanpro, 100—69; Sigo, 80—28; Sabungo, 60—33; Brang, 50—22; Sinnar, 80—34; Stang, 80—30; Samban, 60—34; Tubbia, 80—30; Goon, 40—25; Bang, 40—12; Kuj-juss, 35—0; Lundu, 80—2; Sow, 200—100; Sarambo, 100—60; Bombak, 35—35; Paninjow, 80—40; Singè, 220—220; Pons, 20—0; Sibaduh, 25—25.

and the work of extirpation would have gone on at an accelerated pace, had the remnant been left to the tender mercies of the Pangerans; but chance (we may much more truly say, Providence) led our countryman Mr. Brooke to this scene of misery, and enabled him, by circumstances far removed beyond the grounds of calculation, to put a stop to the sufferings of an amiable people.

There are twenty tribes in Sarāwak, on about fifty square miles of land. The appearance of the Dyaks is prepossessing: they have good-natured faces, with a mild and subdued expression; eyes set far apart, and features sometimes well formed. In person they are active, of middling height, and not distinguishable from the Malays in complexion. The women are neither so good-looking nor well formed as the men, but they have the same expression, and are cheerful and kind-tempered. The dress of the men consists of a piece of cloth about fifteen feet long, passed between the legs and fastened round the loins, with the ends hanging before and behind; the head-dress is composed of bark-cloth, dyed bright yellow, and stuck up in front so as to resemble a tuft of feathers. The arms and legs are often ornamented with rings of silver, brass, or shell; and necklaces are worn,

Total, formerly, 1795—now, 849 families; and reckoning eight persons to each family, the amount of population will be, formerly, 14,360—now, 6792: giving a decrease of population in ten years of 846 families, or 7568 persons!

made of human teeth, or those of bears or dogs, or of white beads, in such numerous strings as to conceal the throat. A sword on one side, a knife and small betel-basket on the other, completes the ordinary equipment of the males; but when they travel they carry a basket slung from the forehead, on which is a palm mat, to protect the owner and his property from the weather. The women wear a short and scanty petticoat, reaching from the loins to the knees, and a pair of black bamboo stays, which are never removed except the wearer be *enceinte*. They have rings of brass or red bamboo about the loins, and sometimes ornaments on the arms; the hair is worn long; the ears of both sexes are pierced, and ear-rings of brass inserted occasionally; the teeth of the young people are sometimes filed to a point and discoloured, as they say that "Dogs have white teeth." They frequently dye their feet and hands of a bright red or yellow colour; and the young people, like those of other countries, affect a degree of finery and foppishness, whilst the elders invariably lay aside all ornaments, as unfit for a wise person or one advanced in years.

In character the Dyak is mild and tractable, hospitable when he is well used, grateful for kindness, industrious, honest, and simple; neither treacherous nor cunning, and so truthful that the word of one of them might safely be taken before the oath of half a dozen Borneons. In their dealings they are very straightforward and correct, and so trustworthy that they rarely attempt, even after a lapse of years, to evade payment of a just debt. On the reverse of this picture there is little unfavourable to be said; and the wonder is, they have learned so little deceit or falsehood where the examples before them have been so rife. The temper of the Dyak inclines to be sullen; and they oppose a dogged and stupid obstinacy when set to a task which displeases them, and support with immovable apathy torrents of abuse or entreaty. They are likewise distrustful, fickle, apt to be led away, and evasive in concealing the amount of their property; but these are the vices rather of situation than of character, for they have been taught by bitter experience that their rulers set no limits to their exactions, and that hiding is their only chance of retaining a portion of the grain they have raised. They are, at the same time, fully aware of the customs by which their ancestors were governed, and are constantly appealing to them as a rule of right, and frequently arguing with the Malay on the subject. Upon these occasions they are silenced, but not convinced; and the Malay, whilst he evades or bullies when it is needful, is sure to appeal to these very much-abused customs whenever it serves his purpose. The manners of the Dyaks with strangers are reserved to an extent rarely seen amongst rude or half-civilised people; but on a better acquaintance (which is not readily acquired), they are open and talkative, and, when heated with their favourite beverage, lively, and evincing more shrewdness and observation than they have gained credit for possessing. Their ideas, as may well be supposed, are very limited: they reckon with their fingers and toes, and few are clever enough to count beyond twenty; but when they repeat the operation, they record each twenty by making a knot on a string.

Like other wild people, the slightest restraint is irksome, and no temptation will induce them to stay long from their favourite jungle. It is there they seek the excitement of war, the pleasures of the chase, the labours of the field, and the abundance of fruit in the rich produce which assists in supporting their families. The pathless jungle is endeared to them by every association which influences the human mind, and they languish when prevented from roaming there as inclination dictates.

The latest accounts received from Sarāwak represent the increasing prosperity of that interesting settlement; and with reference to the gradual advance of the Dyaks, Mr. Brooke observes:—"The peaceful and gentle aborigines—how can I speak too favourably of their improved condition? These people, who, a few years since, suffered every extreme of misery from war, slavery, and starvation, are now comfortably lodged, and comparatively rich. A stranger might now pass from village to village, and he would receive their hospitality, and see their padi stored in their houses. He would hear them proclaim their happiness, and praise the white man as their friend and protector. Since the death of Parembam, no Dyak of Sarāwak lost his life by violence, until a month since, when two were cut off by the Sakarran Dyaks. None of the tribes have warred amongst themselves; and I believe their war excursions to a distance in the interior have been very few, and those undertaken by the Sarambos. What punishment is sufficient for the wretch who finds this state of things so baleful as to attempt to destroy it? Yet such a wretch is Seriff Sahib. In describing the condition of the Dyaks, I do not say that it is perfect, or that it may not be still further improved; but with people in their state of society innovations ought not rashly or hastily to be made; as the civilised being ought constantly to bear in mind, that what is clear to him is not clear to a savage; that intended benefits *may* be regarded as positive injuries; and that his motives are not, and scarcely can be, appreciated! The greatest evil, perhaps, from which the Dyaks suffer, is the influence of the Datus or chiefs; but this influence is never carried to oppression, and is only used to obtain the expensive luxury of 'birds-nests' at a cheap rate. In short, the Dyaks are happy and content; and their gradual development must now be left to the work of time, aided by the gentlest persuasion, and advanced (if attainable) by the education of their children."

CHAPTER IX.

Mr. Brooke's memorandum on the piracy of the Malayan Archipelago. The measures requisite for its suppression, and consequent extension of British commerce in that important locality.

I CANNOT afford my readers a more accurate idea of the present state of piracy in the Malayan Archipelago, of the best mode of suppressing it, and of the vast field which the island of Borneo offers for the extension of British commerce, than by quoting a few of Mr. Brooke's observations on these important subjects, written before the operations of the squadron under command of Rear-Admiral Sir Thomas Cochrane took place, and which have already been narrated in Chapter VII. With reference to the first topic, piracy, Mr. Brooke remarks:

"The piracy of the Eastern Archipelago is entirely distinct from piracy in the Western world; for, from the condition of the various governments, the facilities offered by natural situation, and the total absence of all restraint from European nations, the pirate communities have attained an importance on the coasts and islands most removed from foreign settlements. Thence they issue forth and commit depredations on the native trade, enslave the inhabitants at the entrance of rivers, and attack ill-armed or stranded European vessels; and roving from place to place, they find markets for their slaves and plunder.

"The old-established Malay governments (such as Borneo and Sooloo), weak and distracted, are, probably without exception, participators in or victims to piracy; and in many cases both—purchasing from one set of pirates, and enslaved and plundered by another; and whilst their dependencies are abandoned, the unprotected trade languishes from the natural dread of the better disposed natives of undertaking a coasting voyage.

"It is needless to dwell upon the evil effects of piracy; but before venturing an opinion on the most effectual means of suppression, I propose briefly to give an account of such pirate communities as I am acquainted with.

"The pirates on the coast of Borneo may be classed into those who make long voyages in large heavy-armed prahus, such as the Illanuns, Balagnini, &c., and the lighter Dyak fleets, which make short but destructive excursions in swift prahus, and seek to surprise rather than openly to attack their prey. A third, and probably the worst class, are usually half-bred Arab Seriffs, who, possessing themselves of the territory of some Malay state, form a nucleus for piracy, a rendezvous and market for all the roving fleets; and although occasionally sending out their own followers, they more frequently seek profit by making advances, in food, arms, and gunpowder, to all who will agree to repay them at an exorbitant rate in slaves.

"The Dyaks of Sarebus and Sakarran were under the influence of two Arab Seriffs, who employed them on piratical excursions, and shared in equal parts the plunder obtained. I had once the opportunity of counting ninety-eight boats about to start on a cruise; and reckoning the crew of each boat at the moderate average of twenty-five men, it gives a body of 2450 men on a piratical excursion. The piracies of these Arab Seriffs and their Dyaks were so notorious, that it is needless to detail them here; but one curious feature which throws a light on the state of society, I cannot forbear mentioning. On all occasions of a Dyak fleet being about to make a piratical excursion, a gong was beat round the town ordering a particular number of Malays to embark; and in case any one failed to obey, he was fined the sum of thirty rupees by the Seriff of the place.

"The blow struck by Captain Keppel of her Majesty's ship Dido on these two communities was so decisive as to have put an entire end to their piracies; the leaders Seriff Sahib and Seriff Muller have fled, the Malay population has been dispersed, and the Dyaks so far humbled, as to sue for protection; and in future, by substituting local Malay rulers of good character in lieu of the piratical Seriffs, a check will be placed on the Dyaks, and they may be broken of their piratical habits, in as far as interferes with the trade of the coast.

"The next pirate horde we meet with is a mixed community of Illanuns and Badjows (or sea-gipsies) located at Tampasuk, a few miles up a small river; they are not formidable in number, and their depredations are chiefly committed on the Spanish territory; their market, until recently, being Bruni, or Borneo Proper. They might readily be dispersed and driven back to their own country; and the Dusuns, or villagers (as the name signifies), might be protected and encouraged. Seriff Houseman, a half-bred Arab, is located in Malludu Bay, and has, by account, from fifteen hundred to two thousand men with him. He is beyond doubt a pirate direct and indirect, and occasionally commands excursions in person, or employs the Illanuns of Tampasuk, and others to the eastward, who for their own convenience make common cause with him. He has no pretension to the territory he occupies; and the authority he exerts (by means of his piratical force) over the interior tribes in his vicinity, and on the island of Palawan, is of the worst and most oppressive description. This Seriff has probably never come in contact with any Europeans, and consequently openly professes to hold their power in scorn.

"To my own knowledge Seriff Houseman seized and sold into slavery a boat's crew (about twenty men) of the Sultana, a merchant ship, which was burned in the Palawan passage. Within the last few months he has plundered and burned an European vessel stranded near the Mangsi Isles; and to shew his entire independence of control, his contempt for European power, and his determination to continue in his present course, he has threatened to attack the city of Bruni, in consequence of the Bruni government having entered into a treaty with her Majesty's government for the discouragement and suppression of piracy! This fact speaks volumes; an old-established and recognised Malay government is to be attacked by a lawless adventurer, who has seized on a portion of its territory, and lives by piracy, for venturing to treat with a foreign power for the best purposes. If any further proof of piracy were requisite, it would readily be established by numerous witnesses (themselves the victims), and by the most solemn declaration of the Bruni authorities, that peaceful traders on the high seas have been stopped by the prahus of this Seriff and his allies, their vessels seized, their property plundered, and their persons enslaved: numerous witnesses could attest their having been reduced to slavery and detained in the very household of Seriff Houseman! When, however, the facts of his having sold into slavery the crew of a British vessel (which has been established before the Singapore authorities) comes to be known, I conceive every other proof of the character of this person is completely superfluous.

"The indirect piracy of Seriff Houseman is even more mischievous than what is directly committed; for he supplies the Balagnini (a restless piratical tribe, hereafter to be mentioned) with food, powder, arms, salt, &c. under the agreement that they pay him on their return from the cruise, at the rate of five slaves for every 100 rupees worth of goods. The Balagnini are in consequence enabled, through his assistance, to pirate effectively, which otherwise they would not be able to do; as, from their locality, they would find it difficult to obtain firearms and gunpowder. The most detestable part of this traffic, however, is Seriff Houseman selling, in cold blood, such of these slaves as are Borneons, to Pangeran Usop, of Bruni, for 100 rupees for each slave, and Pangeran Usop re-selling each for 200 rupees to their relations in Bruni. Thus, this vile Seriff (without taking into account the enormous prices charged for his goods in the first instance) gains 500 per cent for every slave, and Pangeran Usop clears 100 per cent on the flesh of his own countrymen, thereby *de facto* becoming a party to piracy, though doubtless veiled under the guise of compassion.

"More might be added on the subject of the piracies committed by this Seriff; and it could easily be shewn that the evils accruing from them affect, not only the peaceful trader, but extend to the peaceful agriculturist; but, for the sake of brevity, I deem it sufficient to add, that he exercises the same malign influence on the north coast as Seriff Sahib exercised on the north-west; and that, having surrounded himself by a body of pirates, he arrogates the rights of sovereignty, defies European power, contemns every right principle, and threatens the recognised and legitimate governments of the Archipelago.

" The Balagnini inhabit a cluster of small islands somewhere in the vicinity of Sooloo; they are of the Badjow or sea-gipsey tribe, a wandering race, whose original country has never been ascertained. At present, as far as I can learn, they are not dependant on Sooloo, though it is probable they may be encouraged by some of the Rajahs of that place, and that they find a slave-market there.

"The Balagnini cruise in large prahus, and to each prahu a fleet sampan is attached, which, on occasion, can carry from ten to fifteen men. They seldom carry large guns, like the Illanuns, but, in addition to their other arms, big lelas (brass pieces, carrying from one to a three-pound ball), spears, swords, &c. They use long poles with barbed iron points, with which, during an engagement or flight, they hook their prey. By means of the fleet sampans already mentioned, they are able to capture all small boats; and it is a favourite device with them to disguise one or two men, whilst the rest lie concealed in the bottom of the boat, and thus to surprise prahus at sea, and fishermen or others at the mouths of rivers. By being disguised as Chinese they have carried off numbers of that nation from the Sambas and Pontiana rivers. The cruising-grounds of these pirates are very extensive; they frequently make the circuit of Borneo, proceed as far as the south of Celebes, and in the other direction have been met off Tringanu, Calantan, and Patani. Gillolo and the Moluccas lie within easy range, and it is probable that Papua is occasionally visited by them. It will readily be conceived how harassing to trade must be the continued depredations of the Balagnini pirates, and more especially to the trade of Bruni, which seems, from the unwarlike habits of the natives, the chosen field of their operations. The number of Borneons yearly taken into slavery is very considerable, as a fleet of six or eight boats usually hang about the island of Labuan, to cut off the trade, and to catch the inhabitants of the city. The Borneons, from being so harassed by these pirates, call the easterly wind 'the pirate wind.' The Balagnini commence cruising on the northwest coast about the middle of March, and return, or remove to the eastern side of the island, about the end of November.

" Of Magindano, or Mindanao, we are at the

present time very ignorant; but we know that the inhabitants are warlike and numerous, and that that part of the island called Illanun Bay sends forth the most daring pirates of the Archipelago. The first step requisite is to gain more information concerning them, to form an acquaintance with some of their better-disposed chiefs, and subsequently we might act against them with a suitable force; but it would be rash and premature, in the present state of our knowledge, to come in contact with them in their own country. On one occasion I met eighteen Illanun boats on neutral ground, and learned from their two chiefs that they had been two years absent from home; and from the Papuan negro-slaves on board it was evident that their cruise had extended from the most eastern islands of the Archipelago to the north-western coast of Borneo.

"Having now enumerated the pirates I have become acquainted with since my residence in Sarāwak, I shall proceed to offer an opinion of the best mode for the suppression of piracy in these seas.

"In the first place, a blow should be struck at the piratical communities with which we are already acquainted, and struck with a force which should convince all other pirates of the hopelessness of resistance; subsequently the recognised Malay governments may be detached from all communication with pirates; and, joining conciliation with punishment, laying down the broad distinction of piracy and no piracy—we may foster those who abandon their evil habits, and punish those who adhere to them.

"A system of supervision will, however, be necessary to carry out these measures; our knowledge of the native states must be improved; and as we become able to discriminate between the good and the bad, our sphere of action may be enlarged, and we may act with decision against all descriptions of pirates; against the indirect as well as the direct pirate; against the receiver of stolen goods as well as the thief; and against the promoter as well as the actual perpetrator of piracy.

"I would especially urge that, to eradicate the evil, the pirate-haunts must be burned and destroyed, and the communities dispersed; for merely to cruise against pirate-prahus, and to forbear attacking them until we see them commit a piracy, is a hopeless and an endless task, harassing to our men, and can be attended with but very partial and occasional success; whereas, on the contrary principle, what pirate would venture to pursue his vocation if his home be endangered—if he be made to feel in his own person the very ills he inflicts upon others?

"A question may arise as to what constitutes piracy; and whether, in our efforts to suppress it, we may not be interfering with the right of native states to war one upon another. On the first point, it appears clear to me, that the plunder or seizure of a peaceful and lawful trader on the high seas constitutes an act of piracy, without any reference to the nation or colour of the injured party; for if we limit our construction of piracy we shall, in most cases, be in want of sufficient evidence to convict, and the whole native trade of the Archipelago will be left at the mercy of pirates, much to the injury of our own commerce and of our settlement of Singapore.

"On the second point, we can only concede the right of war to recognised states; and even then we must carefully avoid introducing the refinements of European international law amongst a rude and semi-civilised people, who will make our delicacy a cloak for crime, and declare war merely for the sake of committing piracy with impunity. On the contrary, all chiefs who have seized on territory and arrogate independence (making this independence a plea for piracy) can never be allowed the right of declaring war, or entering on hostilities with their neighbours; for, as I have before remarked, all native trade must in that case be at an end, as the piratical chiefs, no longer in dread of punishment from European powers, would doubtless declare war against every unwarlike native state which they did not need as a market for the sale of their slaves and plunder.

"Practically acting, however, on the broad principle, that the seizure of any lawful trader constitutes piracy, I consider no injustice could be done to the native states, and no interference occur with their acknowledged rights; for in practice it would be easy to discriminate a war between native nations from the piracies of lawless hordes of men; and without some such general principle, no executive officer could act with the requisite decision and promptitude to ensure the eradication of this great evil.

"With a post, such as is proposed to be established, our measures for the suppression of piracy (after the punishment of Seriff Houseman and the Balagnini) would advance step by step, as our knowledge increased, and with alternate conciliation and severity, as the case might require. By detaching the recognised governments from the practice, and gradually forming amongst the chief men a friendly and English party opposed to piracy, we should, I doubt not, speedily obtain our principal object of clearing the sea of marauders, and ultimately correct the natural propensity of the natives for piracy.

"In order to extend our commerce in these seas generally, and more particularly on the N.W. coast of Borneo, it is requisite, 1st, that piracy be suppressed; 2dly, that the native governments be settled, so as to afford protection to the poorer and producing classes; and, 3dly, that our knowledge of the interior should be extended, and our intercourse with the various tribes more frequent.

"That our commerce may be largely extended is so clear, that I shall not stop to detail the productions of the island of Borneo, as it will suffice here to state generally that all authorities agree in representing it as one of the richest portions of the globe, and in climate, soil, and mineral and vegetable productions, inferior to no portion of the same extent.

"If these opinions be true—and, from my experience, I believe them to be so—it follows that the materials for an extensive and extended trade exist, and only require development; whilst a numerous and industrious though wild population, which inhabits the interior, is debarred from all intercourse with Europeans from the badness of Malay government.

"On the first requisite for the development of commerce I need add nothing further, as it is a duty incumbent on all governments to eradicate piracy at any cost; and in the present case it would not be found a difficult or tedious task.

"A post like Labuan or Balambangan would beyond doubt give an impetus to trade, merely from the freedom from all restrictions, and the absence of all exactions, which the natives would enjoy; and (piracy being checked) countries which now lie fallow would, from their proximity, be induced to bring their produce into market.

"This limited extension is, however, of little moment when compared with the results which must attend our exerting a beneficial influence over the native governments for the purposes of affording protection to the poorer classes, insuring safety to the trader, and opening a field for the planter or the miner.

"The slightest acquaintance with the north-west coast of Borneo would convince any observer of the ease with which these objects might be effected; for the native government, being in a state of decadence, requires protection, and would willingly act justly towards traders and capitalists, and encourage their enterprises, in order to continue on friendly terms with any European power located in their vicinity. The numerous rivers on the coast, with their local rulers, are harassed by the demands of every petty Pangeran; and whilst the sovereign is defrauded of his revenue, which the people would cheerfully pay, and his territory ruined, this host of useless retainers (acting always in his name) gain but very slight personal profits to counterbalance all the mischief they do.

"The principal feature is the weakness of the governments, both of the capital and its dependencies; and in consequence of this weakness there is a strong desire for European protection, for European enterprise, and for any change effected by Europeans. Supposing Labuan to be taken as a naval post, I consider that European capital might with safety be employed in Bruni.

"In the rivers contiguous to Sarāwak, the

presence of Europeans would be hailed with joy, not only by the Dyaks, but by the Malays; and subsequently it would depend on their own conduct to what degree they retained the good will of the natives; but with ordinary conciliation and a decent moral restraint on their actions, I feel assured that their persons and property would be safe, and no obstruction offered to fair trade or to mining operations.

"Supposing, as I have before said, the occupation of Labuan by the English, our influence over the government of Bruni would be complete; and one of our principal objects would be to maintain this ascendancy, as a means of extending our trade.

"Our position at Labuan would, it must be borne in mind, differ from the position we occupied in relation to the native princes in Singapore. In the latter case, the native princes were without means, without followers, and with a paltry and useless territory, and became our pensioners. In the case of Labuan, we shall have an acknowledged independent state in our vicinity; and for the prosperity of our settlement we must retain our ascendancy by the support of the government of Muda Hassim. Let our influence be of the mildest kind. Let us, by supporting the legitimate government, ameliorate the condition of the people by this influence. Let us pay every honour to the native princes; let us convince them of our entire freedom from all selfish views of territorial aggrandisement on the mainland of Borneo; and we shall enjoy so entire a confidence, that virtually the coast will become our own without the trouble or expense of possession. I have impressed it on the Rajah Muda Hassim and Pangeran Budrudeen, that the readiest and most direct way of obtaining revenues from their various possessions will be by commuting all their demands for a stated yearly sum of money from each; and by this direct taxation, to which Muda Hassim and his brother seem ready to accede, the system of fraud and exaction would be abolished, the native mind tranquillised, and the legitimate government would become the protector rather than the oppressor of its dependencies. By this measure likewise, a tone might be imparted to the native chiefs and rulers of rivers; and the people at large taught to feel that, after the payment of a specified sum, a right existed to resist all extra demands. Besides this, these Rajahs are convinced that a certain yearly revenue is what they require, and is the only means by which they can retain their independence; and I have impressed it on their minds that, to gain a revenue, they must foster trade and protect Europeans in their dealings.

"If Labuan were English, and if the sea were clear of pirates, I see no obstacle to bringing these and other measures into immediate operation; and I am assured we should have the sincere and hearty co-operation of the Borneon government.

" Since the advent of Europeans in the Archipelago, the tendency of the Polynesian governments generally has been to decay; here the experiment may be fairly tried on the smallest scale of expense, whether a beneficial European influence may not re-animate a falling state, and at the same time extend our own commerce. We are here devoid of the stimulus which has urged us on to conquest in India. We incur no risk of the collision of the two races; we occupy a small station in the vicinity of a friendly and unwarlike people; and we aim at the development of native countries through native agency.

" If this tendency to decay and extinction be inevitable; if this approximation of European policy to a native state should be unable to arrest the fall of the Borneon government, yet we shall retain a people already habituated to European manners, industrious interior races, and at a future period, if deemed necessary, settlements gradually developed in a rich and fertile country. We shall have a post in time of war highly advantageous as commanding a favourable position relative to China, we shall extend our commerce, suppress piracy, and prevent the present and prospective advantages from falling into other hands; and we shall do this at a small expense.

" I own the native development through their

own exertions is but a favourite theory; but whatever may be the fate of the government of Borneo, the people will still remain; and if they be protected, and enabled to live in quiet security, I cannot entertain a doubt of its becoming a highly productive country, eminently calculated as a field for British enterprise and capital.

"If the development of the resources of the country can be effected by its native rulers, it will be a noble task performed; but if it fail, the people of the coast will still advance and form governments for themselves under British influence.

"In concluding this hasty and general view of the subject, I may remark that commerce might be extended and capital laid out on the north-west coast of Borneo, to an amount to which it is difficult to fix limits, as the country is capable of producing most articles of commerce in demand from this quarter of the world, and the natives (who, as far as we know them, are an unwarlike, mild, and industrious race,) would receive our manufactures, from which they are now in a great measure debarred. I have not alluded to any other countries of the Archipelago; for we must first become acquainted with them; we must become intimate, cultivate an English party, and accustom them to our manners; and probably the same conciliatory policy, the same freedom from design, which has succeeded in Borneo, will succeed elsewhere, if pushed with temper and patience.

"The general principle ought to be—to encourage established governments, such as Borneo and Sooloo, provided they will with all sincerity abandon piracy, and assist in its suppression; but at the same time, by supervision to convince ourselves of the fact, and keep them in the right path; for all treaties with these native states (and we have had several) are but so much waste paper unless we see them carried into execution.

"I have now only to mention the third means for the extension of commerce. Our intercourse with the natives of the interior should be frequent and intimate: these people (beyond where I am acquainted with them) are represented as very numerous, hospitable, and industrious; and a friendly intercourse would develop the resources of their country, draw its produce to our markets, and give the natives a taste for British manufactures. This intercourse, however, must be prudently introduced and carefully advanced; for to bring these wild people into contact with ignorant and arrogant Europeans would produce bloodshed and confusion in a month. In Borneo, it is an advantage that the two races cannot come in collision; for from its climate it precludes all idea of colonisation, and that which is next to an impossibility, the maintaining a good understanding between ignorant civilised men and ignorant savages: it is a field for commerce and capital, but no violent change should be attempted of native customs; and in this way alone, by gradual means, can we really benefit the natives and ourselves. When we consider the amount of produce obtained from the countries of the Archipelago, and their consumption of British manufactures, under the worst forms of government, living in a state of distraction and insecurity, and exposed to the depredations of pirates at sea, we may form some idea how vast may be the increase, should peace and security be introduced amongst them; and judging of the future by the past — by the limited experiment made at Sarāwak — we may hope that the task is neither so difficult nor so uncertain as was formerly supposed."

CHAPTER X.

Proposed British settlement on the north-west coast of Borneo, and occupation of the island of Labuan. Governor Crawfurd's opinions thereon.

THE establishment of a British settlement on the north-west coast of Borneo, and the occupation of the island of Labuan, are measures that have for some time past been under consideration by her Majesty's government; and I am courteously enabled to lay before my readers the valuable opinions of Mr. Crawfurd (late Governor of Singapore) on this subject:

"I am of opinion (Mr. Crawfurd writes) that a settlement on the north-west coast of Borneo,—that is, at a convenient point on the southern shore of the China Sea,—would be highly advantageous to this country, as a coal-depôt for steam-navigation; as a means of suppressing Malayan piracy; as a harbour of refuge for ships disabled in the China Sea; and finally, as a commanding position during a naval war.

"The island of Labuan has been pointed out

for this purpose; and as far as our present limited knowledge of it will allow me to judge, it appears to possess all the necessary qualities for such a settlement.

"The requisite properties are, salubrity of climate, a good harbour, a position in the track of steam-navigation, conveniency of position for ships disabled in typhoons, conveniency of position for our cruisers during war, and a locality strong and circumscribed by nature, so as to be readily capable of cheap defence.

"Labuan lies in about 6^0 of north latitude, and consequently the average heat will be about 83^0 of Fahrenheit; the utmost range of the thermometer will not exceed ten degrees. In short, the year is a perpetual hot summer. It is, at the same time, well ventilated by both monsoons; and being near twenty miles from the marshy shores of the Borneo River, there is little ground to apprehend that it will be found unhealthy, even if those shores themselves had been ascertained to be so, which, however, is not the case; for, in proof of their salubrity, it may be stated, that the town of Borneo is healthy, although it stands, and has stood for centuries, on the flooded banks of the river; the houses being built on posts, and chiefly accessible by boat.

"With respect to harbour, a most essential point, I do not perceive that the island is indented by any bay or inlet that would answer the purpose of one.[1] The channel, however, which lies between it and the mainland of Borneo is but seven miles broad, and will probably constitute a spacious and convenient harbour. The name of the island itself, which means anchorage, I have no doubt is derived from the place affording shelter to native shipping, and those probably, in most cases, fleets of pirate prahus. This channel is again further restricted by four islets, and these, with four more lying to the south-west, will afford shelter in the south-west or mild monsoon; protection is given in the north-east, the severest monsoon, by Labuan itself: and I may add, that the island is, by four degrees of latitude, beyond the extreme southern limit of the typhoons of the Chinese Sea.

"In the channel between Labuan and the main, or rather between Labuan and the islets already mentioned, the soundings on the Admiralty chart shew that vessels drawing as much as eighteen feet water may anchor within a mile of the shore, and the largest vessels within a mile and a half; a convenience for shipping which greatly exceeds that of Singapore. One of the advantages of Labuan will be that it will prove a port of refuge for shipping disabled in the storms of the Chinese Seas. Many examples, indeed some of recent occurrence, might be adduced to shew the need there is of such a port.

[1] Sir Edward Belcher has since surveyed Labuan in her Majesty's ship Samarang, and finding an excellent harbour, named it Victoria Bay. Vide Plan.—H. K.

"Labuan lies nearly in the direct track both of steam and sailing navigation from India to China, during the north-east, the worst and severest of the two monsoons; and is as intermediate a position between Singapore and Hong Kong as can be found, being 700 miles from the former and 1000 from the latter.

"The insular character and narrow limits of Labuan will make it easily and cheaply defensible. The extreme length of the island appears to be about six miles, its greatest breadth about four and a half, and probably its whole area will not be found to exceed thirty square miles.

"From the rude tribes of the immediate vicinity no hostile attack is to be apprehended that would make the present erection of forts or batteries necessary. No Asiatic enemy is at any time to be feared that would make such defences requisite. In five-and-twenty years it has not been found imperative to have recourse to them at Singapore. It is only in case of war with a naval power that fortifications would be required; but I am not informed what local advantages Labuan possesses for their erection. A principal object of such fortifications would be the defence of the shipping in the harbour from the inroads of an enemy's cruisers. At one point the soundings, as given in the Admiralty chart, are stated nine fathoms, within three quarters of a mile of the shore: and I presume that batteries within this distance would afford protection to the largest class of merchantmen. In Singapore Roads no class of shipping above mere native craft can lie nearer than two miles of the shore; so that in a war with an European naval power, the merchant shipping there can only be defended by her Majesty's navy.

"One of the most striking national advantages to be expected from the possession of Labuan would consist in its use in defending our own commerce, and attacking that of opponents, in the event of a naval war. Between the eastern extremity of the Straits of Malacca and Hong Kong, a distance of 1700 miles, there is no British harbour, and no safe and accessible port of refuge; Hong Kong is, indeed, the only spot within the wide limits of the Chinese Sea for such a purpose, although our legitimate commercial intercourse within it extends over a length of 2000 miles. Everywhere else, Manilla and the newly opened ports of China excepted, our crippled vessels or our merchantmen pursued by the enemy's crusiers, are met by the exclusion or extortion of semi-barbarous nations, or in danger of falling into the power of robbers and savages.

"Labuan fortified, and supposing the Borneon coal to be as productive and valuable in quality as it is represented, would give Great Britain in a naval war the entire command of the China Sea. This would be the result of our possessing or commanding the only available supply of coal, that of

Bengal and Australia excepted, to be found in the wide limits which extend east of the continents of Europe and America.

"The position of Labuan will render it the most convenient possible for the suppressing of piracy. The most desperate and active pirates of the whole Indian Archipelago are the tribes of the Sooloo group of islands lying close to the north shore of Borneo, and the people of the north and northeastern coast of Borneo itself: these have of late years proved extremely troublesome both to the English and Dutch traders; both nations are bound by the Convention of 1824, to use their best endeavours for the suppression of piracy, and many efforts have certainly been made for this purpose, although as yet without material effect in diminishing the evil.

" From Labuan, these pirates might certainly be intercepted by armed steamers far more conveniently and cheaply than from any other position that could be easily pointed out: indeed, the very existence of a British settlement would tend to the suppression of piracy.

"As a commercial depôt, Labuan would have considerable advantages by position; the native trade of the vicinity would of course resort to it, and so would that of the north coast of Borneo, of the Sooloo Islands, and of a considerable portion of the Spice Islands. Even for the trade of the Philippines and China, it would have the advantage over Singapore of a voyage by 700 miles shorter; a matter of most material consequence to native commerce.

"With all the countries of the neighbourhood lying west of Labuan I presume that a communication across both monsoons might be maintained throughout the year. This would include a portion of the east coast of the Malay peninsula, Siam, and part of Cochin China.

"Labuan belongs to that portion of the coast of Borneo which is the rudest. The Borneons themselves are of the Malay nation, originally emigrants from Sumatra, and settled here for about six centuries. They are the most distant from their original seat of all the colonies which have sprung from this nation. The people from the interior differ from them in language, manners, and religion, and are divided into tribes as numerous and as rude as the Americans when first seen by Europeans.

"From such a people we are not to expect any valuable products of art or manufacture, for a British mercantile depôt. Pepper is, however, produced in considerable quantity, and the products of the forests are very various, as bees-wax, gum-benjamin, fine camphor, camphor oil, esculent swallows' nests, canes and rattans, which used to form the staple articles of Borneon import into Singapore. The Borneon territory opposite to Labuan abounds also, I believe, in the palm which yields sago, and indeed the chief part of the manufactured article was thirty years ago brought from this country. The Chinese settlers would, no doubt, as in Singapore and Malacca, establish factories for its preparation according to the improved processes which they now practise at those places.

" There may be reason to expect, however, that the timber of the portion of Borneo referred to may be found of value for ship-building; for Mr. Dalrymple states that in his time, above seventy years ago, Chinese junks of 500 tons burthen used to be built in the river of Borneo. As to timber well suited for boats and house-building, it is hardly necessary to add that the north-west coast of Borneo, in common with almost every other part of the Archipelago, contains a supply amounting to superfluity.

"I may take this opportunity of stating, as evidence of the conveniency of this portion of Borneo for a commercial intercourse with China, that down to within the last half century a considerable number of Chinese junks were engaged in trading regularly with Borneo, and that trade ceased only when the native government became too bad and weak to afford it protection. Without the least doubt this trade would again spring up on the erection of the British flag at Labuan. Not a single Chinese junk had resorted to the Straits of Malacca before the establishment of Singapore, and their number is now, of one size or another, and exclusive of the junks of Siam and Cochin China, not less than 100.

"From the cultivation of the land I should not be disposed to expect any thing beyond the production of fresh fruits and esculent vegetables, and, when the land is cleared, of grass for pasture. The seas, in this part of the world, are prolific in fish of great variety and great excellence; and the Chinese settlers are found every where skilful and industrious in taking them.

"Some difficulty will, in the beginning, be experienced with respect to milk, butter, and fresh meat: this was the case at first in Singapore, but the difficulty has in a good measure been overcome. The countries of the Archipelago are generally not suited to pasture, and it is only in a few of them that the ox and buffalo are abundant. The sheep is so no where, and, for the most part, is wanting altogether; cattle, therefore, must be imported. As to corn, it will unquestionably be found far cheaper to import than to raise it. Rice will be the chief bread-corn, and will come in great abundance and cheapness from Siam and Cochin China. No country within 700 miles of Singapore is abundant in corn, and none is grown in the island; yet, from the first establishment of the settlement to the present time, corn has been both cheap and abundant, there has been wonderfully little fluctuation, there are always stocks, and for many years a considerable exportation. A variety of pulses, vegetable oil, and culinary salt, will be derived from the same countries, as is now done in abundance by Singapore.

"The mines of antimony are 300 miles to the south-west of Labuan, and those of gold on the west and the south coasts; and I am not aware that any mineral wealth has been discovered in the portion of Borneo immediately connected with Labuan, except that of coal—far more important and valuable, indeed, than gold or antimony. The existence of a coal-field has been traced from Labuan to the islands of Kayn-arang—which words, in fact, mean coal-island—to the island of Chermin, and from thence to the mainland, over a distance of thirty miles. With respect to the coal of Labuan itself, I find no distinct statement beyond the simple fact of the existence of the mineral; but the coal of the two islands in the river, and of the main, is proved to be—from analysis and trial in steam-navigation—superior to nearly all the coal which India has hitherto yielded, and equal to some of our best English coals. This is the more remarkable as it is known that most surface-minerals, and especially coals, are inferior to the portions of the same veins or beds more deep-seated.

"Nearly as early as the British flag is erected, and, at all events, as soon as it is permanently known to be so, there may be reckoned upon with certainty a large influx of settlers. The best and most numerous of these will be the Chinese. They were settled on the Borneo river when the Borneo government, never very good or otherwise than comparatively violent and disorderly, was most endurable.

" It will be seen by the map that Borneo is, of all the great islands of the western portion of the Archipelago, the nearest to China, and Labuan and its neighbourhood the nearest point of this island. The distance of Hong Kong is but 1000 miles, and that of the island of Hainan, a great place for emigration, not above 800; distances which to the Chinese junks—fast sailers before the strong and favourable winds of the monsoons— do not make voyages exceeding four or five days. The coasts of the provinces of Canton and Fokien have hitherto been the great hives from which Chinese emigration has proceeded; and even Fokien is not above 1400 miles from Labuan, a voyage of seven or eight days. Chinese trade and immigration will come together. The northwest coast of Borneo produces an unusual supply of those raw articles for which there is always a demand in the markets of China; and Labuan, it may be reckoned upon with certainty, will soon become the seat of a larger trade with China than the river of Borneo ever possessed.

"I by no means anticipate the same amount of rapid advance in population, commerce, or financial resources for Labuan, that has distinguished the history of Singapore, a far more centrical position for general commerce; still I think its prospect of success undoubted; while it will have some advantages which Singapore cannot, from its nature, possess. Its coal-mines, and the command of the coal-fields on the river of Borneo, are the most remarkable of these; and its superiority as a post-office[1] station necessarily follows. Then it is far more convenient as a port of refuge; and, as far as our present knowledge will enable us to judge, infinitely more valuable for military purposes, more especially for affording protection to the commerce which passes through the Chinese Sea, amounting at present to probably not less than 300,000 tons of shipping, carrying cargoes certainly not under the value of 15,000,000*l.* sterling.

"Labuan ought, like Singapore, to be a free port; and assuredly will not prosper if it is not. Its revenue should not be derived from customs, but, as in that settlement, from excise duties; upon the nature of these, as it is well known, it is unnecessary to enlarge. They covered during my time, near twenty years ago, and within five years of the establishment of the settlement, the whole charges of a small but sufficient garrison (100 Sepoys), and a moderate but competent civil establishment.

[1] Vide Mr. Wise's Plan for accelerating the communication between Great Britain and China, viz. the conveyance of the mails from Hong-Kong to Suez (*viâ* Ceylon) direct. Submitted to her Majesty's Government, 14th September, 1843; adopted 20th June, 1845.

SUGGESTIONS FOR ACCELERATING THE COMMUNICATION BETWEEN GREAT BRITAIN AND CHINA.

Proposed Route from Hong Kong to London, and vice versâ.	Course.	Distance, Miles.	Average Rate per Hour, Miles.	Interval under Weigh.		Interval at Anchor.		Total Interval.		Duties at Anchor.
				Days.	Hours.	Days.	Hours.	Days.	Hours.	
HONG KONG ... to PULO LABUAN	S. 2° 18′ E.	1009	7	6	—	1	12	7	12	To receive Coal.*
PULO LABUAN ..., SINGAPORE	S. 69 23 W.	707	—	4	6	—	12	4	18	To receive Coal, land and receive Mails.
SINGAPORE ....., MALACCA	{ S. 64 48 W. 19 / N. 51 41 W. 103 }	122	—	—	18	—	6	1	—	To land and receive Mails.
MALACCA ......, PINANG	N. 30 37 W.	222	—	1	8	—	16	2	—	To receive Coal, land and receive Mails.
PINANG ....; CEYLON†	{ N. 82 24 W. 303 / S. 89 45 W. 916 }	1219	—	7	6	1	12	8	18	Ditto Ditto.
CEYLON .... ,, ADEN	As now performed by the Peninsular and Oriental Steam Navigation Co., detention of 2 days included							11	—	
ADEN .... ,, SUEZ	,,			,,		2		8	—	
SUEZ .... ,, ALEXANDRIA	,,			,, all stoppages				3	—	
ALEXANDRIA ..., MALTA	,,			,,				4	—	
MALTA ...., MARSEILLES	H.M. Post-Office Packets			,,				4	—	
MARSEILLES ...., LONDON	Regular course of Post			,,				5	—	

Total interval from HONG KONG to LONDON, and vice versâ, by the proposed Route . . . . Days 59 —

Average interval of transmission of China Correspondence, via Calcutta, and Bombay, during the last Twenty Overland Mails. viz. from 10th October, 1841, to 6th May, 1843 . . . . 89 —

Difference of time in favour of proposed Route . . . . Days 30 —

MEM.—I have adopted an average rate of seven miles per hour as a fair estimate of the speed well-appointed Steam Vessels, of moderate size and power, will be enabled to accomplish and maintain, throughout the proposed Route, at all seasons of the year; for, during the whole distance from Pinang to Aden, and vice versâ, neither monsoon, from the course steered, becomes at any period a directly adverse wind, an advantage which the route hitherto observed does not possess. Assuming that the Honourable East India Company continue the management of the Bombay line, and that the Peninsular and Oriental Steam Navigation Company are encouraged to render their operations more comprehensive, by the establishment of branch steamers between Ceylon and Singapore, to which latter port her Majesty's steam vessels on the China station could convey the mails from Hong Kong, this all-important object might, without difficulty, be attained. The advantages to the Straits settlements, consequent on the adoption of improved arrangements, require no comment; and the practicability of effecting a very considerable acceleration of the communication with China is evident from the simple fact, that the average interval which has occurred in the transmission of letters from China, by the last twenty Overland Mails (irrespective of the unfortunate July mail from Bombay), exceeds the period occasionally occupied by fast-sailing ships, in accomplishing the voyage viâ the Cape of Good Hope.

LONDON, 14th Sept. 1843.‡

P.S.—Oct. 9th. The arrival at Suez on the 16th ult. of the H.C.S. Akbar, in forty-six days from Hong Kong, after accomplishing the passage down the China seas, against the s.w. monsoon—unassisted also by any previously arranged facilities for coaling, exchange of steamers at Aden, and other manifest advantages requisite for the proper execution of this important service, confirms the correctness of my estimate for performing the voyage from Hong Kong to Suez, or vice versâ, viz. forty-three days, including stoppages.

HENRY WISE,
13 Austin Friars.

* The Borneo coal mines would also serve to keep the Hong Kong, Singapore, and Pinang stations supplied with fuel for Steam Vessels carrying the Mails between Hong Kong and Suez direct.
† Receiving at Ceylon the Outward Overland Mail from England, and returning therewith to China.
‡ Date of submitting the above proposed route and estimate to her Majesty's government for consideration.

"The military and civil establishments have been greatly increased of late years; but the revenue, still in its nature the same, has kept pace with them. During my administration of Singapore, the municipal charges fell on the general fund; but they are at present amply provided for from a distinct source, chiefly an assessment on house-property.

"If the military and civil charges of Labuan are kept within moderate bounds, I make no doubt but that a similar excise revenue will be adequate to cover the charges of both, and that in peace at least the state need not be called on to make any disbursement on its account; while during a naval war, if the state make any expenditure, it will be fully compensated by the additional security which the settlement will afford to British commerce, and the annoyance it will cause to the enemy.

"As to the disposal of the land, always a difficult question in a new and unoccupied colony, the result of my own inquiries and personal experience lead me to offer it as my decided conviction that the most expedient plan — that which is least troublesome to the government, most satisfactory to the settler, and ultimately most conducive to the public prosperity — is to dispose of it for a term of years, that is on long leases of 1000 years, or virtually in perpetuity; the object in this case of adopting the leasehold tenure being by making the land a chattel interest, to get rid of the difficulties in the matter of inheritance and transfer, which, under the administration of English law, and in reference more particularly to the Asiatic people who will be the principal landowners, are incident to real property. Town allotments might be sold subject to a considerable quit-rent, but allotments in the country for one entirely nominal. Those of the latter description should be small, proportionate with the extent of the island, and the time and difficulty required in such a climate to clear the land, now overgrown for the most part with a stupendous forest of evergreen trees, and the wood of which is too abundant to be of any value, certainly for the most part not worth the land-carriage of a couple of furlongs.

"A charter for the administration of justice should be as nearly as possible contemporaneous with the cession. Great inconvenience has resulted in all our Eastern settlements of the same nature with that speculated on at Labuan, from the want of all legal provision for the administration of justice; and remembering this, it ought to be guarded against in the case of Labuan.

"Whether in preparing for the establishment of a British settlement on the coast of Borneo, or in actually making one, her Majesty's ministers, I am satisfied, will advert to the merits and peculiar qualifications of Mr. Brooke. That gentleman is unknown to me, except by his acts and writings; but, judging by these, I consider him as possessing all the qualities which have distinguished the successful founders of new colonies; intrepidity, firmness, and enthusiasm, with the art of governing and leading the masses. He possesses some, moreover, which have not always belonged to such men, however otherwise distinguished; a knowledge of the language, manners, customs, and institutions of the natives by whom the colony is to be surrounded; with benevolence and an independent fortune, things still more unusual with the projectors of colonies. Towards the formation of a new colony, indeed, the available services of such a man, presuming they are available, may be considered a piece of good fortune."

CONCLUDING OBSERVATIONS.

THE recent proceedings of Government in following up the impression made upon Malay piracy, as related in these pages; the appointment of Mr. Brooke as British Agent in Borneo, armed with the moral and physical power of his country; the cession of the island of Labuan to the British Crown; and the great advance already made by the English ruler of Sarāwak, in laying broad foundations for native prosperity, whilst extending general security and commerce; all combine to add an interest to the early individual steps which have led to measures of so much national consequence.

Deeply as I felt the influence of that individual on the condition of Borneo, and the Malayan Archipelago generally, whilst employed there, and much as I anticipated from his energetic character, extraordinary exertions, and future views, I confess that my expectations have been greatly increased by the progress of events since that period. It needed nothing to confirm me in the prospects that were sure to result from his enlightened acts—from his prudence and humanity in the treatment of his

Dyak subjects, and the neighbouring and interior independent tribes—from his firm resistance to the Malay tyranny exercised upon the aborigines, and his punishment of Malay aggression, wherever perpetrated. But when I see these elements of good wisely seconded by the highest authorities of England, I cannot but look for the consummation of every benefit desired, much more rapidly and effectively than if left to personal effort, even though that person were a Brooke! If the appearance of H.M.S. Dido on the coast and at Sarāwak produced a salutary effect upon all our relations with the inhabitants, it may well be presumed that the mission of Captain Bethune, and the expedition under Rear-Admiral Sir Thomas Cochrane, must have greatly improved and extended that wholesome state of affairs. Indeed, it is evident, by the complete success which attended Mr. Brooke's official visit to Borneo Proper in H.M.S. Driver, after receiving despatches from Lord Aberdeen appointing him British Agent in the island, carried out by Captain Bethune in November 1844, that the presence of a British force in those seas was alone necessary to enable him to suppress piracy, and perfect his plans for the establishment of a native government, which should not oppress the country, and which should cultivate the most friendly intercourse with us. Thus we find the piratical Pangeran Usop put down, and Muda Hassim exercising the sovereign power in the name of his imbecile nephew, who still retains the title of Sultan. The principal chiefs, and men distinguished by talent and some acquaintance with foreign affairs, are now on our side; and it only requires to support them in order that civilisation may rapidly spread over the land, and Borneo become again, as it was one or two centuries ago, the abode of an industrious, rich, pacific, and mercantile people, interchanging products with all the trading nations of the world, and conferring and reaping those blessings which follow in the train of just and honourable trade wheresoever its enterprising spirit leads in the pursuit of honest gain. As the vain search for the philosopher's stone conducted to many a useful and valuable discovery, so may we be assured that the real seeking for gold through the profitable medium of commerce has been, is, and will be the grand source of filling the earth with comfort and happiness.

Among the numerous visions of this kind which open to our sense whilst reflecting on the new prospects of this vast island—so little known, yet known to possess almost unbounded means to invite and return commercial activity—is the contemplation of the field it opens to missionary labours. When we read Mr. Brooke's description of the aboriginal Dyak, and observe what he has himself done in one locality, within the space of four or five short years, what may we not expect to be accomplished by the zeal of Christian missions, judiciously directed to reclaim such a people from utter barbarism, and induce them to become true members of a faith which teaches forbearance and charity between man and man, and inculcates, with the love and hope of heaven, an abhorrence of despotism and blood, and a disposition to live in good will and peace with all our fellow-creatures? There are here no prejudices of caste, as in India, to impede the missionaries' progress. Mr. Brooke has pointed out what may be effected in this way; and we have only to say amen to his prayer, with an earnest aspiration that it may be speedily fulfilled.

Having enjoyed the pleasure of communicating to the public this satisfactory description of the *status quo* in Borneo to the latest period (September 1845), I venture to congratulate them upon it. Thus far all is well, and as it should be, and promising the happiest issue. But I hope I may not be charged with presumption in offering an opinion from my experience in this quarter, and respectfully suggesting that in addition to a permanent British settlement at Labuan, it will be absolutely necessary to proceed with the suppression of Malay piracy, by steadily acting against every pirate-hold. Without a continued and determined series of operations of this sort, it is my conviction that even the most sanguinary and fatal onslaughts will achieve nothing beyond a present and temporary good. The impression on the native mind is not sufficiently lasting. Their old impulses and habits return with fresh force; they forget their heavy retribution; and in two or three years the memory of them is almost entirely effaced. Till completely suppressed, there must be no relaxation: and well worth the perseverance is the end in view, the welfare of one of the richest and most improvable portions of the globe, and the incalculable diffusion of the blessings of Britain's prosperous commerce and humanising dominion.

In looking forward to the certain realisation of these prospects, I may mention the important circumstance of the discovery of coal in abundance for the purposes of steam navigation. The surveys already made afford assurance of this fact; and the requisite arrangements are in progress for opening and working the mines. It is generally known that the Dutch assert very wide pretensions to colonies and monopolies in those seas. The Treaty between the Netherlands Government and England will be found in the Appendix; and although that important document contains no reference whatever to Borneo, it is most desirable for the general extension of commerce that no national jealousies, nor ideas of conflicting interests, nor encroaching and ambitious projects, may be allowed to interfere with or prevent the beneficial progress of this important region. With such a man as Mr. Brooke to advise the course most becoming, disinterested, and humane. for the British empire to pursue, it is not too much to say that if the well-being of these races of our fellow-creatures is defeated or postponed, the crime will not lie at our door. Our sacrifices to extinguish Slavery throughout the universe is a sure and unquestionable pledge that we will do our utmost to extirpate the horrid traffic in these parts; and, together with the uprooting of piracy, it is the bounden duty of both Holland and Great Britain to unite cordially in this righteous cause. The cry of nature is addressed to them; and if rejected, as sure as there is justice and mercy in the Providence which overrules the fate of nations, no blessing will prosper them; and wealth, and dominion, and happiness will pass away from them for ever. Mr. Brooke invokes their co-operation; and his noble appeal cannot be withstood.

The central position of Labuan is truly remarkable. That island is distant from

> Hong Kong . . . 1009 miles.
> Singapore . . . . 707 ,,
> Siam . . . . . 984 ,,
> Manilla . . . . . 650 ,,

On the other hand, Mr. Brooke's territory of Sarāwak is distant from

> Singapore . . . . 427 miles.
> Labuan . . . . . 304 ,,
> Hong Kong . . . 1199 ,,

How direct and central are these valuable

possessions for the universal trade of the East!—and how expedient to have a fair knowledge of their geographical and navigable capabilities! To help forward these desiderata, the maps which illustrate this work have been carefully constructed; and in order that they might be more available to men-of-war as well as to merchantmen, the use of mixed foreign and barbarous names has been superseded[1] by such plain English as 'point,' 'cape,' 'bay,' 'river,' 'mount,' 'bluff,' &c.

[1] At the recommendation of one of our ablest hydrographers, Captain F. Beaufort, R.N., F.R.S., after the maps were engraved with the old unintelligible titles of Tanjong, Pulo, Gunong, Songi, &c.

APPENDIX.

APPENDIX.

No. I.

Proposed exploring Expedition to the Asiatic Archipelago, by JAMES BROOKE, *Esq.* 1838.

THE voyage I made to China opened an entirely new scene, and shewed me what I had never seen before, savage life and savage nature. I inquired, and I read, and I became more and more assured that there was a large field of discovery and adventure open to any man daring enough to enter upon it. Just take a map and trace a line over the Indian Archipelago, with its thousand unknown islands and tribes. Cast your eye over the vast island of New Guinea, where the foot of European has scarcely, if ever, trod. Look at the northern coast of Australia, with its mysterious Gulf of Carpentaria; a survey of which it is supposed would solve the great geographical question respecting the rivers of the mimic continent. Place your finger on Japan, with its exclusive and civilised people; it lies an unknown lump on our earth, and an undefined line on our charts! Think of the northern coast of China, willing, as is reported, to open an intercourse and trade with Europeans, spite of their arbitrary government. Stretch your pencil over the Pacific Ocean, which Cook himself declares a field of discovery for ages to come! Proceed to the coast of South America, from the region of gold-dust to the region of furs — the land ravaged by the cruel Spaniard and the no less cruel Buccanier—the scene of the adventures of Drake and the descriptions of Dampier. The places I have enumerated are mere names, with no specific ideas attached to them: lands and seas where the boldest navigators gained a reputation, and where hundreds may yet do so, if they have the same courage and the same perseverance. Imagination whispers to ambition that there are yet lands unknown which might be discovered. Tell me, would not a man's life be well spent—tell me, would it not be well sacrificed, in an endeavour to explore these regions? When I think on dangers and death, I think of them only because they would remove me from such a field for ambition, for energy, and for knowledge.

Borneo, Celebes, Sooloo, the Moluccas, and the islands of the Straits of Sunda and Banka, compose what is called the Malayan group; and the Malays located on the seashores of these and other islands may with certainty be classed as belonging to one people. It is well known, however, that the interior of these countries is inhabited by various tribes, differing from the Malays and each other, and presenting numerous gradations of early civilisation: the Dyaks of Borneo, the Papuans of New Guinea, and others, besides the black race scattered over the islands. Objects of traffic here as elsewhere present interesting subjects of inquiry; and whilst our acquaintance with every other portion of the globe, from the passage of the Pole to the navigation of the Euphrates, has greatly extended, it is matter of surprise that we know scarcely any thing of these people beyond the bare fact of their existence, and remain altogether ignorant of the geographical features of the countries they inhabit. Countries which present an extended field for Christianity and commerce, which none surpass in fertility, rich beyond the Americas in mineral productions, and unrivalled in natural beauty, continue unexplored to the present day, and, spite of the advantages which would probably result, have failed to attract the attention they so well deserve. The difficulty of the undertaking will scarcely account for its non-performance, if we consider the voluntary sacrifices made on the shrine of African research, or the energy displayed and the sufferings encountered by the explorers of the Polar regions: yet the necessity of prosecuting the voyage in an armed vessel, the wildness of the interior tribes, the lawless ferocity of the Malays, and other dangers, would prevent most individuals from fixing on this field for exertion, and points it out as one which could best and most fully be accomplished by Government or some influential body.

It is not my object to enter into any detail of the past history of the Malayan nations, but I may refer to the undoubted facts that they have been in a state of deterioration since we first became acquainted with them; and the records of our early voyagers, together with the remains of antiquity still visible in Java and Sumatra, prove that once flourishing nations have now ceased to exist, and that countries once teeming with human life are now tenantless and deserted. The causes of such lamentable change need only be alluded to; but it is fit to remark, that whilst the standard of education is unfurled, and dreams are propagated of the progressive advancement of the human race, a large part of the globe has been gradually relapsing and allowed to relapse into barbarism. Whether the early decay of the Malay states, and their consequent demoralisation, arose from the introduction of Mahommedism, or resulted from the intrigues of European ambition, it were useless to decide; but we are very certain that this "Eden of the Eastern wave" has been reduced to a state of anarchy and confusion, as repugnant to every dictate of humanity as it is to the prospect of commercial advantage.

Borneo and Celebes, and indeed the greater portion of the islands of the Malayan Archipelago, are still unknown, and the apathy of two centuries still reigns supreme with the enlightened people of England; whilst they willingly make the most expensive efforts favourable to science, commerce, or Christianity in other quarters, the locality which eminently combines these three objects is alone neglected and alone uncared for. It has unfortunately been the fate of our Indian possessions to have laboured under the prejudice and contempt of a large portion of the well-bred community. Whilst the folly of fashion requires an acquaintance with the deserts of Africa, and a most ardent thirst for a knowledge of the usages of Timbuctoo, it at the same time justifies the most profound ignorance of all matters connected with the government and geography of our vast acquisitions in Hindoostan. The Indian Archipelago has fully shared this neglect; and even the tender philanthropy of the present day, which originates such multifarious schemes for the amelioration of doubtful evils, which shudders at the prolongation of apprenticeship for a single year in the west, is blind to the existence of slavery in its worst and most aggravated form in the east. Not a single prospectus is spread abroad; not a single voice is upraised to relieve the darkness of Paganism, and the horrors of the eastern slave-trade. Whilst the trumpet-tongue of many an orator excites thousands to the rational and charitable objects of converting the Jews and reclaiming the gipsies; whilst the admirable exertions of missionary enterprise in the Ausonian climes of the

South Sea have invested them with worldly power as well as religious influence; whilst we admire the torrent of devotional and philosophical exertion, we cannot help deploring that the zeal and attention of the leaders of these charitable crusades have never been directed to the countries under consideration. These unhappy countries have failed to rouse attention or excite commiseration, and as they sink lower and lower, they afford a striking proof how civilisation may be dashed, and how the purest and richest lands under the sun may be degraded and brutalised by a continued course of oppression and misrule. It is under these circumstances that I have considered individual exertion may be usefully applied to rouse the zeal of slumbering philanthropy, and to lead the way to an increased knowledge of the Indian Archipelago. Such an exertion will be made at some cost and some sacrifice; and I shall here quit the general topic, and confine myself to the specific objects of my intended voyage.

It must be premised, however, that any plan previously decided on must always be subject during its execution to great modifications in countries where the population is always rude and often hostile, and where the influence of climate is sometimes so fatally opposed to the progress of inquiry. Local information likewise frequently renders such a change both advisable and advantageous; and circumstances as they spring up too often influence us beyond the power of foresight, more especially in my own case, where the utmost care would still leave the means very inadequate to the full accomplishment of the proposed undertaking. With a small vessel properly equipped, and provided with the necessary instruments for observation, and the means for collecting specimens in natural history, it is proposed in the first instance to proceed to Singapore, which may be considered as head-quarters for the necessary intervals of refreshment and repose, and for keeping open a certain communication with Europe. Here the best local information can be obtained, interpreters procured, the crew augmented for any particular service; and here, if needful, a small vessel of native construction may be added to the expedition, to facilitate the objects in view. An acquaintance may likewise be formed with the more respectable Bugis merchants, and their good-will conciliated in the usual mode, viz. by civility and presents, so as to remove any misconceived jealousy on the score of trading rivalry, and to induce a favourable report of our friendly intentions in their own country, and at the places where they may touch. The Royalist will probably reach Singapore in the month of March 1839, at the latter end of the north-west, or rainy monsoon. The delay consequent on effecting the objects above mentioned, besides gaining a general acquaintance with the natural history and trade of the settlement, and some knowledge of the Malay language, will usefully occupy the time until the setting in of the south-east, or dry monsoon. It may be incidentally mentioned, however, that in the vicinity of Singapore there are many islands imperfectly known, and which, during the intervals of the rainy season, will afford interesting occupation. I allude, more especially, to the space between the Straits of Rhio and those of Duryan, and likewise to the island called Bintang, which, although laid down as one large island, is probably composed of small ones, divided by navigable straits; a better acquaintance with which might facilitate the voyage from Singapore to the more eastern islands, by bringing to light other passages beside those of Rhio and Duryan; and, at any rate, would add something to our geographical knowledge in the immediate vicinity of our settlement. On the commencement of the healthy season I propose sailing from Singapore, and proceeding without loss of time to Malludu Bay, at the north end of Borneo. This spot has been chosen for the first essay; and in a country, every part of which is highly interesting, and almost unknown, the mere fact of its being a British possession gives it a prior claim to attention.

The objects in view may be briefly mentioned. 1. A general knowledge of the Bay, and the correct position of various points,—more especially the two principal headlands at its entrance, so as to determine its outline. The westernmost of these headlands, called Sampanmange, will likewise determine the extreme north point of Borneo. 2. Inquiries for the settlement of Cochin Chinese, reported, on Earl's authority, to be fixed in the vicinity of Bankoka: an intercourse will, if possible, be opened with this settlement, if in existence. 3. The rivers which flow into the bay will be carefully and minutely explored, and an attempt will be made to penetrate into the interior as far as the lake of Kini Ballu. 4. For the same purpose, every endeavour will be used to open a communication with the aboriginal inhabitants of the country, and every means employed to conciliate their good opinion; and (if the ceremony exists in this part of the island) to enter into the bonds of fraternity (described by Mr. Dalton) with some of the chiefs.

I speak with great diffidence about penetrating into the interior of this country, for I am well aware of the insurmountable difficulties which the hard reality often presents, which are previously overlooked and easily overcome in the smoothness of paper, or the luxury of a drawing-room. The two points to be chiefly relied upon for this purpose are, a friendly intercourse with the natives, and the existence of navigable rivers. It is mentioned by Sir Stamford Raffles, on native authority, that a land-communication, of not more than forty miles, exists between Malludu Bay and Lake Kini Ballu; but neither this computation, nor any other derived from the natives, however intelligent otherwise, can be relied on; for the inhabitants of these countries are generally ignorant of any measure for distance; and their reckoning by time is so vague, as to defy a moderately-certain conclusion. The fact, however, of the vicinity of the lake to the bay may be concluded; and it follows, as a reasonable inference, that the river or rivers flowing into the bay communicate with the lake. The existence of such rivers, which were from the locality to have been expected, is vouched for by Captain Forrest. "Most of this north part of Borneo (he says), granted to the English East India Company by the Sooloos, is watered by noble rivers: those that discharge themselves into Malludu Bay are not barred." It is by one or other of these rivers that I should hope to penetrate as far as the lake and mountain of Kini Ballu, and into the country of the Idaan. I have not been able to learn that any Malay towns of importance are situated in the bight of Malludu Bay, and their absence will render a friendly communication with the aborigines a matter of comparative ease. The advantages likely to result from such friendly relations are so evident, that I need not dwell upon them; though the mode of effecting such an intercourse must be left to the thousand contingencies which govern all, and act so capriciously on the tempers of the savage races. The utmost forbearance, and a liberality guided by prudence, so as not to excite too great a degree of cupidity, appear the fundamental rules for managing men in a low state of civilisation. The results of an amicable understanding are as uncertain as its commencement; for they depend on the enterprise of the individual, and the power of the native tribe into whose hands he may have fallen. I will not, therefore, enter into a visionary field of discovery; but it appears to me certain that, without the assistance of the natives, no small party can expect to penetrate far into a country populous by report, and in many parts thickly covered with wood. Without entertaining any exaggerated expectation, I trust that something may be added to our geographical knowledge of the sea-coast of this bay, its leading features, productions, rivers, anchorages, and inhabitants, the prospect of trade, and the means of navigation; and although my wishes lead me strongly to penetrate as far as the lake of Kini Ballu, yet the obstacles which may be found to exist to the fulfilment of this desire will induce me to rest satisfied with the more moderate and reasonable results.

It may not be superfluous to notice here, that a foregone conclusion appears to be spread abroad regarding the aboriginal (so called) inhabitants of Borneo, and that they are usually considered and mentioned under the somewhat vague appellation of Dyaks. They are likewise commonly pronounced as originating from the same stock as the Arafuras of Celebes and New Guinea, and radically identical with the Polynesian race. The conclusion is not in itself highly improbable, but certainly premature, as the facts upon which it is built are so scanty and doubtful as to authorise no such structure. On an island of the vast size of Borneo, races radically distinct might exist; and at any rate, the opposite conclusion is hardly justifiable from the specimens of language or the physical appearance of the tribes of the southern portion of the country. We have Malay authority for believing that there are many large tribes in the interior, differing greatly in their degree of civilisation, though all alike removed from the vicinity of a superior people. We have the Dyaks of the south; the Idaan of the north; the Kagins; and a race little better than monkeys, who live in trees, eat without cooking, are hunted by the other tribes, and would seem to exist in the lowest conceivable grade of humanity. If we may trust these accounts, these latter people resemble in many particulars the Orang Benua, or aborigines of the peninsula; but the Dyaks and Idaans are far superior, living in villages, cultivating the ground, and possessing cattle. Besides these, likewise, we have the names of several other tribes or people; and, in all probability, many exist in the interior with whom we are unacquainted.

There are strong reasons for believing that the Hindoo religion, which obtained so extensively in Java and Sumatra, and yet survives at Bali and Lombock, was likewise extended to Borneo; and some authors have conceived grounds for supposing a religion anterior even to this. If only a portion of these floating opinions should be true, and the truth can only be tested by inquiry, we may fairly look for the descendants of the Hindoo dynasty as well as an aboriginal people. It never seems to have occurred to any one to compare the Dyaks with the people of Bali and Lombock. We know indeed but little of the former; but both races are fair, good-looking, and gentle. Again, respecting the concluded identity of the Dyaks and the Arafuras, it is clear we have a very limited knowledge indeed of the former; and, I may ask, what do we know of the Arafuras?

In short, I feel as reluctant to embrace any preconceived theory as I am to adopt the prevailing notion on this subject; for it requires a mass of facts, of which we are wholly deficient, to arrive at any thing approaching a reasonable conclusion. To return, however, to the proceedings of the Royalist, I would remark, that it depends greatly on the time passed in Malludu Bay whether our next endeavour be prosecuted at Abai on the western, or Tusan Abai on the eastern coast. The object in visiting Abai would be chiefly to penetrate to the lake, which, on the authority of Dalrymple and Burton, is not far distant thence, by a water-communication; but should any success have attended similar efforts from Malludu Bay, this project will be needless, as in that case the enterprise will have been prosecuted to the westward, and reach to the vicinity of Abai. As Kaminis is the limit of the British territory to the westward, so Point Kaniungan, situated to the southward of the bay of Sandakan, forms the eastern boundary; and a line drawn from coast to coast between these points is represented as including our possessions. A reference to the chart will shew the extent to be considerable; and the eastern coast from Malludu Bay to Point Kaniungan is so very little known, that it is highly desirable to become acquainted with its general features and conformation, and to seek thence the means of gaining an inlet into the interior, should it be denied at Malludu Bay.

The reported proximity of Kini Ballu to Malludu Bay, and likewise to Abai, would (supposing it is anything like the size it is affirmed to be) lead us to expect that it cannot be far distant from the eastern coast; and it is but reasonable to conclude that some rivers or streams discharge themselves into the sea in the numerous indentations that abound on this shore. However this may be, the coast, with its bays and islands and bold headlands, is one of great interest, and almost unknown; and the careful inspection of it as far as Point Kaniungan will, I trust, add something to our knowledge. The longitude of Point Kaniungan and Point Unsang will likewise determine the eastern extremity of Borneo.

Much more might be added on this topic, especially of the reported communication by a line of lakes from Malludu Bay to Banjamassim, which, if true, would in all probability place some of these lakes near particular points of the east coast, as the whole line, from the relative position of the two extremes, must be on the eastern side of the island. These reports, and the various surmises which arise from them, are rather matters for verification than discussion; and I will therefore only add that, tempted by success, I shall not devote less than a year and a half to this object; but, in case of finding a sickly climate, or meeting with a decidedly hostile population, I shall more easily abandon the field, and turn to others of not less interest, and perhaps of less risk.

Equal to Borneo in riches, and superior in picturesque beauty to any part of the Archipelago, is the large and eccentric country of the Bugis, called Celebes. So deep are the indentations of its coasts, that the island may be pronounced as being composed of a succession of peninsulas, nearly uniting in a common centre in the district of Palos; and thus, by the proximity of every part to the sea, offering great facilities for brief and decisive interior excursions. The Dutch are in possession of Makassar, and had formerly settlements on the north-west coast and in the bay of Sawa. Their power appears, however, never to have been very extensively acknowledged; and at present I have not been able to meet with any account of the condition of their factories. This information will probably be gained at Singapore. Avoiding the Dutch settlements, I propose limiting my inquiries to the northern and north-eastern portion of the island, more especially the great bay of Gunong Tella. It is impossible to state here the direction of these inquiries, or any definite object to which they should be turned, as I am acquainted with no author who speaks of the country save in a general and vague manner. It is reported as rich, fertile, mountainous, strikingly beautiful, and possessed of rivers; abounding in birds, and inhabited, like Borneo, by wild tribes in the interior, and by the Bugis on the sea-shores and entrance of rivers. The character of the Bugis, though so variously represented, gives me strong hopes of rendering them, by care and kindness, useful instruments in the prosecution of these researches; for all writers agree that they are active, hardy, enterprising, and commercial; and it is seldom that a people possessing such characteristics are deaf to the suggestions of self-interest or kindly feeling. The arrogance, and especially the indolence, of the Malays counteracts the influence of these strong incentives; and the impulse which governs such rude tribes as the Dyaks and Arafuras is a dangerous weapon, which cuts all ways, and often when least anticipated. The Badjows, or sea-gipsies, are another race on whom some dependence may be placed. Mr. Earl, who had a personal acquaintance with this tribe, and could speak their language, always expressed to me a degree of confidence in their good faith, which must have had some grounds.

I may here conclude the first stage of the expedition, during the progress of which the head-quarters will be fixed at Singapore. During some of the intervals I hope to see Manilla, and to acquire a cursory knowledge of the unexplored track at the southern extremity of Celebes, called in Norie's general chart the Tiger Islands.

The time devoted to the objects above mentioned must, as I have before said, be regulated by the degree of fortune which attends them; for, cheered by success, I should not readily abandon the field; yet, if persecuted by climate, or other serious detriments, I shall frequently shift the ground, to remove myself beyond such evil influence. It is scarcely needful to continue a detail of projects so distant, having already carved out for myself a work which I should be proud to perform, and which is already as extended as the chances of human life and human resolves will warrant. The continuation of the voyage would lead me to take the Royalist to Timor or Port Essington, thence making excursions to the Arru Isles, Timor Laut, and the southern shores of New Guinea. That part of the coast contiguous to Torres Straits I am particularly desirous of visiting; as it has been suggested to me by Mr. Earl, and I think with reason, that a better channel than the one we are at present acquainted with may be found there. That such a channel exists, and will be discovered when the coast is surveyed, I entertain but little doubt; but the navigation is hazardous, and must, from the westward, be attempted with great caution.

My own proceedings must, of course, be regulated by the discoveries previously made by Captain Wickham or others; and as this gentleman has orders to survey Torres Straits, the field may be well trodden before I reach it. The rest of the voyage I shall consider as one merely of pleasure, combining such utility as circumstances will permit. It is probable that I shall visit our Australian settlements; glance at the islands of the Pacific; and return to Europe round Cape Horn. Before concluding, I may observe, that there are points of inquiry which may be useful to the studies of the learned, which (provided the process be moderately simple) I shall be willing to make, and I shall always be happy to receive any directions or suggestions regarding them. I allude to observations on the tides, to geology, to the branches of natural history, &c. &c., for the general inquirer often neglects or overlooks highly interesting facts, from his attention not having been called to them. The specimens of natural history will be forwarded home on every visit to Singapore; and the information will be sent to the Geographical Society, and may always, if it be of any value, be used as freely as it is communicated. In like manner, the objects of natural history will be open to any person who is at all interested in such pursuits. I cannot but express my regret, that from pecuniary considerations as well as the small size of the vessel, and the limited quantity of provision she carries, I am unable to take a naturalist and draughtsman; but I should always hail with pleasure any scientific person who joined me abroad, or who happened to be in the countries at the time; and I may venture to promise him every encouragement and facility in the prosecution of his pursuits. I embark upon the expedition with great cheerfulness, with a stout vessel, a good crew, and the ingredients of success as far as the limited scale of the undertaking will permit; and I cast myself upon the waters—like Mr. Southey's little book—but whether the world will know me after many days, is a question which, hoping the best, I cannot answer with any positive degree of assurance.

No. II.

Sketch of Borneo, or Pulo Kalamantan, by
J. HUNT, *Esq.*

(Communicated, in 1812, to the Honourable Sir Thomas Stamford Raffles, late Lieutenant-Governor of Java.)

THE island of Borneo extends from 7° 7' north to 4° 12' south latitude, and from 108° 45' to 119° 25' east longitude; measuring at its extreme length nine hundred miles, at its greatest breadth seven hundred, and in circumference three thousand. It is bounded on the north by the Solo seas, on the east by the straits of Macassar, on the south by the Java, and on the west by the China seas. Situated in the track of the most extensive and valuable commerce, intersected on all sides with deep and navigable rivers, indented with safe and cápacious harbours, possessing one of the richest soils on the globe, abounding in all the necessaries of human life, and boasting commercial products that have in all ages excited the avarice and stimulated the desires of mankind; with the exception of New Holland, it is the largest island known. Of the existence of this extensive territory, so highly favoured by Providence, and enriched by the choicest productions of nature, there remains scarce a vestige in the geographical descriptions of the day; and its rich products and fertile shores, by one tacit and universal consent, appear abandoned by all the European nations of the present age, and handed over to the ravages of extensive hordes of piratical banditti, solely intent on plunder and desolation.

The natives and the Malays, formerly, and even at this day, call this large island by the exclusive name of Pulo Kalamantan, from a sour and indigenous fruit so called. Borneo was the name only of a city, the capital of one of the three distinct kingdoms on the island. When Magalhaens visited it in the year 1520, he saw a rich and populous city, a luxuriant and fertile country, a powerful prince, and a magnificent court: hence the Spaniards hastily concluded that the whole island, not only belonged to this prince, but that it was likewise named Borneo. In this error they have been followed by all other European nations. The charts, however, mark this capital " Borneo Proper," or in other words, the only place properly Borneo: this is the only confession of this misnomer that I have met with amongst Europeans. The natives pronounce Borneo, Bruni, and say it is derived from the word Brani, courageous; the aboriginal natives within this district having ever remained unconquered.

The aborigines of Borneo, or Pulo Kalamantan, still exist in the interior in considerable numbers; there are various tribes of them, speaking different dialects. Some of them acknowledge Malay chiefs, as at Landa, Songo, Mantan, &c. Several communities of them still remain under independent chiefs of their own nation; and every where their origin, their language, their religion, their manners and customs, are totally distinct and apparent from those of the Islams, or Malays, who have settled on the island. About Pontiana and Sambas they are called Dayers; at Benjarmasing, Biajus; at Borneo Proper, Moruts; farther northward, Orang Idan. Their original history is as much enveloped in obscurity as that of the Monocaboes of Malaya, the Rejangs and Battas of Sumatra, or the Togals of the Philippines. On a nearer acquaintance with their language, customs, traditions, &c. perhaps an affinity in origin may be discovered among all the original possessors of the eastern isles. The Moruts and Orang Idan are much fairer and better featured than the Malays, of a more strong and robust frame, and have the credit of being a brave race of people. The Dayer is much darker, and approaches nearer in resemblance to the Malay. The Biajus I never saw. The few particulars which I have been able to collect of these people I shall briefly state: They live in miserable small huts; their sole dress consists of a slight wrapper round their waists, sometimes made of bark, at others from skins of animals, or perhaps of blue or white cloth; they eat rice or roots, and indeed any description of food, whether beast, reptile, or vermin: they are extremely filthy; this and bad food give them a cutaneous disorder, with which they are very generally afflicted. Several tribes of them smear themselves with oil and pigments, which gives them the appearance of being tattooed. Whether this is intended to defend them against the bites of insects, to operate as a cure or prevention of this epidemic, or to adorn their persons, I cannot take upon me to decide. They believe, it is said, in a Supreme Being, and offer sacrifices of gratitude to a beneficent Deity. Polygamy is not allowed among them; no man has more than one wife: they burn their dead. They are said to shoot poisoned balls or arrrows through hollow tubes; and whenever they kill a man, they preserve the skull to exhibit as a trophy to commemorate the achievement of their arms. They are said to have no mode of communicating their ideas by characters or writing, like the Battas. Driven from the sea-coast of Borneo into the mountains and fastnesses in the interior, they are more occupied in the chase and the pursuits of husbandry than in commerce. They, however, barter their inland produce of camphor, gold, diamonds, birds-nests, wax, and cattle, for salt (which they hold in the highest degree of estimation, eating it with as much *goût* as we do sugar), china porcelain, brass and iron cooking utensils, brass bracelets, coarse blue and white cloth, Java tobacco, arrack (which they also like), parangs, hardware, beads, &c. Some tribes of them are said to pull out their front teeth and substitute others of gold, and others adorn themselves with tigers' teeth. The greatest numbers and most considerable bodies of these men are found near Kiney Balu and about Borneo Proper.

The Malays represent them as the most savage and ferocious of men; but to be more savage or ferocious than a Malay is a thing utterly impossible. Their representations may be accounted for. These aborigines have always evinced a strong disposition and predilection for liberty and freedom; they have either resisted the yoke of the Malay, or have retired to their mountains to enjoy this greatest of all human blessings. The Malay, unable to conquer them, lays plans for kidnapping as many as he can fall in with. Every Dayak so taken is made a slave of, his children sold, and his women violated. The Malay, hence, is justly considered by them as the violater of every law, human and divine; and whenever any of these people meet with one, they satiate their vengeance, and destroy him as the enemy of their race, and as a monster of the human kind. The Portuguese missionaries found these people very tractable converts, and very large bodies of them are very easily governed by a single Malay chief, as at Landa, Songo, and Matan. I have seen very large bodies of them at Kimanis and Maludu, but none of them possessing the ferocity of a Malay.

The Islams, or Malayans, who now possess the sea-coasts of Borneo (as well as the sea-coasts of all the eastern islands), are said to be colonies from Malacca, Johore, &c. planted in the fourteenth century; at this period, according to Mr. Poivre, " Malacca was a country well peopled, and was consequently well cultivated. This nation was once one of the greatest powers in the eastern seas, and made a very considerable figure in the theatre of Asia: they colonised Borneo, Celebes, Macassar, Moluccas, &c." The Malays on Borneo are like the Malays every where else, the most atrocious race of beings on the earth; and from their general character, and imprudent institutions, both political and religious, are fast mouldering in self-decay, or mutual destruction.

From the earliest date that I have been able to trace, the island of Borneo was always divided into three distinct kingdoms. The kingdom of Borneo, properly so called, extended from Tanjong Dato in latitude 3° 15′ north to Kanukungan point, in the straits of Macassar, 1° 15′ north, which included the whole north part of the island. The kingdom of Sukadana (from *suka*, happiness, and *dunia*, the world, or earthly paradise), extending from Tanjong Dato to Tanjong Sambar, which belonged to the king of Bantam (when or how acquired I have not learned): and the remainder of the island from Tanjong Sambar to Kanukungan point aforesaid, to the kingdom of Benjarmassing (from *bendar*, a port of trade, and *masing*, usual, or the ordinary port of trade).

When the Portuguese first visited Borneo, in 1520,

the whole island was in a most flourishing state. The numbers of Chinese that had settled on her shores were immense; the products of their industry, and an extensive commerce with China in junks, gave her land and cities a far different aspect from her dreary appearance at this day, and their princes and courts exhibited a splendour and displayed a magnificence which has long since vanished.

Pigofetta says, there were twenty-five thousand houses in the city of Borneo Proper, and that it was rich and populous. Much later accounts describe the numbers of Chinese and Japanese junks frequenting her ports as great; but in 1809 there were not three thousand houses in the whole city, nor six thousand Chinese throughout that kingdom, and not a junk that had visited it for years. But the ports of Borneo have not dwindled away more than Acheen, Johore, Malacca, Bantam, Ternate, &c. All these places likewise cut a splendid figure in the eyes of our first navigators, and have since equally shared a proportionate obscurity.

Were the causes required which have eclipsed the prosperity of Borneo and the other great emporiums of eastern trade that once existed, it might be readily answered—a decay of commerce. They have suffered the same vicissitudes as Tyre, Sidon, or Alexandria; and like Carthage—for ages the emporium of the wealth and commerce of the world, which now exhibits on its site a piratical race of descendants in the modern Tunisians and their neighbours the Algerines—the commercial ports of Borneo have become a nest of banditti, and the original inhabitants of both, from similar causes, the decay of commerce, have degenerated to the modern pirates of the present day.

In exact proportion as the intercourse of the Europeans with China has increased, in precise ratio has the decrease of their direct trade in junks become apparent. The Portuguese first, and subsequently the Dutch, mistress of the eastern seas, exacted by treaties and other ways the Malay produce at their own rates, and were consequently enabled to undersell the junks in China. But these powers went further; by settling at ports on Borneo, or by their guardas de costas, they compelled the ports of Borneo to send their produce, calculated for the China market, to Malacca and Batavia, which at length completely cut up the direct trade by means of the Chinese junks.

The loss of their direct intercourse with China affected their prosperity in a variety of ways. First, by this circuitous direction of their trade, the gruff goods, as rattans, sago, cassia, pepper, ebony, wax, &c. became too expensive to fetch the value of this double carriage and the attendant charges, and in course of time were neglected; the loss of these extensive branches of industry must have thrown numbers out of employment. But the loss of the direct intercourse with China had more fatal effects; it prevented large bodies of annual emigrants from China settling upon her shores; it deprived them of an opportunity of visiting the Bornean ports, and exercising their mechanical arts and productive industry; and of thus keeping up the prosperity of the country in the tillage of the ground, as well as in the commerce of her ports. The old Chinese settlers by degrees deserted these shores; and, to fill up the chasms in their revenues by so fatal a change, the Rajas have been tempted to turn their views to predatory habits, and have permitted their lands to run to jungle, by dragging their wretched labourers from agricultural employments to maritime and piratical enterprises.

The first material alteration in the sovereignty of the territorial possession took place in the kingdom of Borneo Proper, when her Raja was obliged to call in the aid of the Solos, to defend him against an insurrection of the Maruts and Chinese. In consideration of this important aid, the Raja of Borneo Proper ceded to the Sultan of Solo all that portion of Borneo then belonging to him, from Kimanis in latitude 5° 30' north, to Tapean-durian, in the straits of Macassar, which includes the whole north of Borneo. After this period, the power and fortunes of the Sultan of Solo rapidly declined. The Spaniards succeeded in conquering all their islands. Solo, the capital, was taken and fortified; the Sultan and his court made prisoners. When the English captured Manilla, they found this Sultan incarcerated. They agreed to relieve him from prison, and reinstate him on the musnud of his forefathers, under the express stipulation, that the whole of the aforesaid territory of Borneo, ceded to Solo by the Raja of that kingdom, should be transferred to the English East India Company, together with the south of Palawan, and the intermediate islands. These terms were joyfully acceded to by the Sultan of Solo, and signed, sealed, and delivered by him to the late Alexander Dalrymple, in the year 1763.

The kingdom of Sukadana was ceded by the Raja of Bantam (in what year I know not) to the Dutch East India Company. Whether the kingdom of Benjarmasing was ever actually ceded to the Dutch or not, I have not been able to learn. But the occupancy of her capital, the military government of the country, by the erection of forts, and a permanent standing force, since transferred to the English arms, give to the East India Company, actually or virtually, the entire sovereignty and rule over the whole of this large island, with the exception of the piratical port of Borneo Proper, and the portion of territory yet annexed thereto.

The Portuguese, at a very early period, established themselves at Benjarmasing: at Borneo Proper there still remain two bastions and a curtain of a regular stone fort built by them: they had also one on the isle of Laboan, since destroyed. They fixed themselves at old Sambas, from which they were driven by the Dutch in the year 1690, and nearly about this period from all their establishments on Borneo.

When, or from what causes, the Dutch were induced to evacuate Sambas, I know not, nor have I learned the period when they fortified themselves at Benjarmasing and Pasir, but believe it could not have taken place before the middle of the last century. They, however, settled at Pontiana in 1786, and built a fortified wall round the palace and factory, but were compelled to withdraw from it when the war broke out with the English in 1796. The ports at Benjarmasing, when evacuated, were sold by the Dutch to the Sultan, and are since said to have been re-purchased from him by the English. The Dutch obtaining the cession of the kingdom of Sukadana from the Raja of Bantam, and their subsequent measures in different parts of this territory, will shew that they had extensive views of firmly establishing themselves on this island; and waking from an age of lethargy, at last began to see the great advantages and unbounded resources these rich possessions were capable of affording them, without any cost or expense whatever. The year they withdrew from Pontiana they had it in contemplation to take repossession of Sambas, and to unite all the ports, as well as the interior, under the Raja of Pontiana, in trust for them. Some letters to this effect were written by the Dutch government to the late Raja.

That the English were not insensible to the value and importance of the once valuable commerce of Borneo may be inferred, not only from the number of the Honourable Company's regular ships annually despatched to her ports prior to the year 1760 (vide Hardy's Shipping Register), but from the efforts they have repeatedly made to establish themselves on her shores. There still exist the remains of a British factory at Borneo Proper. Before the year 1706, they had made two successive attempts to fortify themselves at Benjarmasing; twice they have attempted an establishment on the sickly island of Balambangan (lying north of Borneo, near Maludu); and in 1775, the Honourable Company's ship Bridgewater was sent to Passir with similar views.

The failure of these British attempts, as well as the exclusion of all other powers from the ports of Borneo, may be principally attributed to the sordid desire of the Dutch of monopolising the whole produce of the eastern Archipelago, and their rooted jealousy in opposing the establishment of every other power in the vicinity of Java, or that of the Spice Islands.

These considerations and feelings have induced them to commit the most flagrant crimes, not only against the natives of these regions, but against every European power. Their infamous massacres at Amboyna, Banda, Bantam, &c. have been historically recorded to their eternal disgrace. By their intrigues at Benjarmasing, the British attempts at a settlement twice failed; and Forrest, in his Voyage to New Guinea, says, that the Sulos were by Dutch instigation induced to cut off the infant establishment of Balambangan, in 1775. They frustrated the attempts of the Bridgewater at Pasir; and even the massacre of the garrison of Pulo Condore was effected by Javanese soldiers supplied by the governor of Batavia. The English, from their strong desire of having a port in the China seas, hastily pitched upon the most unhealthy spots for that purpose, viz. Balambangan and Pulo Condore.

The father of the present Sultan of Pontiana was the descendant of an Arab, residing at Simpan, near Matan. By the advice and concurrence of the Dutch, he was induced, about forty-two years ago, to settle on the unfrequented shores of the river Pontiana, or Quallo Londa, with promises of early co-operation and assistance, as well as of rendering it the mart of the trade and capital of all Sukadana. As soon as Abdul Ramman (the name of the first Sultan) had succeeded in attracting around him several Chinese, Buguese, and Malay settlers, and in building a town, the Dutch (in 1786) came with two armed brigs and fifty troops to establish their factory. To make good their promises to Abdul Ramman (the treaty I have never seen), they immediately overthrew the chief of Mompava, and gave his country in trust to this ally: they shortly after invested the ancient city of Sukadana, burned it to the ground, transferred the inhabitants to Pontiana, or dispersed them and their chief into the interior. The Dutch likewise placed the present Rajas on the musnuds of Songo, Landa, &c. and kept up a force at the former, with the express stipulation that the whole of their produce should be sent from each of their respective districts to the Dutch factory of Pontiana. They had it in contemplation, in 1795, to take re-possession of Sambas, and wrote to Abdul Ramman as to the preparatory measures requisite, when the English war, as before observed, obliged them to abandon Pontiana.

This Abdul Ramman, the first Sultan or chief of Pontiana, reigned thirty-five years, and died in 1807, leaving his eldest son, the present Sultan Kasim, now forty-six years of age, his successor; who has a second brother, called Pangeran Marko, aged thirty-eight, and Pangeran Hosman, thirty-six years, besides four sisters, one of whom married the present Raja of Matan, and about seventy half brothers and sisters, the natural children of his father, with an extensive sub-progeny. The present Sultan has three sons (Abibuker, heir-apparent, twenty-one years old, Ali, and Abdul Ramman), and four daughters, lawfully begotten. None of the royal family make use of either opium, betel, or tobacco, in any shape whatever; and the present Sultan has much the appearance of an Arab. The grandfather of the present Sultan was from Arabia, a Sayed Suriff; one of his relations was fixed at Palimbang, whose name is unknown to me, and the other, Shad Fudyel, at Acheen, who has been long dead.

The wet season commences from September, and ends in April, when heavy rain, hard squalls, and much thunder and lightning are experienced. From April till September is called the dry season, but even in this portion of the year seldom a day elapses without a smart shower or two. The monsoons on the northerly shores of

Borneo are found to correspond with those prevalent in the China seas, viz. from the N. E. from October to April, and from the S. W. the rest of the year. To the southward, about Benjarmasing, the monsoons are the same as in the Java seas, *i. e.* westerly from October to April, and easterly the rest of the year. Those parts of Borneo near or upon the equator have variable winds all the year, and land and sea-breezes close in shore.

This country is by no means so warm as one would be led to imagine by its proximity every where to the line: this arises from the perpetual refreshing showers and the land and sea-breezes, the former being wafted over innumerable rivers. In the month of November, the thermometer at Pontiana ranges from 78° to 82°.

During the wet season, the rivers swell and overflow the adjacent shores, and run down with such continued rapidity, that the water may be tasted fresh at sea at the distance of six or seven miles from the mouths: these overflowings fertilise the banks and adjacent country, and render the shores of Borneo, like the plains of Egypt, luxuriantly rich. Susceptible of the highest possible culture, particularly in wet grain, in the dry season the coast, from these overflowings, presents to the eye the richest enamelled fields of full-grown grass for miles around. It is at this season that whole herds of wild cattle range down from the mountains in the interior to fatten on the plains, but during the wet season they ascend to their hills.

The whole of the north, the north-west, and the centre of Borneo is extremely mountainous. The greatest portion of the ancient kingdom of Borneo Proper is extremely elevated. That of Kiney Baulu, or St. Peter's Mount, in latitude 6° north, is perhaps one of the highest mountains known. The country about Sambas, Pontiana, and Sukadana is occasionally interspersed with a few ranges of hills, otherwise the land here might be deemed low. But to the southward and more particularly to the east, in the Straits of Macassar, it is very low. The shore in these latter places is extremely moist and swampy, but the interior is said to be dry.

The common charts of Borneo will shew the innumerable rivers that water this vast island in every possible direction; but it is worthy of remark, that all the principal rivers on this island have their main source in a large lake in the vicinity of that stupendous mountain before mentioned, Kiney Baulu. The river Benjarmasing takes its rise from thence, and after traversing in all its windings a distance of 1500 miles, intersecting the island into two parts, falls into the Java sea. Its rise and fall is said to be twelve feet, and it has only nine feet at low water on the bar. It is said to have numberless villages scattered on its banks; but I have obtained no particular accounts of them, or their produce.

The great river of Borneo Proper is certainly the finest on the island. It is a deep navigable and majestic stream; it has three fathoms upon the bar at low water; the rise and fall is, I believe, fifteen feet; there are docks here for Chinese junks of five or six hundred tons, and a first-rate ship of war might get up far above the town. The country too is populous, productive, and healthy. The southern branch of this river has been well surveyed, but the branch leading to the Marut country is little known; it has its source in Kiney Baulu.

In the ancient kingdom of Sukadana, the five principal rivers are the Sukadana, the Lava, the Pogore, the Pontiana, and the Sambas. The former rivers communicate inland, and their main source is in Kiney Baulu. The whole of these rivers are deep and navigable for seventy or eighty miles; but have all of them mud flats at their mouths, which would not admit of the entry of vessels exceeding fourteen feet at high water springs.

The third most considerable river on Borneo is the Kinabatangan, lying in the north of the island, and emptying itself into the Sulo seas. It is said to be deep and navigable much farther than the Benjarmasing river; it has several mouths, but it has never been surveyed. The rivers Kuran, Passir, and a variety of others that fall into the Straits of Macassar, are said to be noble streams, navigable for vessels of large burthen; but I have no accurate information of them. The harbour of Sandakan is one of the finest in the world: a correct chart of the same is published. The harbour of Tambisan, near Cape Unsing, is equal to Pulo Pinang, and calculated for careening and building ships; a tolerable chart of these is also published. The harbours of Pulo Laut, Punangan, Maludu, and several others in the Straits of Macassar, afford good anchorage and complete shelter for shipping.

Situated as Borneo is, immediately under the equator, every thing that can be produced in vegetation by the combined influence of heat and moisture is here displayed in the highest luxuriance and super-excellence. All the Oriental palms, as the cocoa-nut, the areca, the sago, &c. abound here. The larger grasses, as the bamboo, the canna, the nardus, assume a stately growth and thrive in peculiar luxuriance. Pepper is found wild every where, and largely cultivated about Benjarmasing and the districts of Borneo Proper. The *laurus cinnamomum* and *cassia odoriferata* are produced in abundance about Kimanis.

In no part of the world does the camphor-tree flourish in equal perfection as in the districts of Maludu and Payton, in the north of Borneo. The ebony, the dammar, the tree that yields the finest dragon's blood in the world, all abound here. The cotton and coffee trees are found in all parts of Borneo, though not much attended to. The chocolate nut of Sulo is preferred at Manilla to that from South America. The tree that yields the clove-bark, and the nutmeg, and clove, thrive luxuriantly, though never tried to any extent.

The woods about Pontiana for carpentry and joinery are, kayu bulean, chena, mintangore, laban, ebony, iron wood, dammar, and dammar laut, &c. &c. The pine abounds in the bay of Maludu, teak at Sulo. The fruit-bearing trees which enrich and adorn the Indian continent offer, on the Bornean shore, all their kindred varieties, nurtured by the bountiful hand of luxuriant nature. The durian, mangustin, rambutan, proya, chabi, kachang, timon, jambu, kniban, besides the nanka or jack, tamarind, pomplemose, orange, lemon, and citron, all the kindred varieties of the plantain, banana, melon, annanas, pomegranate, &c. are found on Borneo.

The garden-stuffs met with are, onions, garlic, yams, pumpkins, brinjals, greens, beans, cucumbers; and turnips, cabbages, and potatoes would succeed, were there Europeans to attend to them.

The elephant was said to be seen about Cape Unsing, where several teeth are still found; but it is conceived this animal is extinct on the island. There are no dromedaries nor camels; nor are horses, asses, or mules met with on Borneo (the former are seen at Sulo). None of the larger breed of the feline species are found here, as the lion, tiger, leopard; nor the bear, the wolf, the fox, nor even a jackal or dog, that I ever saw. The orang outang, or the man of the woods, is the most singular animal found in these regions. The rivers swarm with alligators, and the woods with every variety of the monkey tribe. The names of other animals on Borneo are, the bodok or rhinoceros, pelando or rabbit, rusa or stag, kijang or doe, minjagon, babi utan or wild hog, tingileng, bintangan, &c. There are buffaloes, goats, bullocks, hogs, besides the rat and mouse species; a dog I never saw on Borneo.

There are few snakes on the sea-coast, owing to the moisture; plenty, however, are found in the interior. The musquito, the fly, the frog, and the noisy beetle, with other insects and vermin found in Malay countries, abound here.

The coasts and rivers abound with excellent and wholesome fish in the greatest variety, and of the most delicious flavours; but such is the miserable state of society, that few Malays have either the inclination or the inducement to venture beyond the mouths of their rivers in quest of them; and even there they are more indebted to the industry of the Chinese with their fishing-stakes than to their own labour for the supply of their markets. The names of their fish are, the kakab, klabaw, jilawat, lai-is, pattain, udang or prawn, shrimp, talang, sinanging, bawan, rowan, taylaon, duri, bleda, tingairy, alu-alu, pako, jumpul, pari or skait, boli ayam, tamban or shad, belut or eel, iyu or shark, lida or sole, batu batu, kabab batu, klaoi, krang or cockle, tiram or oyster, tipy and lapis pearl oysters, cupang or muscle, all the varieties of the turtle, with several other sorts.

The ornithology of Borneo is somewhat limited. There are the bayan, nuri, dara, pepit or sparrow, tukukur or turtle-dove, berkey, kandang, kiridi, gogaw or crow, seyrindit, layang or swallow, kalilawan. The Chinese rear ducks; the tame fowl abounds; but the turkey, goose, and peafowl are seldom met with.

The principal gold-mines on Borneo are in the vicinity of Sambas. There is a mountain called Guning Pandan, about eighty miles inland; from this branch out three rivers, one leads to Mompava, one to Batu Bulat near Tanjong Mora, and one to Landa; the whole intermediate area between the above rivers is of a firm yellow argillaceous schistus, or ferruginous quartz, interspersed with horn and vitreous ores, of a remarkable dark reddish colour, abounding with the richest veins of gold, and equal if not superior to any mine extant. There are only fifty parets or mines now wrought in the whole kingdom of Sukadana, thirty of which are in the Sambas district, each mine having at least three hundred men, Chinese, employed in them. Their pay, one with another, is four dollars per mensem.

The mines are rented from the Raja at the rate of fifty bunkals of gold per mine per annum, besides a capitation tax of three dollars per head on every Chinaman. There are thirty thousand Chinese in the Sambas districts, and they feel themselves strong enough to oppose or evade this tax; it hence becomes a perpetual contest between greedy extortion on the one side, and avaricious chicane on the other; there are besides about twelve thousand Malays and Dayers.

The Laurat gold-mines are situated to the eastward of the town of Sambas, and are particularly rich and productive. The mines of Siminis are one day's journey from Sambas, up a small creek leading from Sambas river, below the town; and the mines are abundant. Salako is up a river fifteen miles south of the Sambas river; it lies nearly forty miles up, but communicates with Sambas by another river: here the metal is found more abundant than any where else; and twenty thousand Chinese are found in this district. Mantrado is three days' journey up the Mompava river; it is under an independent Malay prince. Some accounts make the population of this district great, near fifty thousand Dayers, Malays, and Chinese; but perhaps half the number may be nearer the truth; these are chiefly employed on the gold-mines, and in producing food for the miners: these mines, however, do not produce that quantity which they might under Chinese management. Mandore is about a day's journey from Pontiana, and belongs to the Sultan; it is reckoned a very rich mine, though but recently wrought. There are as yet only twelve parets of about two hundred men each, but it is capable of extension. Likewise are found in this district some very rich specimens of copper-ore; it has not as yet been wrought, gold being deemed a much more productive article. The Sultan wishes, however, he had some boring utensils and an experienced miner, to enable him to decide whether it would be worth working under the peculiar circumstances above mentioned. Numbers of Chinese are settled in this district, and the population is annually increasing.

About three days' journey up the Pongole river lies the district of Songo, with a population of twenty-five thousand souls, Dayers, and a few Chinese, under a Malay and an independent prince. The population is chiefly employed on the rich mines of gold in the neighbourhood, which is particularly pure and abundant; but the mines are not wrought with the same industry as those under Chinese management. The Dutch thought it of so much consequence as to keep a force at Songo, and to place the present Raja on that musnud. About two days' journey farther up lies another gold-district called Santam, the inhabitants of which are principally Dayers. Beyond Santam, and higher up on the same river, lies the town of Sukadow, abounding in gold, the inhabitants of which are also Dayers.

Matan belongs to the Raja of that name: he had the title of Raja of Sukadana, until driven out of the latter place by the Dutch, seventeen years ago. There are ten thousand Dayers in this district, and a few Chinese and Malays. The mines of gold are abundant, and capable of becoming highly productive, as well as the mines of iron and unwrought tin; but the Sultan is much addicted to the use of opium, and hence neglects a valuable country, capable, under better management, of becoming the most valuable district on all Borneo.

About three days' journey from Pontiana lies the celebrated mountain of Landa, which, after Golconda, is the most valuable diamond-mine in the world. There are at least thirty thousand people, principally Dayers, employed on the mines and agriculture; it belongs to a Malay prince, raised to that musnud twenty-five years ago by the Dutch, through the agency of the present Sultan of Pontiana: here also much gold is produced; and much more might be had under proper management.

There is a very valuable gold-mine in the north of Borneo, at a place called Tampasuk, situated in the district ceded to the English by the Sultan of Sulo; but having become the principal pirate-port on the coast, the working of the mines has been discontinued.

The whole produce of the gold-mines of Sukadana is said to be annually about twenty piculs, or a million of dollars, at twenty-five dollars a bunkal; but no calculation of this sort can possibly be correct. Living, as the Chinese do, under the rapacity of despotic and ferocious freebooters, who are actuated by no one principle of honour, justice, or good faith, it is their interest to conceal the riches they amass, not only to preserve themselves from the clutches of these tyrants, but as the most compact substance to transport to their native shores, to which they repair with the fruits of their industry, by the annual junks that arrive at Pontiana, leaving the mines to new settlers: from two to three hundred leave Pontiana every year.

The standard of Slakow gold at Pontiana is affixed at twenty-three Spanish dollars the bunkal, of two dollars weight. The Songo and Laurat is twenty-five dollars the said bunkal.

Not having had an opportunity to inspect any of the gold-mines personally, I know not if the ores readily melt of themselves, or whether they require the aid of any fluxes before they yield the metal; but I believe the principal attention of the miners is directed to the rich veins of pure native gold, and that no operation is performed beyond that of pulverising, and simple washing; all the gold about Pontiana being in dust, though some I have met with in Borneo Proper was run into bars. About Landa, where the diamonds are found, the whole of the stratum is observed to be a clay of a red burnt appearance, nearly to the same degree as that of burnt bricks, which gives to the rivers hereabouts a peculiar tinge. Whether this has been formed by the action of subterraneous fires, or is the effect of volcanoes or earthquakes, I cannot decide; the latter are said to be frequently felt at Pontiana and at Sambas; and the former are said to exist in the central mountains of Borneo.

From the slovenly manner in which the diamonds are sought for by the Dayers, they seldom collect them of a size exceeding three or four carats weight each. When rough the Landa diamond has a white or yellow hue; but none are found of that inky and flinty tinge, so valuable in some of the Golconda diamonds. But that Landa does produce them of a very considerable size, the extensive and valuable specimens in Java, as well as the quantities annually sent to Batavia, will evince. The king of Matan is at this instant in possession of a diamond weighing 367 carats: the value of which, according to the old mode of calculation, would be $(367+367+2)=365,378l$. The Sultan of Pontiana says, however, that a much larger price was offered for it by the Dutch government of Java. He refused, it is said, twenty-five laks of dollars, two sloops of rice, fifty pieces of cannon, and a hundred muskets. Several from twenty to thirty carats have been dug up. At Mompava there are said to be very rich coppermines; but from want of population, a vigorous government, and scientific mineralogists, little is to be hoped from them at the present day. At Pulo Bongorong, near Borneo Proper, there is plenty of loadstone found.

About one degree north of Sambas there is a country called Sarāwak, belonging to the Raja of Borneo Proper; there is a vast district abounding in tin, in veins as rich and as plentiful as those wrought on Banca: but they have been neglected for a series of years; they were partially wrought before those of the latter were discovered, in the beginning of the last century. The tyranny of that government, the want of hands, and the contiguity of rich and valuable gold-mines, have together caused their utter neglect; and there is little probability of more favourable results, except under a change of government, and a happier order of things.

In the Matan districts there is an extensive and most

valuable iron-mine, producing pure metal without any admixture of ore: it is fully equal in quality to the best Swedish iron; they run it into shot, and much of it is exported; but the gold-mines in its vicinity, and the want of a proper government, are obstacles to its further productiveness and utility. At Maday, on the north-east coast of Borneo, in the province of Mangidara, there is a very rich mine of gold. Pasir and Coti, in the Straits of Macassar, produce considerable quantities of gold; and gold and diamonds are brought down by the river to Benjarmasing. I have, however, no accurate information on the subject, and can simply note the general fact.

There are several fine specimens of crystal found at Kimanis and Sulo: they call them water diamonds. To give full effect to the mines in the kingdom of Sukadana, says the Sultan of Pontiana, and to raise the excess of food required for the additional hands, would together give employment to at least a million of Chinese. Under the British flag, he thinks thousands of new settlers will find their way in the annual junks.

All that extensive range, from Cape Unsing, passing by the Tawi Tawi islands and Sulo, as far as Baselan, is one vast continued bed of pearl-oysters, principally of the Behoren or mother-of-pearl-shell species; these are called by the natives *tipi*. There is likewise an extensive bed of the Ceylon oyster, called by the Malays *kapis;* the principal banks of the latter are found in Maludu Bay. The Sulo pearls have, from time immemorial, been the most celebrated, and praised as the most valuable of any in the known world. Pigofetta, the companion of Magalhaens, mentions having seen in 1520 two Sulo pearls in the possession of the Raja of Borneo as large as pullet eggs. Very large ones, from one to two hundred *chaw* weight, are at all times to be purchased at Sulo; and there are altogether sold here to the China junks, the Spaniards, &c. more than two laks of dollars worth annually. The quantity of mother-of-pearl shell, *communibus annis*, sold there is two thousand piculs, at six dollars a picul. The fishery is partly carried on by the Malays, and partly by the Chinese; the large pearls they endeavour to conceal as much as possible, from a law that all pearls above a certain size of right belong to the Sultan. " The small narrow guts," says Dalrymple in his account of the Sulo seas, " about Tawi Tawi, are the most rich and valuable fishery in the world." I have had an opportunity of inspecting the banks about Manar and Tutacoryn, as well as all the banks in the Sulo seas; but the former have not banks near as extensive, equalling in the quantity of oysters, in productiveness, size, or richness, the Sulo pearl, nor are they to be compared in any way to the Sulo beds. Still the Ceylon fishery has netted the British Government from one to two laks of pagodas for permitting it to be fished fourteen days annually. As this portion of Borneo belongs to the English, a much greater revenue might be drawn from these vast sources of wealth, under proper management.

As there are no people of sufficient opulence to contract for so vast a fishery, the Company might undertake it themselves; three or four gun-boats would be necessary to protect the fishermen; and a small fort should be erected at Tambisan or Tawi Tawi. But it is necessary to observe, the Sulo people do not practise diving at all, as is the case at Beharen and Ceylon, but only comprehend the slow method of dredging for the tipy with a thing like the fluke of a wooden anchor. It would be a desirable thing, in the event of prosecuting this valuable fishery as a national concern, to obtain forty or fifty Arab divers from Beharen, and perhaps an equal number of Chulias from Nagore and Negapatam, from the number employed annually on the Ceylon fishery. These men would teach the Malay the superiority of diving, which can, in fourteen days' fishing, bring in to government a revenue of two laks of pagodas, pay the expenses of the fishery, and enrich all parties concerned; whilst the Malayan operose plan of dredging perhaps affords but a precarious subsistence. But had they divers, from the extent of the banks, instead of fourteen days in the year, they might, one after another, be fished the whole year round, and never be exhausted. The Chinese fishermen, though laborious, possess no enterprise, and can never be prevailed on to dive, from apprehension of the sharks. The Caffris from New Guinea and the Arroes would be superior to them.

The Sultan of Sulo, in 1810, proposed to me to bring over one hundred Chulia divers from Negapatam on our joint expense and profit; and the divers agreed to go over on receiving each twenty-five rupees advance, their victuals being found, and one-fourth of the produce of oysters allowed them, as at Ceylon. Circumstances, however, occurred to prevent an undertaking which I think must have turned out highly lucrative. They dredge the banks all the year round. The water on the Tahow, Maludu, and Tawi Tawi banks, is from seven to ten fathoms deep; in other places they fish in fifteen fathoms water.

The Malays of Borneo understand the art of cutting, polishing, and setting their diamonds. Gold and silver filagree works they excel in; gunpowder is manufactured at Pontiana; brass cannon is cast at Borneo Proper; iron-shot is run from their mine. They can manufacture and repair krises, and clean their arms. Their carpentry extends to the building and repairing of prows, and the erecting of a hut. Their industry is farther exerted in collecting birds-nests and wax; in cutting rattans and felling timber; in the pearl and tripan fisheries; or as mariners in commercial or piratical pursuits. The tillage of the ground and the edible fisheries are often left to the more indefatigable industry of the Chinese. For the exercise of every other useful occupation also, the mechanical and scientific arts, and the labour of the mines, these indolent savages are indebted solely to the superior industry and civilisation of the Chinamen.

The amusements of the Malays in other parts are unpractised on the shores of Borneo: the only ones I ever saw were flying the kite, swimming, and the songs of their women; this latter is confined to the Rajas.

Wherever a water-communication on Borneo presents, the indolence of the Malay will not permit him to think of the construction of a road. In the interior, however, there are pathways in all directions; about Mompava, where the river is narrow and shallow, they have constructed several roads. Being a people much occupied in maritime pursuits, they prefer, like the amphibious Dutch, travelling by rivers, or the innumerable cuts, canals, and creeks, which every where intersect the country: besides, their prows afford more protection from surprise, and they conceive their town as safer by being surrounded by a jungle and situated in a swamp; nor have they any conception beyond water-carriage.

Their laws neither depend upon the Koran nor any written code, human or divine, beyond the whim and caprice of the chief (assassin) and his gang of desperadoes.

The Sultan of Pontiana has, however, established the following regulations:

Punishments for murder:—Life for life, except when the parties can commute the same by fine.

* * * * *

A proclamation is publicly affixed announcing the law, that if any person be found adulterating gold-dust, or uttering it, so depreciated, with a view to defraud, the perpetrator shall lose his right arm, and the adulterated gold shall be confiscated.

For theft:—Five dollars per head is given by the Sultan to any one bringing in the head of a thief: if brought in alive, he is suspended by the heels and flogged as far as nature can bear short of death, and the punishment repeated *ad libitum*.

Prisoners taken from an enemy, whether found in arms or not, are made slaves of, or suffer death, at the option of the captor.

The Malay government is said to exhibit the feudal system in its most perfect form. The chief, or Raja, issues his orders to the Pangerans, or princes of the blood; to the Datus, or nobles of royal descent; or to the Orang Kayas, or wealthy vassals. All these obey and follow him to war, free of expense, when the king is sufficiently powerful to enforce it; but whenever the vassal feels himself strong enough to throw off the yoke, and to assert his independence, he sets up for himself. These vassals exact the same obedience from their slaves or villains, who pay the like deference only so long as they are compelled to observe and obey them. The property acquired by a slave he is often allowed to enjoy unmolested during his lifetime; but at his death, his master administers to the estate as heir, executor, and sole legatee.

In fact, it is a government that inspires on all sides one universal distrust; that rules by precedents of oppression without a view to protection. The chiefs dread the power of their vassals, who, in return, apprehend every thing from the rapacity of the governing power; whilst the bulk of the people, having no property to lose, are still compelled to appear abroad armed to defend their very persons from the outrage and violence of the next assassin they meet.

Where governments not only tolerate murder, rapine, thefts, piracies, conflagrations, with every outrage violating the happiness and safety of society, but they are the first to set the example and to consecrate the atrocity—where the people are taught no one principle of morality or religion—where the arts and sciences are wholly unknown or despised—where the amusements and sociabilities of human life are totally disregarded—where the bounties and comforts of nature are rather dispensed with than enjoyed—and where the absolute necessaries to existence and the decorations of life are more scanty and wretched than yet discovered amongst the rudest set of barbarians extant; if, from the experience of the past, expectations of the future are to be formed, we may safely infer that every vestige of Malay government and dominion will be engulfed in the vortex of self and mutual destruction. Such a system of society has in itself the seeds of dissolution, and is rapidly verging to an inherent decay and general oblivion; which it will doubtless meet, unless some beneficent power arrest its baneful impetus, and direct its feverish energies through channels calculated to promote the happiness and to consolidate the welfare of the inhabitants of these scattered regions.

Should so fortunate an occurrence ever fall to the lot

of Borneo—should a strong and a wise government ever be established on her shores; a government that will religiously respect property and secure to industry the fruits of her labour; that will, by a wise system of laws, protect the peaceable and punish the violator of the laws of a well-organised society; that will direct their industry to useful purposes, and check their propensities to violence and plunder—such a government, in a short series of years, would behold, as if by magic, a paradise burst from her wilds, see cultivation smile upon her jungles, and hail a vast and increasing population, blessing the hand that awoke them to life, to happiness, and to prosperity. That so felicitous a change is not the mere reverie of a glowing imagination, or the sheer effusion of benevolence alone, is easily demonstrable.

Whoever has seen the Egyptian fertility of the soil from the moistness of the climate, the numberless rivers meandering around and intersecting the country in all directions, with the mild temperature of the climate from similar causes—whoever considers the vast extent and inexhaustible wealth of her innumerable mines of pure native gold, her block-tin, her copper, her iron, her diamonds, &c., her various valuable fisheries of pearl and tripan—whoever views her ports, her harbours, and her productive shores, at the threshold of the over-teeming population of China, and at the same moment recollects that the country abounds in various valuable products in the highest possible estimation, and of increasing demand in the empire of China—must easily conceive what a tempting field and rich harvest this land of promise holds out to their industry and cupidity under such a system of laws and government as we have deemed a *sine quâ non*.

If, under the present codes of tyranny, oppression, and

general ferocity, where nothing is permanent but violence and desolation—if, under such a system of barbarism, a hundred thousand Chinese (which is the fact) have found inducements sufficiently strong to settle on her shores, what might we not hope and expect from the overburdened population of that vast empire under a happier order of things? The astonishing number of Chinese settled within a few years at Pulo Pinang, on a contracted soil, possessing no peculiar advantages but from a free trade and equitable laws impartially administered, is both a fact and an illustration; and what might not Borneo hope for from a happier soil, greater inducements, and other physical advantages? Java, under the despotism of the Dutch, with the character of a sickly climate, and the remembrance of the cruel massacre of sixty thousand innocent Chinese, could still boast a hundred thousand of these people at the period it fell to the British arms; and withal, let it be remembered that these shores were once blessed with the industry of these people to a far greater extent under a happier period of her history.

Whatever, indeed, might prove the work of ages in various other parts of the globe would, under the present circumstances of the Chinese empire, be instantaneous on these shores; and their habits of industry and civilisation, when once rooted to the soil, would soon spread their genial influence to the extensive population of the interior; unite them in the bonds of social life; cement them in the general prosperity; and render these extensive shores a valuable appendage and an increasing resource to the wealth and power that brought about so happy a revolution in their affairs.

For a considerable series of years past, the piratical ports of Borneo, &c. have been in the habit of committing depredations upon the commerce of British India, in the capture of her ships, the insulting of her flag, the offering of outrageous violence to the persons and lives of her mariners, merchants, &c., and this too with the most perfect impunity; no retribution having been exacted, no reprisals made, no remonstrance presented, and, in fact, no notice taken of their atrocious depredations. Hence these desperadoes, from inference and experience of the past, have been led to conclude, that whatever was practicable would be tolerated; that wherever they had the means or opportunity of overpowering, it was their duty, as it was to their advantage, to seize it to their own use, without any other apprehensions of the consequences than what might arise in the attempt.

Under this discouraging aspect of affairs, there was but little more left to the commercial community of India than either to abandon the valuable commerce of Borneo wholly; or, if allured to it by a prospect of gain, to proceed in armed vessels at an increased expense and high insurance, so as to cover the extraordinary risks. These enhanced prices either operated as a prohibition to the trade, or circumscribed it so much, that an occasional capture excited no surprise, and was frigidly dismissed as a matter of course.

But, from the prodigious accession of territorial possession, including the whole of the vast Dutch empire in the east, the communications between these and British India have necessarily increased a thousand fold; consequently the recent alarming depredations upon our commerce, the serious obstacles to a safe communication, almost tantamount to a blockade of our eastern ports by these pirates, imperiously call upon the British government to adopt the most energetic means and decisive measures to crush their power and annihilate their resources, either by extirpating them wholly, or placing them and their possessions under such future control and checks, as shall prevent the possibility of a revival of a power capable of recurring to enormities that have so long outraged and disgraced the British flag in the eastern seas.

The idea of extirpating whole hordes of piratical states, were it possible, must, from its cruelty, be incompatible with the liberal principles and humane policy of a British government. The simple burning down of a Malay town can prove no serious impediment to future piratical enterprises: constructed, as they are, of bamboos, mats, and atap leaves, a town is almost rebuilt in the same period of time as it takes to destroy it. The Dutch, who had centuries of dear-bought experience, knew there was no other mode of prevention and radical cure than building small redoubts at the principal towns, and keeping up an adequate force to check piratical enterprises, and to turn their restless minds to exertions of industry; satisfied if, with the attainment of these objects, they covered the expenses of the establishment. This is the true history of the innumerable little forts on Celebes, Borneo, Timor, and all the eastern isles.

The principal piratical ports that still exist, besides those of Lingin, Rhio, and Billiton, are—1st, Pangeran Annam, at Sambas; 2d, Port Borneo Proper, and four hundred prows at Tampasuk, both under the Raja of Borneo Proper; 3d, the Pasir pirates; 4th, the Sulo pirates; 5th, the Illano, or pirates on the isle of Magindano.

I shall, from memory, cite such few of their depredations as I recollect.

In 1774, says Forrest, the British were expelled from their infant settlement of Balambangan by an insurrection of the Sulos, who, finding the garrison weak and sickly, unprepared and off their guard, murdered and plundered them, and set fire to their settlement: this was in return for having released their Sultan from prison, and re-established him on the musnud of his ancestors. In 1800, Captain Pavin and a boat's crew were cruelly murdered in the palace of the Sultan of Sulo whilst the commander was drinking a cup of chocolate: they fired upon the ship Ruby, but did not succeed in capturing her. In 1810, they plundered the wreck of the ship Harrier of a valuable cargo: several of her crew are still in slavery at Bagayan Sulo. In 1788, the ship May of Calcutta, 450 tons burden, Captain Dixon, was cut off at Borneo Proper: they were invited up to the town with the ship, and whilst at dinner, the Sultan and his people fell upon them, and murdered Captain Dixon, three officers, and ten Europeans; the lascars were retained in slavery, the valuable cargo plundered, and the ship burnt. In 1803, the ship Susanna of Calcutta, Captain Drysdale, was cut off near Pontiana by the Sambas and Borneo pirates; the Europeans were all massacred, and the vessel taken. In 1769, Captain Sadler, with his boat's crew, was murdered by the Sambas pirates off Mompava, having a prodigious quantity of gold-dust: they did not succeed in cutting off the ship. In 1806, Mr. Hopkins and crew, of the Commerce, were murdered by the pirates of Borneo Proper: the ship was plundered by them and the Sambas pirates. In 1810, Captain Ross was cut off. In 1811, Captain Graves was cut off by the Pasir pirates with a rich cargo. In 1812, the enormities of Pangeran Annam have out-heroded Herod: these are too recent to require recapitulation.

Independent of his depredations on the Coromandel, a Portuguese ship, &c., nine Europeans of the Hecate have been seized and made slaves; two have been since murdered; two have escaped; and five are hamstrung and otherwise maimed. Mrs. Ross and her son are still in slavery there.

The Tampasuk pirates, belonging to the Raja of Borneo Proper, aiding and abetting Pangeran Annam against the English, are Datu Akop, Datu Aragut, and Datu Jumbarang, with ten large men-of-war prows: there is also there the Raja Endut, a Siak chief.

Matan is under an independent Raja, who was formerly styled Sultan of Sukadana; but about seventeen years ago the Dutch burnt down his city. At length, by some pecuniary aid received from the late Sultan of Pontiana, he was enabled to re-establish his affairs as Raja of Matan; and, in consideration of this aid, entered into a treaty of alliance, which stipulated, that on his daughter's marriage with the grandson of the late, and son of the present, Sultan of Pontiana, he would cede his kingdom and large diamond as a marriage-portion: the parties yet remain single. Under the head mineralogy we have pointed out how valuable a country this might become under better management. Iron, gold, tin, and diamonds, abound here; also much wax, pepper, rattans, garu, and about two pikuls of the finest birds-nests, which sells at twenty-eight dollars the catty at Pontiana. Most of the trade finds its way to Pontiana, Benjar, or Java, in prows. The population is about ten thousand Dayers, &c.

Sukadana, once the most celebrated city on Borneo, as the name implies, a terrestrial paradise, the capital of a kingdom and a great mart of trade, since burnt down and destroyed by the Dutch, exhibits nothing but ruins.

There still remain numberless delicious fruit-trees, and a country still susceptible of general cultivation, being yet clear of jungle and morass. It is utterly abandoned: that it has not been rebuilt is owing to the Raja of Pontiana, at whose suggestion it was destroyed, and whose interest it was to keep it down, having himself risen upon its ashes.

There are no towns of any importance between Matan and Pontiana. The rise of this dynasty of Sultans has been noted in another place; it is, however, almost the only power that has been expressly raised, supported, and that still exists, by commerce. It is situated in latitude 4° north of the equator. The river has two mouths to it; the northern mouth is the deepest, the most direct, and of the greatest breadth; there are in this branch only two reaches up to the town. The city is no more than fifteen miles from the mouth of the rivers; its site is on the junction of the Matan and Landa rivers. About two-thirds of the way up it is fortified; first, with a battery on piles in the centre of the stream, mounting five guns; on the left bank is another with wooden pales, mounting likewise five guns; on the opposite bank is a third, similar to the foregoing, with a like number of cannon; and, lastly, on the same bank is their grand battery, constructed of stone, mounting five eighteen pounders, at the batu, or rock. Here the mausoleum of the royal family is erected, containing the tomb of the late Sultan. The whole of this side of the river exhibits the marks of infant cultivation. The jungle has been, in part, cleared away, and here and there a solitary hut greets the eye. The Sultan's palace has a battery of eleven guns of all sizes; none of these are calculated to make any serious resistance. So sensible is the Sultan of this that he has commenced staking round with piles a low swampy island, just detached from the palace. On this stands the grand mosque. He proposes throwing mud and stones within the ranges of piles, and planting upon them the heaviest calibred cannon; it is a commanding site, and capable of being rendered formidable. There are no roads about Pontiana; the town is situated in the midst of a swamp, so low that the tide at high water overflows the lower parts of the houses, and this, with the addition of a country overrun with impenetrable jungle, renders it extremely unhealthy, and a most disagreeable residence.

The campo China contains about two thousand souls, and lies on the left bank of the Matan river, abreast of the palace; the campo Buguese, on the right bank of the Landa; and the campo Malayu adjoins the palace. The whole population is about seven thousand souls: no Dayers are found hereabouts. The whole of the districts under Pontiana produce about three hundred coyans of rice, the average selling price of which is from fifty-five to seventy Spanish dollars the coyan. The king's revenue is forty thousand dollars per annum. The Chinese plead poverty, but some of the Buguese are pointed out as wealthy. The quantity of gold that finds its way to Pontiana is annually from three to four piculs. The imports there consist of opium, iron, steel, salt, rice, hardware, cutlery, blue and white gurras, salampories, Java cloths, gunpowder, besides China produce of all possible descriptions. They make their returns in gold, diamonds, birds-nests, wax, rattans, garu, ebony, agar-agar; besides pepper, sago, camphor, cassia, tripan, &c. brought here by the prows: five Chinese junks annually visit Pontiana, bringing down produce amounting to about fifty thousand dollars. The depredations of the Pangeran Annam prevent an extension of this most useful of all trades to this country. One or two Siamese junks arrive annually. The Tringanu, Timbilan,

Karimata, and Borneo Proper prows trade here; and before Java fell to the British arms, the Buguese from the eastward traded here to a considerable amount.

The stone walls built by the Dutch still encompass the palace. The piles on which their factory stood are yet discernible, but the buildings have been pulled down. Should the English hoist their flag here, a new factory must be erected; the most eligible situation for which would be where the mosque now stands, or the mosque itself might be converted into one, and another rebuilt elsewhere; but to this the Sultan has insuperable objections. In an English fort, to think to have a mosque open to the ingress of a large body of Malays at all times is wholly incompatible with a certain reserve and security required from it. Besides, as the island is small, and soldiers at times inconsiderate, they might profane or defile its holy precincts, and thus lay the foundation of perpetual disputes, or even a serious rupture. The fort and factory, if built at all at Pontiana, must hence be fixed in some detached place. The Sultan is building a new palace and covering it with tiles; a novelty in this quarter. There is but a scanty supply of fowls, and buffaloes and the necessaries of life are scarce and dear. It is altogether the most uncouth and dreary spot under the sun, though the Sultan prefers it to Sambas and Mompava.

Their naval force consists of two small ships, two brigs, fifty prows large and small, and about one thousand men. There is water on the bar to admit vessels drawing nine feet water. The roadstead with seven fathoms water on it lies seven miles from the river's mouth. Care must be taken not to mistake the Pongole river seen from the offing, and which lies ten miles farther southward. The only stock procurable here were hogs at ten dollars the picul, and water shipped off in China tank-boats at four and a half dollars the tun.

The next port is Mompava, about sixteen miles to the northward of Pontiana, and the second port belonging to the Sultan. The river is shallow, narrow, extremely serpentine, and constantly running down with great rapidity. The country around is a paradise in comparison with Pontiana. It is upon an elevated site, and, wherever the eye reaches, it is clear of jungle, and of fine rich mould, susceptible of the highest culture. There is a walk up to the town about eight miles from the mouth of the river; here the fishing-stakes nearly extend across the river, besides two miserable forts, mounting each five or six pounders, to defend the river. The population is seven thousand men, Malays, Buguese, and Dayers, and about two thousand Chinese. Formerly the territory of Mompava extended as far as 1° north latitude. This territory belonged to a chief or Raja, reduced by the Dutch twenty-five years ago, shortly after they settled at Pontiana; the territory thus conquered was delegated in trust to the Raja of Pontiana. The Sambas Raja has forcibly taken possession of a part of it. Sultan Kassim, of Pontiana, governed this district during his father's lifetime. On his accession to the musnud, five years ago, he placed a half-brother there, a stupid fellow, about twenty-five years of age. This man, about eight months ago, was trying to establish his independence, which he found he could not maintain. It has the same trade as Pontiana, but the regulations of the Sultan do not admit of any vessel's touching here for that purpose. The palace is extensive, paled round with a sort of a fortification. The campo China, in October last, was in part burnt down by the people of Sambas, to the number of four hundred houses. There is a variety of roads hereabouts; one leading to Sambas, one to Landa, one to Mintrada, &c. Groves of cocoanut-trees mark the site of ancient villages, since demolished; and indicate that it once enjoyed a superiority and pre-eminence of which it has been despoiled. In point of susceptibility of cultivation, it is a full half century beforehand with Pontiana; it is capable of great improvement, and much grain might be raised with very little trouble.

There is a considerable mud-flat at the mouth of the Sambas river, extending four or five miles out, but no regular bar. Vessels drawing thirteen feet may get in at high-water springs; nine feet is the least water, and there is thirteen at the flood. In the offing there is a rise and fall of seven feet. At the entrance of the river neither shore must be too closely hugged, having ledges of rocks near them. Twelve miles above the bar the river branches into two parts; the broad or northern branch is called the Borneo river, having its source in Kiney Baulu; the other, leading to the town of Sambas, is named the Landa river, having its source in the diamond-mines: where these two unite below there was formerly a fort. The Landa river is extremely serpentine, deep to the very bushes on both sides, and quite clear of danger up to the town, except near Siminis creek, about ten miles below the fort; here a reef of rocks runs across the stream, and as the fair way over them is somewhat intricate, the channel ought to be buoyed before attempted to be passed. The Barracouta, drawing thirteen feet, just scraped them at high water.

About five or six leagues up the Landa branch, and about thirteen from the sea, stands the town and palace of Sambas, on the confluence of the Landa and Salako rivers. The fort on the right bank of the Landa is about a league below the town, built of two rows of large piles, the interstices being filled up with mud and stones, apparently mounting five guns, eighteens and twelves in the lower tier, and an equal number of smaller calibre on the second or more elevated range. A boom or dam of fishing-stakes was constructed across the river one eighth of a mile below the fort, a large armed prow was moored in the centre of the river, mounting two long twelves, and a masked battery opposite to the right, the number of guns unknown. The reach which these forts command is a mile and a half. The land makes an elbow where these forts are, which obliged the Barracouta to haul athwart the river, to get her broadside to bear. The whole of this Landa river is very narrow, but near the forts not one-third additional to her length. Both sides of this river towards the fort appear tolerably clear from the mast-head, interspersed with pleasant hills, inhabited by the Chinese. The tides are pretty regular, six hours and six hours, running a knot and a half per hour. This river is too serpentine and narrow to admit sailing up; sweeps, towing, or tiding it up are the only modes that can be resorted to. The great branch of Borneo river, before mentioned, when up it twenty miles, divides into two; the branch running north being called Tampasan river, the other still retaining the name of Borneo. The Tampasan branch leads to old Sambas; it is from hence they get their supplies of rice and provisions, by the two cuts above the town of Sambas, which re-unites the Landa and Borneo streams. There are roads from the great branch leading to the town, fort, and palace. Since the Dutch abandoned Sambas, three Sultans have reigned on this musmud (within fifty years orthereabouts). There are four Pangerans, Annam being the most daring of the whole. His naval force consists of the Portuguese ship of 400 tons, one brig, and eight or ten large fighting prows, besides his allies from Borneo Proper, with ten large prows. The population amounts to twelve thousand Dayers and Malays, and thirty thousand Chinese.

Under the head mineralogy we have given a detailed account of the principal sources of its industry. Sambas produces, besides gold, ten piculs of birds-nests annually (of an inferior quality), much ebony, rattans, wax, &c. The trade here is much the same as at Pontiana, and susceptible of a tenfold increase: it is every way superior to the latter for the capital of a large mart. The country is better cleared, and hence susceptible of more easy cultivation; the land more elevated and less swampy, consequently healthier; the river deeper and farther navigable; the population more dense, and, the land being clear of jungle, more capable of being increased. Besides, it is the vicinage of the most considerable gold-mines on all Borneo. The Sultan of Pontiana would make it his capital if desired; his apprehensions of the power of the Sambas princes lead him to give the preference to Pontiana.

The town of Calaca, belonging to the Raja of Borneo Proper, lies north of Tanjong Datu; it is the principal port of trade south of the capital, and the mart of the Sedang country. Here much grain is produced, one hundred piculs of black birds-nests, two hundred pikuls of wax, some gold, pepper, camphor, &c., but the tin-mines, before mentioned, are utterly neglected. There are several other towns upon each o the rivers along this coast; the principal ones are Silat, Bacalo, Pasir, and Baram. They produce nearly the same articles as the above, which are, however, sent on to the capital as fast as collected.

It is here necessary to observe, that all the rocks and shoals laid down on this coast do not exist at all; such as Volcano Island, the Byhors, Krenpel, the whole Slykenburgh, five Comadas, &c. Having beat up this coast twice, and carefully surveyed the whole, I can declare a finer and clearer coast does not anywhere exist. The old chart, published by A. Dalrymple, is much more correct than the recent ones. The numbers of immense drifts and floating isles hereabouts must have given birth to all these imaginary dangers.

The town of Borneo Proper, the capital of the kingdom of the same name, lies in latitude 5° 7' north; it is situated fifteen miles up one of the finest rivers in the world, with three fathoms low water on the bar, and a rise and fall of fifteen feet. A correct plan of the river and town is published by Mr. Dalrymple. Here are mud docks for vessels of 500 or 600 tons. The town consists of about three thousand houses, built on stakes, in the middle of the river, with a population altogether of fifteen thousand souls, Chinese, Malays, Moruts, &c.

The palace is slightly fortified; but the Raja of Pontiana says, the Raja of Borneo Proper is preparing the means of defence, apprehending the resentment of the English in vindicating the rights of their flag, so frequently insulted by them with impunity; however, as there is sufficient water for a line-of-battle ship to the city, nothing need be apprehended from them. The remains of a stone fort up the river are still seen, but the one on Pulo Laboan is destroyed. Both banks of the river are planted with pepper, which formerly produced sixty thousand pikuls annually; these are now running to decay from want of commerce. The Chinese junks, for years past, have ceased touching here, from the numberless piratical depredations committed upon them; and the Portuguese, from Macao, have attempted to renew the trade from time to time, but at length, in 1808, their agent withdrew to Macao, a large ship having been cut off, and the crew murdered, the year preceding. They now have no other resource but piracy; and the produce, such as it is, finds its way in prows to Tringan, Sambas, Pontiana, Lingin, and Malacca. Very large quantities of the finest camphor in the world is procurable here; it comes down from the Morut country, by the great river; a great deal of wax, some gold, much birds-nest of an inferior quality, any quantity of sago, cassia, clove-bark, pepper, betel-nut, rattans, camphor-oil, &c., tripan, tortoise-shell, &c.

The hills hereabouts are clear of jungle, and wear a beautiful appearance, and, without the aid of history, bear evident marks of a more extensive population and culture. There are plenty of black cattle, buffaloes, goats, fruits and vegetables of all kinds, abundance and variety of fish, turtle, &c. The articles best suited for this market are coarse China, white cangyans, brass plates, China crockery, brass wire, tea, sugar-candy, coarse China silks and satins, blue and white coarse guras, and salampories, coarse ventipallam handkerchiefs, arcot chintzes, iron and steel, quallies, cooking utensils, and other articles suited to a Malay market, all coarse; no opium. The Borneo catty is two and a half lbs.

The English have been very desirous of a port in the China seas for ages past, but have generally appeared to stumble on the most unhealthy and ill-adapted places possible, such as Balambangan, Pulo Condore, &c.; and even the principal object of Lord Macartney's embassy was the obtaining of a cession of this nature. But if a capital harbour, a navigable and majestic river, a productive country, a healthy site, population ready formed, and a commerce all sufficient to pay the expenses of an establishment (within one hundred miles of Balambangan), is required, the East India Company ought to have pitched upon Borneo Proper. It was once a most flourishing country, and a very short period under British auspices would render it the first mart in the east for China-Malayan commerce. There are large populous towns of Moruts, and Orang Idan, who abhor the Malays, but who would be soon reconciled to a milder and less traitorous government.

Kimanis lies in latitude 5° 8′ north; this is the first port on this coast ceded to the English by the Sultan of Sulo. The town lies ten miles up the river, at the foot of some of the most beautiful hills I ever saw, and is inhabited by thirty-five thousand Orang Idan. The river is small and almost choked up at the mouth. This province has the following sea-ports in it, viz. Kimanis, Benome, Papal, and Pangalat, each governed by Orang Kayas, and still continue to send their produce to Borneo Proper, consisting of ten pikuls of birds-nest annually, two hundred pikuls of wax, two pikuls of camphor, and cassia, sago, betel-nut, and pepper, as much as required; tripan, camphor-oil, and rice; with fruit, fish, and provisions, of sorts which are cheap and plentiful. The articles mentioned as fit for Borneo answer here, only their produce is had about fifty per cent cheaper.

The province of Kiney Baulu has the following seaports: Putatan, Mangatal, Innanam, Labatuan, Mangabong, Tawaran, Sulaman, Ambung, Abai, Tampasuk, and Padasan. The whole of this province is tremendously high. The stupendous mountain of Kiney is about fifteen miles from Tampasuk, which at present is the most considerable pirate-port in the Malay seas, and belongs to the Raja of Borneo Proper. The pirates frequenting this place have committed such depredations hereabouts, as to have induced the English to call the north of Borneo, Pirates' Point. These desperate banditti originally resided at Tawaran, but were compelled to leave it from the resentment of whole tribes of Orang Idan. The whole of this province is very fertile; it is the source of all the great rivers on the island, and is more populous with the aborigines of the country than perhaps the rest of the island put together. The gold-mines of Tampasuk have been mentioned; there are also mines of rock-crystal. Tawaran and several other places abound in goats and cattle. Abai has a small harbour, and the whole of this coast is accurately laid down by Lieutenant James Burton, in the sloop Endeavour. There are produced in this province much wax, tortoise-shell, very fine camphor, sago, rattans, and a red birds-nest (which comes from Mantanane isle, to Pandasan). They send their produce to Borneo Proper. The pirates are commanded by Datus from Borneo Proper. The lake in the vicinity of Kiney Baulu is said to be delightful; it is many miles in circumference, well cultivated, populous, and productive. It is said to be very cold, from the extreme elevation, and the inhabitants are almost as fair as Europeans. There is a valuable coral-tree somewhere hereabouts.

The Bay of Maludu, on the north of Borneo, is thirty miles in length and from four to six in breadth, with numberless rivers flowing into it. There is no danger on the right-hand shore going up, but what is seen; on the larboard shore considerable coral-reefs are met with. Laurie and Whittle's chart of it is tolerably correct. The principal towns are, Sungy Bassar, nearly at the head of the bay, and

Bankaka, on the left; the former, under Sheriff Mahomed, sends its produce to Sulo; the latter under Orang Kayas, trade with Borneo Proper. The British, when last at Balambangan, threw up a small redoubt on the Bankaka side, with a view to supplies of rice and provisions; and this part is tranquil and a good roadstead, being sheltered from the swell brought in by the sea-breeze.

The rich and valuable fishery of copis or Ceylon oyster in this bay has been mentioned; it might be rendered of considerable value. The whole of the rivers for miles up abound in rattans; Mr. A. Dalrymple thinks four thousand tons might be easily cut down every year without exhausting it, and sent by junks to China. There are forests of beautiful pines of stately growth, well calculated for the largest masts, and in high esteem at China. There is no quarter of the world which abounds more in that species of the sea-turtle (called by the Malays pakayan) which yields the shell; any quantity may be had on all the shores and isles of this bay.

The interior abounds in camphor, which can be had in any quantities; so vastly abundant is it, and so little does the Orang Idan know of the extreme value of this commodity, that a bamboo of camphor may be procured in exchange for a bamboo of salt. The petty towns are Sandeck, Bowengun, Patasan, Pone, and Milawi. It produces in one year two hundred pikuls of wax, fifty pikuls of tortoise-shell, ten pikuls of best camphor, and as much inferior; ten pikuls of birds-nest, at ten dollars the catty; 1st camphor, twenty-five; rattans, one dollar per pikul; tortoise-shell, one dollar the catty; wax, twenty the pikul. Articles required are the same as at Borneo Proper. Rice, provisions, fish, and fruits, are abundant and cheap; the sugar-cane also.

The province of Paytan is the principal district for camphor of any in the world. Whole forests for miles every where meet the eye, and the produce from them is the finest that can be conceived, large and transparent as Chin-chew sugar-candy. The principal towns are Pitan, Kinarubatan, Kulepan, and the famous town of Sugut. The coast is so full of coral-reefs, and has been so very indifferently surveyed, that it is only frequented by prows: there is a road from Sugut to Bankaka in Maludu Bay. Much wax, tripan, sago, &c. is produced here.

Labuk has the towns of Camburcan, Labuk, and Songsohi; its produce is somewhat similar to that of Paytan, with the addition of clove-bark and birds-nests.

Sandakan. This celebrated harbour has been already mentioned as one of the finest in the world. The towns within it are Towsam, Duyom, Lu, Bukean, Dom or Doung, Seagally-hood and Tong luly luku; all these are governed by Datus from Sulo, who have expressly settled here to collect the prodigious quantities of birdsnests abounding in this district. They are procured here at ten dollars the catty, and sent to Sulo, with tripan, wax, &c. The Sulos are very jealous of any ships going in here, and will leave no attempt untried in cutting off a vessel going in, although an English port.

In the province of Mangidora lies the great river Kinnabatingan, which is navigable a vast way up, with several towns of Orang Idan on its shores. The other towns are Salasany Supabuscul, Tambesan, which forms also an elegant harbour, Laboan or Saboan, Tuncu, Salurong, Giong, and Maday, which has a gold-mine, before mentioned. The whole of this province it is said will produce above one hundred pikuls of the finest birds-nests, much black ditto, some camphor, tripan, honey, wax, dammer, Buru mats, fine spars; sago and pepper were formerly largely cultivated here. The pearl-banks of Tawi Tawi have been mentioned.

Tirun. The sea-ports of this last-mentioned and valuable province, ceded to the English by the Sulos, are chiefly inhabited by Buguese people. The towns are Sibuku, Sambakung, Leo or Ledong, Sikatak, Sabellar, Kuran or Barrow, Talysion Dumaung, Tapeandurian. The principal ports are Kuran and Sibucu; they produce a large quantity of very fine white birdsnest, a quantity of black ditto, much dammer, sago, tripan, wax, rattans, camphor, honey, Buru mats, gold, &c. The people of Tapeandurian are represented as very ferocious, and the sea-coast hereabouts requires surveying.

The ports of Pasir and Coti originally belonged to the king of Benjarmasing; very fine birds-nest is procured here at twenty dollars the catty; much gold, tripan, wax, &c.

Were Borneo to be settled, I think the principal factory ought to be at Borneo Proper; the second at Sambas; the third at Benjarmasing; the fourth at Pasir; the fifth at Tabesan or Sandakan.

In looking over the map of the world, it is a melancholy reflection, to view so large a portion of the habitable globe as all Borneo abandoned to barbarism and desolation; that, with all her productive wealth and advantages of physical situation, her valuable and interesting shores should have been overlooked by all Europeans; that neither the Dutch nor the Portuguese, with centuries of uncontrolled power in these seas, should have shed a ray of civilisation on shores bordering upon their principal settlements; that her ports and rivers, instead of affording a shelter to the extensive commerce of China, should at this enlightened period of the world hold out only terror and dismay to the mariner; and that all that she should have acquired from the deadly vicinage and withering grasp of Dutch power and dominion has been the art of more speedily destroying each other and rendering themselves obnoxious to the rest of mankind. Now that her destinies are transferred to the enlightened heads and liberal hearts of Englishmen; now that her fortunes are embarked under the administration of a wise and liberal government; we may confidently hope that a happier order of things will, under the blessing of an all-ruling Providence, speedily restore these extensive shores to peace, to plenty, and to commerce; and we ardently trust that another age may not be suffered to pass away without exhibiting something consolatory to the statesman, the philosopher, and the philanthropist.

No. III.

Treaty between His Britannic Majesty and the King of the Netherlands, respecting Territory and Commerce in the East Indies. Signed at London, March 17, 1824.

In the name of the most holy and undivided Trinity.

His Majesty the King of the United Kingdom of Great Britain and Ireland, and his Majesty the King of the Netherlands, desiring to place upon a footing mutually beneficial their respective possessions and the commerce of their subjects in the East Indies, so that the welfare and prosperity of both nations may be promoted in all time to come, without those differences and jealousies which have, in former times, interrupted the harmony which ought always to subsist between them; and being anxious that all occasions of misunderstanding between their respective agents may be, as much as possible, prevented; and in order to determine certain questions which have occurred in the execution of the Convention made at London on the 13th of August, 1814, in so far as it respects the possessions of his Netherland Majesty in the East, have nominated their Plenipotentiaries, that is to say:

His Majesty the King of the United Kingdom of Great Britain and Ireland, the Right Honourable George Canning, a member of his said Majesty's most honourable Privy Council, a member of Parliament, and his said Majesty's principal Secretary of State for Foreign Affairs;—and the Right Honourable Charles Watkin Williams Wynn, a member of his said Majesty's most honourable Privy Council, a member of Parliament, Lieutenant-Colonel Commandant of the Montgomeryshire Regiment of Yeomanry Cavalry, and President of his said Majesty's Board of Commissioners for the affairs of India:

And his Majesty the King of the Netherlands, Baron Henry Fagel, member of the Equestrian Corps of the Province of Holland, Counsellor of State, Knight Grand Cross of the Royal Order of the Belgic Lion, and of the Royal Guelphic Order, and Ambassador Extraordinary and Plenipotentiary of his said Majesty to his Majesty the King of Great Britain; and Anton Reinhard Falck, Commander of the Royal Order of the Belgic Lion, and his said Majesty's Minister of the Department of Public Instruction, National Industry, and Colonies:

Who, after having mutually communicated their full powers, found in good and due form, have agreed on the following Articles.

ARTICLE I. The high contracting parties engage to admit the subjects of each other to trade with their respective possessions in the Eastern Archipelago, and on the continent of India, and in Ceylon, upon the footing of the most favoured nation; their respective subjects conforming themselves to the local regulations of each settlement.

ARTICLE II. The subjects and vessels of one nation shall not pay, upon importation or exportation, at the ports of the other in the Eastern Seas, any duty at a rate beyond the double of that at which the subjects and vessels of the nation to which the port belongs are charged.

The duties paid on exports or imports at a British port on the continent of India, or in Ceylon, on Dutch bottoms, shall be arranged so as in no case to be charged at more than double the amount of the duties paid by British subjects, and on British bottoms.

In regard to any article upon which no duty is imposed, when imported or exported by the subjects or on the vessels of the nation to which the port belongs, the duty charged upon the subjects or vessels of the other shall in no case exceed six per cent.

ARTICLE III. The high contracting parties engage that no treaty hereafter made by either, with any native power in the Eastern Seas, shall contain any article tending, either expressly or by the imposition of unequal duties, to exclude the trade of the other party from the ports of such native power: and that if, in any treaty now existing on either part, any article to that effect has been admitted, such article shall be abrogated upon the conclusion of the present treaty.

It is understood that before the conclusion of the present treaty, communication has been made by each of the contracting parties to the other of all treaties or engagements subsisting between each of them respectively and any native power in the Eastern Seas; and that the like communication shall be made of all such treaties concluded by them respectively hereafter.

ARTICLE IV. Their Britannic and Netherland Majesties engage to give strict orders as well to their civil and military authorities as to their ships of war, to respect the freedom of trade, established by Articles I., II., and III.; and in no case to impede a free communication of the natives in the Eastern Archipelago with the ports of the two governments respectively, or of the subjects of the two governments with the ports belonging to native powers.

ARTICLE V. Their Britannic and Netherland Majesties in like manner engage to concur effectually in repressing piracy in those seas: they will not grant either asylum or protection to vessels engaged in piracy, and they will in no case permit the ships or merchandise captured by such vessels to be introduced, deposited, or sold in any of their possessions.

ARTICLE VI. It is agreed that orders shall be given by the two governments to their officers and agents in the East, not to form any new settlement on any of the islands in the Eastern Seas, without previous authority from their respective governments in Europe.

ARTICLE VII. The Molucca islands, and especially Amboyna, Banda, Ternate, and their immediate dependencies, are excepted from the operation of the I., II., III., and IV. Articles, until the Netherland government shall think fit to abandon the monopoly of spices; but if the said government shall at any time previous to such abandonment of the monopoly allow the subjects of any power other than a native Asiatic power to carry on any commercial intercourse with the said islands, the subjects of his Britannic Majesty shall be admitted to such intercourse upon a footing precisely similar.

ARTICLE VIII. His Netherland Majesty cedes to his Britannic Majesty all his establishments on the continent of India; and renounces all privileges and exemptions enjoyed or claimed in virtue of those establishments.

ARTICLE IX. The factory of Fort Marlborough, and all the English possessions on the island of Sumatra, are hereby ceded to his Netherland Majesty: and his Britannic Majesty further engages that no British settlement shall be formed on that island, nor any treaty concluded by British authority with any native prince, chief, or state therein.

ARTICLE X. The town and fort of Malacca, and its dependencies, are hereby ceded to his Britannic Majesty; and his Netherland Majesty engages for himself and his subjects, never to form any establishment on any part of the peninsula of Malacca, or to conclude any treaty with any native prince, chief, or state therein.

ARTICLE XI. His Britannic Majesty withdraws the objections which have been made to the occupation of the island of Billiton and its dependencies by the agents of the Netherland government.

ARTICLE XII. His Netherland Majesty withdraws the objections which have been made to the occupation of the island of Singapore by the subjects of his Britannic Majesty.

His Britannic Majesty, however, engages that no British establishment shall be made on the Carimon Isles, or on the islands of Battam, Bintang, Lingin, or any of the other islands south of the Straits of Singapore, nor any treaty concluded by British authority with the chiefs of those islands.

ARTICLE XIII. All the colonies, possessions, and establishments which are ceded by the preceding articles shall be delivered up to the officers of the respective sovereigns on the 1st of March, 1825. The fortifications shall remain in the state in which they shall be at the period of the notification of this treaty in India; but no claim shall be made on either side for ordnance, or stores of any description, either left or removed by the ceding power, nor for any arrears of revenue, or any charge of administration whatever.

ARTICLE XIV. All the inhabitants of the territories hereby ceded shall enjoy, for a period of six years from the date of the ratification of the present treaty, the liberty of disposing as they please of their property, and of transporting themselves, without let or hindrance, to any country to which they may wish to remove.

ARTICLE XV. The high contracting parties agree that none of the territories or establishments mentioned in Articles VIII., IX., X., XI., and XII., shall be, at any time, transferred to any other power. In case of any of the said possessions being abandoned by one of the present contracting parties, the right of occupation thereof shall immediately pass to the other.

ARTICLE XVI. It is agreed that all accounts and reclamations arising out of the restoration of Java and other possessions to the officers of his Netherland Majesty in the East Indies,—as well those which were the subject of a Convention made at Java on the 24th of June, 1817, between the commissioners of the two nations, as all others, shall be finally and completely closed and satisfied on the payment of the sum of one hundred thousand pounds, sterling money, to be made in London, on the part of the Netherlands, before the expiration of the year 1825.

ARTICLE XVII. The present treaty shall be ratified, and the ratifications exchanged at London within three months from the date hereof, or sooner if possible.

In witness whereof, the respective plenipotentiaries have signed the same, and affixed thereunto the seals of their arms.

Done at London, the seventeenth day of March, in the year of our Lord one thousand eight hundred and twenty-four.

GEORGE CANNING.
CHARLES WATKIN WILLIAMS WYNN.

Note addressed by the British Plenipotentiaries to the Plenipotentiaries of the Netherlands.

London, March 17, 1824.

In proceeding to the signature of the Treaty which has been agreed upon, the plenipotentiaries of his Britannic Majesty have great satisfaction in recording their sense of the friendly and liberal spirit which has been evinced by their excellencies the plenipotentiaries of his Netherland Majesty; and their conviction that there is, on both sides, an equal disposition to carry into effect, with sincerity and good faith, the stipulations of the treaty in the sense in which they have been negotiated.

The differences which gave rise to the present discussion are such as it is difficult to adjust by formal stipulation: consisting, in great part, of jealousies and suspicions, and arising out of the acts of subordinate agents, they can only be removed by a frank declaration of intention, and a mutual understanding as to principles between the governments themselves.

The disavowal of the proceedings whereby the execution of the Convention of August 1814 was retarded, must have satisfied their excellencies the Netherland plenipotentiaries of the scrupulous regard with which England always fulfils her engagements.

The British plenipotentiaries record, with sincere pleasure, the solemn disavowal on the part of the Netherland government, of any design to aim either at political supremacy or at commercial monopoly in the Eastern Archipelago. They willingly acknowledge the readiness with which the Netherland plenipotentiaries have entered into stipulations calculated to promote the most perfect freedom of trade between the subjects of the two crowns, and their respective dependencies in that part of the world.

TREATY BETWEEN ENGLAND AND

The undersigned are authorised to express the full concurrence of his Britannic Majesty in the enlightened views of his Majesty the King of the Netherlands. Aware of the difficulty of adapting, at once, to a long-established system of monopoly, the principles of commercial policy which are now laid down, the undersigned have been authorised to consent to the exception of the Molucca Islands from the general stipulation for freedom of trade contained in the treaty. They trust, however, that, as the necessity for this exception is occasioned solely by the difficulty of abrogating, at the present moment, the monopoly of spices, its operation will be strictly limited by that necessity.

The British plenipotentiaries understand the term Moluccas as applicable to that cluster of islands which has Celebes to the westward, New Guinea to the eastward, and Timor to the southward; but that these three islands are not comprehended in the exception; nor would it have included Ceram, if the situation of that island, in reference to the two principal spice isles, Amboyna and Banda, had not required a prohibition of intercourse with it so long as the monopoly of spices shall be maintained.

The territorial exchanges which have been thought expedient for avoiding a collision of interests render it incumbent upon the plenipotentiaries of his Britannic Majesty to make, and to require, some explanations with respect to the dependants and allies of England in the island from which she is about to withdraw.

A treaty concluded in the year 1819, by British agents, with the king of Acheen, is incompatible with the 3d article of the present treaty. The British plenipotentiaries therefore undertake, that the treaty with Acheen shall, as soon as possible, be modified into a simple arrangement for the hospitable reception of British vessels and subjects in the port of Acheen. But as some of the provisions of that treaty (which has been communicated to the Netherland plenipotentiaries) will be conducive to the general interests of Europeans established in the Eastern Seas, they trust that the Netherland government will take measures for securing the benefit of those provisions. And they express their confidence, that no measures hostile to the king of Acheen will be adopted by the new possessor of Fort Marlborough.

It is no less the duty of the British plenipotentiaries to recommend to the friendly and paternal protection of the Netherland government the interests of the natives and settlers subject to the ancient factory of England at Bencoolen.

This appeal is the more necessary, because, so lately as the year 1818, treaties were made with the native chiefs, by which their situation was much improved. The system of forced cultivation and delivery of pepper was abolished; encouragement was given to the cultivation of rice; the relations between the cultivating classes and the chiefs of the districts were adjusted; the property in the soil was recognised in those chiefs; and all interference in the detailed management of the interior was withdrawn, by removing the European residents from the out-stations, and substituting in their room native officers. All these measures were calculated greatly to promote the interests of the native inhabitants.

In recommending these interests to the care of the Netherland government, the undersigned request the plenipotentiaries of his Netherland Majesty to assure their government that a corresponding attention will be paid, on the part of the British authorities, to the inhabitants of Malacca and the other Netherland settlements which are transferred to Great Britain.

In conclusion, the plenipotentiaries of his Britannic Majesty congratulate their excellencies the Netherland plenipotentiaries upon the happy termination of their conferences. They feel assured that, under the arrangement which is now concluded, the commerce of both nations will flourish, and that the two allies will preserve inviolate in Asia, no less than in Europe, the friendship which has, from old times, subsisted between them. The disputes being now ended, which, during two centuries, have occasionally produced irritation, there will henceforward be no rivalry between the English and Dutch nations in the East, except for the more effectual establishment of those principles of liberal policy which both have this day asserted in the face of the world.

The undersigned request their excellencies the plenipotentiaries of his Netherland Majesty will accept the assurances of their distinguished consideration.

GEORGE CANNING.
CHARLES WATKIN WILLIAMS WYNN.

Reply of the Netherland Plenipotentiaries to the Note of the Plenipotentiaries of Great Britain.

London, March 17, 1824.

The undersigned, plenipotentiaries of his Majesty the King of the Netherlands, have found in the note which is just delivered to them by their excellencies the British plenipotentiaries, a faithful recapitulation of the communications which had taken place at the time when circumstances, independent of the will of the negotiators, caused a suspension of their conferences.

Summoned to resume a work, the completion of which has ever been desired with equal sincerity by both parties, the undersigned have not failed to recognise in their colabourers in this work that spirit of equity and conciliation which facilitates the arrangement of the most complicated questions, and to which they cannot do justice at a time more fitting than that which is about to sanction, by the signature of a formal treaty, the resolutions, adopted after a most strict examination, as eminently useful for the maintenance of a good understanding even among the inferior agents of the contracting powers.

This essential aim and principal tendency of the treaty is evident to all who read its different articles with attention. What is therein expressly stipulated ought to suffice for the removal, by common consent, of all uncertainty which might present itself in the sequel. However, as the British plenipotentiaries have considered it necessary to enter into some further details, the undersigned, who, on their part, are sensible of the importance of leaving nothing doubtful in so important a matter, have no difficulty in following them through these details, and in supplying, by a concise display of their view of the subject, the answer which is due from them to the aforesaid note of their excellencies.

The 7th article contains an exception to the general principle of liberty of commerce. The necessity of that exception, already admitted by England in the conferences of 1820, rests upon the existence of the system which respects the exclusive trade in spice. Should the determinations of the government of the Netherlands lead to the abandonment of that system, the rights of free trade will be immediately restored, and the whole of that Archipelago, which has been very justly described as comprised between Celebes, Timor, and New Guinea, will be open to all lawful speculations, on the footing to be established by local ordinances, and, so far as particularly concerns the subjects of his Britannic Majesty, in conformity with the grounds sanctioned by the treaty for all the Asiatic possessions of the two contracting powers.

On the other hand, so long as the exception in question remains in force, the ships which traverse the Moluccas must refrain from touching at any ports but those whereof the description has been officially communicated to the maritime powers some years back; except in cases of distress, in which it is superfluous to add, that they will find in all places where the flag of the Netherlands may be flying those good offices and succours which are due to suffering humanity.

If the government of Great Britain conceives it to be a real advantage that by disengaging itself, according to the principles sanctioned by the treaty which is about to be signed, from the connexions which were formed by its agents four or five years ago in the kingdom of Acheen, it secures, by some new clause, the hospitable reception of British vessels and subjects in the ports of that kingdom; the undersigned hesitate not to declare, that, on their part, they do not see any difficulty in it, and conceive that they may assert, at the same time, that their government will apply itself, without delay, to regulate its relations with Acheen, in such a manner, that that state, without losing anything of its independence, may offer both to the sailor and the merchant that constant security which can only be established by the moderate exercise of European influence.

In support of the information contained in the last note of the British plenipotentiaries, on the subject of Bencoolen, their excellencies have communicated to the undersigned the two conventions respectively signed on the 23d of May and the 4th of July, 1818, by the lieutenant-governor of that establishment, on the one side, and by the chiefs of some neighbouring tribes, on the other. They have likewise communicated a despatch of the governor-general in council, dated Fort William, the 9th of May, 1823, and according to which the British government has abolished at Fort Marlborough the monopoly of pepper, encouraged the cultivation of rice, and placed on a firm and uniform footing the relations of the different classes of natives, as well among themselves as with their chiefs. But inasmuch as the undersigned are not wrong in supposing that the object of these arrangements has been the security of the agricultural prosperity of the colony, and the removal of the vexations which often result from the immediate contact of the native population with the subordinate authorities of a foreign government, they experience great satisfaction in saying, that, far from having cause to dread retroactive measures, the individuals interested in the existing order of things may, on the contrary, cherish the hope that the new government will respect their acquired rights and their welfare; and, what the undersigned are above all things desirous to guarantee, that it will cause the articles of the above-mentioned conventions to be observed, on the faith of which the inhabitants of Pasummah, Ulu Manna, and the other colonists in the interior, have recognised the authority, or accepted the protection, of the British East India Company; saving, however, the power of substituting, with the full consent of the parties interested, other analogous conditions, if circumstances should render a change necessary.

With respect to the equitable and benign intentions of the British government towards the inhabitants of Malacca, and the other Dutch establishments ceded by the treaty, the plenipotentiaries of his Majesty the King of the Netherlands accept the assurance thereof with unlimited confidence; and the same sentiment prevents them from insisting that the orders and instructions which shall be addressed to the English authorities in India, relative to the surrender of Fort Marlborough, and its dependencies, should be conceived in such clear, precise, and positive terms, that no cause of uncertainty, or any pretext for delay, may be discovered in them:—being persuaded that the British plenipotentiaries, after having accomplished their labours with so much moderation and equity, will take care that the result of their common exertions be not compromised by any regard to subordinate interests and secondary considerations. This result the British plenipotentiaries themselves have described in their last note; and it only remains for the undersigned to congratulate themselves on having contributed thereto, and to unite their wishes with those of their excellencies, that their respective agents in their Asiatic possessions may ever shew themselves sensible of the duties which two friendly nations, animated with truly liberal views, have to fulfil, both with reference to each other, and also towards the natives whom the course of events or treaties have placed under their influence.

The undersigned avail themselves of this opportunity of renewing to their excellencies the British plenipotentiaries the assurance of their most distinguished consideration.

H. FAGEL.
A. R. FALCK.

No. IV.

Official Letters.

From the Resident Councillor at Singapore to the Honourable the Acting Governor of Prince of Wales Island, Singapore, and Malacca.

Singapore, 17th February, 1843.

Sir,—I esteem it my duty to transmit a copy of a deposition taken by me relative to an act of piracy perpetrated near Poolow Tingie. There is no doubt whatever that, unless some protection is afforded to the trading boats from Cochin China, the loss of life and plunder of property will follow to the same extent, if not more so, than during the past season. On this important subject I have had occasion to write officially.

It is to be feared the Malays at Poolow Tingie are deeply implicated in the acts of piracy which are annually committed in that proximity.

I have, &c.

T. Church,
Resident Councillor.

Hoy, Nakodah of a Cochin China tope, of thirty-five coyans, left Cochin China eleven days since, bound for Singapore, with a cargo consisting of thirty-five coyans of rice, two peculs of raw silk, 600 mats, three pigs. Our crew consisted of fifteen hands. We had no arms of any kind on board. Six days after having left Cochin China we reached near Poolow Tingie, when we fell in with five sampans, having on board about thirty Malays; the Malays were armed with spears, creeses, swords, and muskets. We were boarded by them, and two of our number killed. They took the silk, and a small part of the rice, and then scuttled our prau. Myself and twelve companions were taken by the pirates to Poolow Tingie, where they reside at this season of the year. We were then allowed to take to our sampans, with strict injunctions not to proceed to Singapore; we, however, were compelled to come here by the wind and current. We were five days without food and water.

S. GARLING,
Acting Governor.

Before me,
T. CHURCH,
Resident Councillor at Singapore,
17th February, 1843.

Admiralty, 13th October, 1843.

SIR,—Having laid before my Lords Commissioners of the Admiralty your letter of the 26th June, 1843, No. 164, with its enclosure from Captain the Honourable Henry Keppel, of the Dido, reporting the repulse of the attacks of certain piratical praus, on two occasions, by Lieut. F. W. Horton, and the officers and men employed under him, in three boats of the Dido, I am commanded to acquaint you that their Lordships are satisfied with the manner in which Lieutenant Horton, and the officers and men employed with him, repelled the attack made upon them.

JOHN BARROW.

Vice-Admiral Sir WM. PARKER, G.C.B.
Singapore.

Admiralty, 16th October, 1843.

SIR,—Having laid before my Lords Commissioners of the Admiralty your letter of the 13th July, 1843, No. 183, with its enclosures, from Captain the Honourable Henry Keppel, of the Dido, reporting the spirited conduct of Lieutenant Hunt, and the officers, seamen, and marines of that ship, who accompanied him in a native-built boat, which was attacked by two piratical praus, off Cape Datu, in the island of Borneo; also detailing the proceedings of the boats of the Dido, with ninety-five officers and men, who were detached, under the command of Lieutenant Wilmot Horton, to the river Sarebus, where they effected the destruction of certain forts, and three settlements of pirates; I am commanded to acquaint you that their Lordships are pleased to express their approbation of the gallant and spirited conduct of the officers and men employed on these occasions in executing the judicious arrangements made by Captain Keppel.

JOHN BARROW.

Vice-Admiral Sir Wm. Parker, G.C.B.
Singapore.

Cornwallis, in Madras Roads,
10th May, 1844.

SIR,—I have much pleasure in transmitting herewith the copies of two letters which I have received from the Secretary of the Admiralty, conveying their Lordships' approbation of the gallant and spirited conduct of the officers and men of the Dido, who were employed in the boats of that ship, on the coast and rivers of Borneo. And

I desire you will communicate the same to the officers and men accordingly.

I am, Sir, your very humble servant,
W. PARKER, Vice-Admiral.

Captain the Hon. Henry Keppel,
Her Majesty's ship Dido.

From the Governor of Prince of Wales Island, Singapore, and Malacca, to Captain J. R. SCOTT, commanding the Hon. East India Company's steamer Phlegethon.

Singapore, 13th September, 1844.

SIR,—I have the honour to acknowledge the receipt of your letter of this date, enclosing the copy of a communication to your address, from Captain the Honourable Henry Keppel, commander of her Majesty's ship Dido, expressing the high sense he entertains of your zeal and attention, and the service rendered by the Honourable East India Company's steamer Phlegethon during the recent operations on the coast of Borneo, which I will not fail to submit to the supreme government.

That success would attend the expedition against the pirates on the N.W. coast of Borneo, was to be anticipated, from the approved experience and acknowledged gallantry of your commander, Captain the Honourable Henry Keppel; but such an unprecedented result as the destruction of the main strongholds of men who have been the scourge of these seas for years past, and whose courage and cruelties are proverbial, could only have been effected by the most untiring zeal, energy, and enterprise from all concerned; more especially when it is remembered that these strongholds were situated between fifty and 100 miles up a difficult river, in which every obstacles were thrown, with a view of retarding your progress; and that the pirates were commanded by their chieftains, Seriff Sahib and Seriff Mulak.

It affords me the highest gratification to notice here what will be specially laid before the supreme government, the honourable testimony borne to the determined valour of Mr. Coverley, first officer, and Mr. Simson, second officer of the Phlegethon, by Captain the Honourable Henry Keppel, who observes, in his public despatch, when speaking of the gallant conduct of all engaged, and the creditable and efficient state of the Phlegethon's boats, that these officers were the two first on the heights of Undop, in leading to which the first lieutenant of the Dido was killed.

I have the honour to be, Sir,
Your most obedient servant,
W. J. BUTTERWORTH,
Governor of P. W. Island, Singapore, and Malacca.

Admiralty, February 28th, 1845.

SIR,—I am commanded by my Lords Commissioners of the Admiralty to acquaint you, that they have received with much satisfaction your letter detailing the measures you had taken for the suppression of piracy on the coast of Borneo and up the Sakarran river. Their Lordships desire also to express their approbation at the gallantry and perseverance displayed by the officers, seamen, and marines under your orders, in overcoming the force and numbers opposed to them, and the many obstacles they had to contend with; and my Lords desire that you will, as far as may be in your power, convey to those employed under you in this enterprise the expression of their Lordships' satisfaction. My Lords, however, have to lament the loss on this occasion of a promising and gallant officer, Lieutenant Wade, R.N., and also that of Mr. Steward, who so generously lent his valuable services to the expedition; a loss, however, which their Lordships think might have been still more severe but for the discretion and the judicious conduct of those conducting the attack.

W. A. B. HAMILTON.

Captain the Hon. Henry Keppel.

No. V.

Admiral Sir Thomas Cochrane's Despatches.

From the London Gazette, Friday, Nov. 28th, 1845.

Admiralty, Nov. 27th, 1845.

Despatches have been received at this office from Rear-Admiral Sir Thomas Cochrane, C.B., Commander-in-chief of her Majesty's ships and vessels on the East India Station, of which the following are copies or extracts:—

Agincourt, off Pulo Laboan, coast of Borneo,
August 13th, 1845.

SIR,—I arrived off the river Bruné (Borneo Proper) on the 6th inst.

If their Lordships will be good enough to refer to a paragraph towards the conclusion of the memorandum addressed to me by Mr. Brooke, under date the 3d of July, 1845, they will find a statement of two natives of India having been detained as slaves in the capital itself for two years, continuing under captivity in the presence of the British men-of-war, and from which slavery they made their escape on board the Hon. East India Company's steam-vessel Phlegethon on her last visit there, only a few weeks since.

Under such a glaring disregard of the understanding entered into with the Sultan in respect of slavery, I felt, in conjunction with Mr. Brooke, that it would not be right to permit this transaction to pass without, in the first instance, holding the Sultan responsible for it; and Pangeran Bedurudeen having stated that Pangeran Usop was the real offender, everything should be kept quiet until my arrival in the capital; on the following day I went with the steamers to visit this singular capital, or what is called city, being a miserable collection of bamboo-houses, elevated upon piles, surrounded by water, except at low tide, when under many of them you perceive the bare mud; the poverty of the buildings being singularly and inexplicably contrasted with the manners, dresses, and deportment of the higher orders.

I visited the Sultan with all due ceremony, and, by previous understanding with the Rajah Muda Hassin and his brother Bedurudeen, the visit was entirely complimentary; but after my departure, on the same evening, and following morning, Mr. Brooke had several meetings with those persons. The Sultan stated he was quite ready to punish Pangeran Usop if I would afford my assistance in accomplishing it. It appeared that Usop (I suppose from conscious guilt) concluded he was the object sought, and had, on the day of my visit, told the Sultan that if called on to answer on the score of piracy, he would defend himself to the last.

In answer to my address to the Sultan, I received the accompanying documents (Nos. 2 and 3), one calling for assistance, the other for personal protection; a subaltern's guard was accordingly sent to the Sultan's residence; and it was settled, through Mr. Brooke, that the Sultan should call on Usop to present himself before him, unarmed, to answer for his conduct, and if he did not do so, his residence was to be attacked.

The Sultan's commands were accordingly conveyed to him, which not having been replied to within a given time, a shot was fired over his house, to which he promptly replied by a salvo from his battery, when a fire in earnest was opened upon him, and a few minutes sent him and all his adherents off to the woods, and the marines landed and took possession of his house, where, among other things, twenty handsome brass guns, of various calibre, were found, and 150 half-barrels of gunpowder.

The guns the Sultan requested me to keep; but reserving two of the smallest, for the purpose of sale, to produce funds to remunerate the two natives (now serving on board the Pluto) for their four years' captivity, I sent the remainder to the Sultan, with a message, through Mr. Brooke, to say, that we never accepted any remuneration for the protection of friends who were disposed faithfully to carry out the engagements they had entered into.

I learn from Mr. Brooke, who has been in communication with Muda Hassin and his brother since the flight of Usop and destruction of his property, that the occurrence has given great confidence to the well-disposed party, and that it will equally depress Usop's adherents in the town, of whom there were not a few; and I look for a double result from his punishment—namely, that while it assures the legitimate government of all proper support, they will equally perceive the rod that hangs over them should they be found wanting in their own conduct.

I have, &c.
THOMAS COCHRANE,
Rear-Admiral and Commander-in-Chief.

To the Secretary of the Admiralty, London.

Agincourt, at Sea, in lat. 8° 14′ N., long. 116° 4′ E.
August 26th, 1845.

SIR,—Following out the intentions referred to in my despatch from Laboan (No. 142), of the 13th of August, I left that anchorage on the 15th instant, and reached the northern end of Borneo on the 17th.

Having heard from various sources that Scheriff Osman had, for the last twelvemonth, been making preparations against a probable attack, that he had strongly fortified one of the branches of a river in Maloodoo-bay, and was of a character, and supported by resolute adherents not likely to yield without a sharp struggle, I made corresponding arrangements for attack; and having anchored the Agincourt and frigates in a safe position, in the hitherto little known fine bay of Maloodoo, I hoisted my flag on board the Vixen steam sloop, and, attended by the Cruiser and Wolverine brigs, and the Hon. East India Company's steam vessels Pluto and Nemesis, proceeded to the head of the bay, carrying deep water until within a couple of miles of the river's mouth, when the Vixen and brigs were obliged to anchor, and not far within them the Pluto, drawing only six feet, grounded on the bar.

It being hopeless to attempt to make a further progress in these small vessels, I directed Captain Talbot, assisted by Acting Captain Lyster, and Commanders Fanshawe and Clifford, to take command of the gun and other boats of the squadron, filled with as many marines and small-arm men as they could with propriety carry, and proceed up that branch of the Maloodoo stated by the pilots to be in the occupation of Scheriff Osman; and should their statements prove correct, to ascertain as far as possible the strength of his position and amount of force, either attacking the Scheriff on his refusal to surrender, should he feel equal to the enterprise, or falling back to some suitable position, while he communicated with me in the event of his not considering his force sufficient to guarantee success.

The accompanying letter and report from Captain Talbot will convey to their Lordships a gratifying narration of his success, and prove the soundness of my judgment in selecting this officer for the important duty confided to him.

Their Lordships will not fail to unite with me in deep regret at the heavy loss we have incurred; but when the great strength of the position is referred to, and that the force was for one hour exposed to the steadily sustained fire of eleven heavy guns, within little more than 200 yards of our own position, it is rather astonishing than otherwise, and a source of thankfulness that the casualties were not more numerous.

Their Lordships will not fail to notice the valorous conduct of Acting Captain Lyster, and those immediately under him, upon this occasion; who, undaunted by the fire with which they were assailed, steadily worked at a remarkably well-constructed boom for above an hour before he could effect an opening, and on the success of whose exertions mainly depended the advance of the force, who, in ignorance of any other manner of approaching the forts than by the river, could not be brought forward until this object was accomplished; and while I feel persuaded their Lordships will be fully alive to such meritorious conduct, I deeply lament that death has removed from their Lordships' power of reward that promising young officer, Mr. Leonard Gibbard, mate of the Wolverine, who bravely worked by Captain Lyster's side; the wound he received on that occasion having, unfortunately for his country and his friends, proved fatal on the following day.

I sent up the same evening a small detachment of gun-boats, under Commander Giffard, to burn such prahues and boats, and parts of the forts or town, as might have remained not completely destroyed, and to render unserviceable any iron guns, and to bring down with him any brass ordnance that might be there.

Two or three chiefs are known to have fallen on the present occasion, and there is every reason to believe that Scheriff Osman, so formidable to all the neighbouring country, and whose valour was worthy of a better cause, is among the number slain; at least I have certain information that he was carried off badly wounded; but whether dead or living, I consider his influence to be entirely annihilated, and his confederacy with various piratical chiefs in the Archipelago broken up; for his power as much depended upon his being the encourager of other piratical tribes, and their supplier with goods in exchange for slaves, as in the force naturally at his command. I may add that, among many other articles of European workmanship, a bell belonging to the ship Guilhelm Ludwig, of Bremen, was found in the town. This vessel was supposed to have been wrecked on the Garsi Isles, about October or November last, but nothing has been heard of the crew.

I have, &c.
THOMAS COCHRANE,
Rear-Admiral Commander-in-Chief.

To the Secretary of the Admiralty, London.

Her Majesty's Steam-vessel Vixen, Maloodoo Bay,
August 20th, 1845.

SIR,—I have to report the proceedings of the expedition you did me the honour to place under my command.

Your Excellency's flag having been flying on board the Vixen, you are aware of its progress to the anchorage at the head of the Maloodoo Bay; I commence, therefore, the details from that period.

The force, consisting of 530 seamen and marines (the details of which I annex), conveyed in 24 boats, of which nine were gunboats, left the Vixen at 3 o'clock p.m. on the 18th instant, and after some little difficulty on hitting on the channel, was anchored off the mouth of the Songybasar a little after sunset. Here we were joined by a boat from the Pluto, carrying Agincourt's field-piece.

The tide serving, about 11 o'clock p.m. weighed, and passing the bar, anchored within it; at daylight on the 19th we proceeded up the river in two divisions; after proceeding about two miles, I was informed by the Bruné pilots we were nearing the town. I therefore went ahead with Captain Lyster to reconnoitre. On coming to an abrupt turn in the river, about three miles higher, we found ourselves suddenly in front of the position, which consisted of two stockaded forts of eight and three guns each, commanding the reach. About 200 yards below the forts was a boom across the river, apparently well constructed. The forts appeared to us to stand on a tongue of land, from which we were separated by the river, which at that point divided into two branches, and the pilots declared such to be the case; that turning to the right we observed was still further defended by a floating battery. There appeared, therefore, to be no means of carrying the position but by forcing the boom.

On rejoining the force, arrangements were made for the gun-boats to advance to the boom, to cover the party appointed to cut through it, the remainder of the force to hold themselves in readiness to act when ordered. We had approached the boom to within one hundred yards, when a flag of truce was observed to be coming towards us.

Conceiving the object of the enemy was merely to gain time, I sent back a message, 'that unless Scheriff Osman came to me in half an honr I should open fire.' This being conveyed to the fort, the flag returned with an offer to admit me with two boats, that I might visit the Scheriff. I declined, and the flag retired; the moment it was clear of the line of fire the three-gun battery opened, and the cannonade became general on both sides.

The boom was composed of two large-sized trees, each supporting a chain cable, equal to 10 or 12 inches, firmly bolted and secured around the trunk of a tree on each bank; a cut in the right bank allowed a canoe to pass, but was impassable to any of our boats.

One hour nearly elapsed before we could in any way remove the obstacle, during which time the fire of the enemy was well sustained, all the guns being laid for the boom. I need hardly mention it was briskly returned from our side, both from guns and small arms; and some rockets well thrown by a party which had been landed on the right bank, appeared to produce considerable effect.

As soon as the passage was open for the smaller boats, they passed through rapidly, and embarked the marines from the large boats across the boom; ultimately the whole force passed through. The enemy immediately quitted their defences, and fled in every direction. The marines and small-arm men having cleared the town, the marines were formed as a covering party, and parties of seamen were pushed up both banks of the river, but met with no opposition; at the same time preparations were made for spiking the guns and destroying the stockades and town; in a short time these were completed, and the whole in flames, as well as three large proas, and several smaller ones.

Being anxious to save the tide, and conceiving that the object contemplated by your Excellency was accomplished, I ordered the force to be re-embarked, and proceeded down the river to the Vixen.

When your Excellency considers the strength of the enemy's position, and the obvious state of preparation in which we found him, you will be prepared to learn that this service has not been performed without considerable loss. I regret very much to state it at six killed and 15 wounded; the loss on the part of the enemy was unquestionably very great, but the surrounding jungle afforded the enemy the means of carrying away their dead, according to their custom in such cases. Nevertheless, some of those left on the field we recognised as persons of considerable influence.

Whilst I record my admiration of the gallantry and steadiness of the whole force under a galling fire, sustained for a long period, I must particularly mention Captain Lyster, who directed his attention to the boom, and by whose personal exertions that obstacle was overcome.

Mr. Gibbard, mate of her Majesty's ship Wolverine, was, I grieve to say, mortally wounded by an early shot, when gallantly working at the boom with an axe.

I beg leave to point out to your Excellency the conduct of Mr. Williamson, Malay interpreter to Mr. Brooke; he was with me during the attack, and was exposed to the whole of the fire.

I have, &c.,
CHARLES TALBOT, Captain.

His Excellency Rear-Admiral Sir Thomas Cochrane, C.B.
Commander-in-Chief.

Detail of the naval force employed in the attack on and the destruction of Maloodoo, under the command of Captain Charles Talbot, Her Majesty's Ship Vestal, on the 19th day of August, 1845.

Her Majesty's ship Agincourt's gig, Captain Lyster; Mr. Creswell, midshipman; one petty officer, and five seamen.

Gun-boat (launch), Lieut. Lowther; Mr. Whepple, assistant-surgeon; Mr. Burnaby, midshipman; Mr. Barton, midshipman; 1 petty officer, and 18 seamen.

Gun-boat (barge), Lieut. Paynter; Mr. May, mate; Mr. Patrick, assistant-surgeon; 1 petty officer, and 14 seamen.

(Pinnace, with rockets), Mr. Reeve, mate; 3 petty officers, and 18 seamen.

(Cutter), Mr. Simcoe, midshipman; 11 seamen.

Gun-boat, manned from Agincourt, Hon. East India Company's steam-vessel Nemesis, with 1st company small-armed men (1st cutter), Lieut. Reid; Mr. Hathorn, midshipman; 1 petty officer, and 10 seamen.

Gun-boat (2d cutter), Mr. Young, mate; 1 petty officer, and 10 seamen.

Gun-boat, with Agincourt's field-piece men, Pluto's (cutter), Lieut. Heard; 2 petty officers, and 15 men.

Her Majesty's ship Vestal's (barge), Lieut. Morritt, senior lieutenant; gun-boat, Mr. Pym, second master; 1 petty officer, and 13 seamen.

(Pinnace), Lieutenant Pasco; Mr. Ward, assistant-surgeon; Mr. Sanders, midshipman; 1 petty officer, and 13 men.

Her Majesty's ship Vestal's gun-boat (cutter), Mr. Durbin, mate; 11 seamen; (gig), Mr. Ecles, clerk, 5 seamen.

Her Majesty's ship Dædalus, gun-boat (launch), Mr. Wilkinson, second master; 1 petty officer, and 18 seamen; (barge), Lieut. Randolph, senior lieutenant; Mr. Huxham, midshipman; 2 petty officers, and 17 seamen; (pinnace), Mr. Nolloth, mate; Mr. Balcomb, midshipman; 1 petty officer, and 12 seamen; (cutter), Mr. Protheroe, midshipman; 1 petty officer, and 8 seamen.

Her Majesty's steam-vessel Vixen's gun-boat (pinnace), Lieut. Wilcox, senior lieutenant; Mr. Dent, mate; 1 petty officer, and 15 men; (first cutter), Mr. W. Sainsbury, midshipman; 9 seamen; (second cutter), Lieut. Bonham; 11 seamen.

Her Majesty's sloop Cruiser's gun-boat (pinnace), Lieut. Rodney, senior lieutenant; Mr. Cotter, midshipman; 1 petty officer, and 12 men; (gig), Commander Fanshawe; 1 petty officer, and 4 seamen; (cutter), Mr. Tuke, midshipman; 1 petty officer, and 8 seamen.

Her Majesty's sloop Wolverine's (pinnace), Lieut. Hillier, senior lieutenant; Mr. Johnson, midshipman; 1 petty officer, and 12 seamen; (gig), Commander Clifford; 1 petty officer, and 4 seamen; (cutter), Mr. Gibbard, mate; 1 petty officer, and 4 men.

Abstract of the foregoing detail.

Agincourt—officers, 15; petty officers, 10; seamen, 99. Total, 124.

Vestal—officers, 8; petty officers, 2; seamen, 42. Total, 52.

Dædalus—officers, 6; petty officers, 5; seamen, 55. Total, 66.

Vixen—officers, 4; petty officers, 1; seamen, 35. Total, 40.

Cruiser—officers, 4; petty officers, 3; seamen, 24. Total, 31.

Wolverine—officers, 4; petty officers, 3; seamen, 24. Total, 31.

Grand total—officers, 41; petty officers, 24; seamen, 279. Total, 344."

Royal Marines employed.

Captain Hawkins, her Majesty's ship Agincourt.
Lieut. Hambly, her Majesty's ship Dædalus.
Lieut. Dyer, her Majesty's ship Vestal.
Lieut. Kennedy, her Majesty's ship Agincourt.
Lieut. Mansell, her Majesty's ship Agincourt.
Eight sergeants, 8 corporals, 3 fifers, 178 privates.

Abstract.

Captain, 1; lieutenants, 4; sergeants, 8; corporals, 8; fifers, 3; privates, 178. Total, 202.

Total number of seamen, 344; marines, 202. Grand total, 546.

CHARLES TALBOT,
Captain Her Majesty's ship Vestal.

No. VI.

Memoir of Lieutenant Wade.

LIEUTENANT CHARLES FRANCIS WADE,[1] whose melancholy death is recorded in these pages, was the third son of the Rev. Thomas Wade of the county of Tipperary, and from an early period of life displayed a strong predilection for that profession in which Providence ordained that he should pass a short, yet honourable career. His family did not encourage this disposition, having no interest to ensure its successful enterprise; but the youth, when in London, having casually heard that the late Earl of Huntingdon was about to proceed to the West Indies in command of H.M.S. Valorous, immediately waited upon his lordship, and volunteered his services. Though he had no previous acquaintance nor introduction, the frankness

---

[1] The previous career of my lamented shipmate, Lieutenant Wade, was so full of honour, and so exemplary of the Nelson spirit—the glory and means of glory to the British navy, and of safety to the British nation—that I trust I may be excused in devoting a few pages of my book to his memory. My information is derived from officers under whom and companions with whom he served, and who admired and loved him: and had it pleased God to spare his life, and opportunity had been afforded him, he must have left the heroic name of a very distinguished man.—H. K.

of his manners, and the good sense he exhibited at the boyish age of fourteen, so won upon the noble earl, that he at once became his patron and friend, and he was appointed to the Valorous, and sailed in her on her destination. On her being ordered home, he was transferred to the Barham, flag-ship on the West India station; and by his good conduct strongly recommended himself to her commander, the Honourable Elphinstone Fleming, to whom, as well as to Lord Huntingdon, he expressed his grateful attachment through life. At a later time, whilst he was serving as mate on board H.M.S. Ocean at Sheerness, it was suggested to him by several of his naval friends, that he might distinguish himself by joining the British Legion in Spain: he accordingly accepted the rank of captain of artillery in the British Legion under Colonel Colquhoun, R.A.

In 1837 he returned from this employment, after two years' gallant devotion to it, and memorialised the government for promotion in the navy as a reward for his services. In this he respectfully represented his meritorious actions in common with the navy at sea and the marines and other forces in the field, with both of which he had fought in several very sharp engagements; in honour of which he had received the Spanish crosses of St. Ferdinand and Isabella Catolica, and a gold medal for commanding the guns which breached the walls of the town of Irun, through which a party of troops entered, and under so heavy a fire, that he had two-thirds of his gun-detachment killed and wounded. In short, his conduct throughout was of the most gallant description, though a slight wound was the only mark he bore of having fought in almost every affair between the Legion and the Carlists during the period of his stay. His preceding eight years in the West Indies, his having been afloat from 1824 to 1835, and his having passed his examination for a lieutenant in 1830, with a high character from every officer under whom he had served, were truly urged as a farther title to the favour he solicited. Lord Minto, then First Lord of the Admiralty, consequently appointed him to the Rhadamanthus in the Mediterranean; and in the June following, at the coronation of her Majesty, he obtained his commission as lieutenant. In 1840 he joined H.M.S. Curaçoa in the Pacific; and here an incident occurred which may serve to shew the intrepid and chivalrous temper which formed so distinguished a feature in his character. Cruising not far from the southern tropic, and a few leagues from the meridian of the island that became the refuge of the descendants of Christian and his comrades, another island was seen, which was thought to be a discovery. The nature of the shore and the sea that broke against it forbade any attempt at landing from a boat, but access to a swimmer seemed possible; and it being considered desirable that the new-found territory should be examined and possession of it taken, Lieutenant Wade volunteered to perform this service, and to swim on shore with the union-jack secured to him. He succeeded in landing, explored the island sufficiently to ascertain that it had neither inhabitants nor shipwrecked mariners upon it, and that it had already been visited by a British ship of war. He then returned safely on board; but the consequences of the adventure were serious, for it was followed by a severe attack of rheumatic fever, occasioned by having remained so long in wet clothes; and finding there was no hope of regaining his health at sea, he quitted his ship, with regret, at San Blas, and returned through Mexico to England.

MEMOIR OF LIEUT. WADE.

In December 1842, hardly recovered from the effects of the disease, but determined to deserve and to obtain promotion, he was appointed first lieutenant of the Samarang, then fitting for the survey of the Indian Seas. In March 1844 he joined for a short time H. M. S. Driver; and on the 5th June following was appointed first of the Dido.

It is not easy to express in adequate language, says one who knew him intimately, the qualities by which poor Wade was distinguished, and how much he was beloved by all his acquaintance. Brave and enterprising, yet gentle, affectionate, and considerate of others; firm in principle, and exact in the performance of every duty, but unpretending, generous, and loyal; there seemed to be united in him all the properties which, joined to skill in his profession, would have ensured to him an eminent place in the brilliant annals of his service. But he was of those who fall in the front, and who die too soon for their own glory.

To his family and intimate friends his amiable, generous, and affectionate manners endear his memory; and although they must mourn his loss, yet they have the consolation of knowing that his whole conduct was influenced by a sincere Christian spirit, and that he was not less willing to devote his life to the service of his country than to manifest in his whole conduct the exalted principles by which he was ever influenced.

No. VII.

Memoir of Mr. George Steward.

THE late George Steward, who fell in August 1844, whilst fighting as a volunteer in the expedition against the pirates of Borneo, commanded by Captain Keppel, was the youngest of seven children of the late Timothy Steward, Esq. of Yarmouth. Having shewn an early predilection for the sea, a midshipman's berth was procured for him in the maritime service of the Honourable East India Company, in which he rose with as much rapidity as its regulations would admit; but unfortunately for him, precisely at the period when he became eligible for, and had secured, the command of a first-class ship, the act of parliament was passed which abolished the mercantile privileges, and consequently extinguished the maritime service, of the Honourable East India Company, whose officers thereupon retired on pensions. Not being disposed to continue at sea as a private adventurer, Mr. Steward remained unemployed for several years; but in 1842 his adventurous and daring spirit led him to embrace the proposition of his friend and brother-officer, Mr. Henry Wise, now connected with the East India and China trade, to undertake the charge of a commercial expedition to the infant settlement established at Sarāwak under the auspices of Mr. Brooke. In the month of March 1843 he left England in the Ariel, a smart fast-sailing brig, purchased, fitted out, and armed by himself and Mr. Wise, in pursuance of the mercantile operation referred to, and for the additional security of Mr. Brooke. The vessel arrived at Singapore in the following July. Here Mr. Steward was informed that the Borneo Seas were swarming with pirates; and the master of the brig having left her at that port, Mr. Steward assumed the command. On his arrival at Sarāwak, he received from Mr. Brooke a welcome, the cordiality of which was enhanced by their recognising each other as schoolfellows. Of the enterprise, intelligence, liberal mind, and friendly disposition of Mr. Brooke, Mr. Steward has, in his correspondence, spoken with the utmost warmth, and to him he was at all times indebted for much valuable assistance and counsel. At Sarāwak Mr. Steward remained until he unfortunately joined the expedition against the pirates, in which his life was sacrificed. In his *last* letter to England he spoke, fearlessly, of an expected descent of the pirates, of having fortified his *iron* house, and of the anticipated and much-desired visit of H. M. S. Dido to that settlement. The subsequent acts of his career are related by Captain Keppel.

THE END.

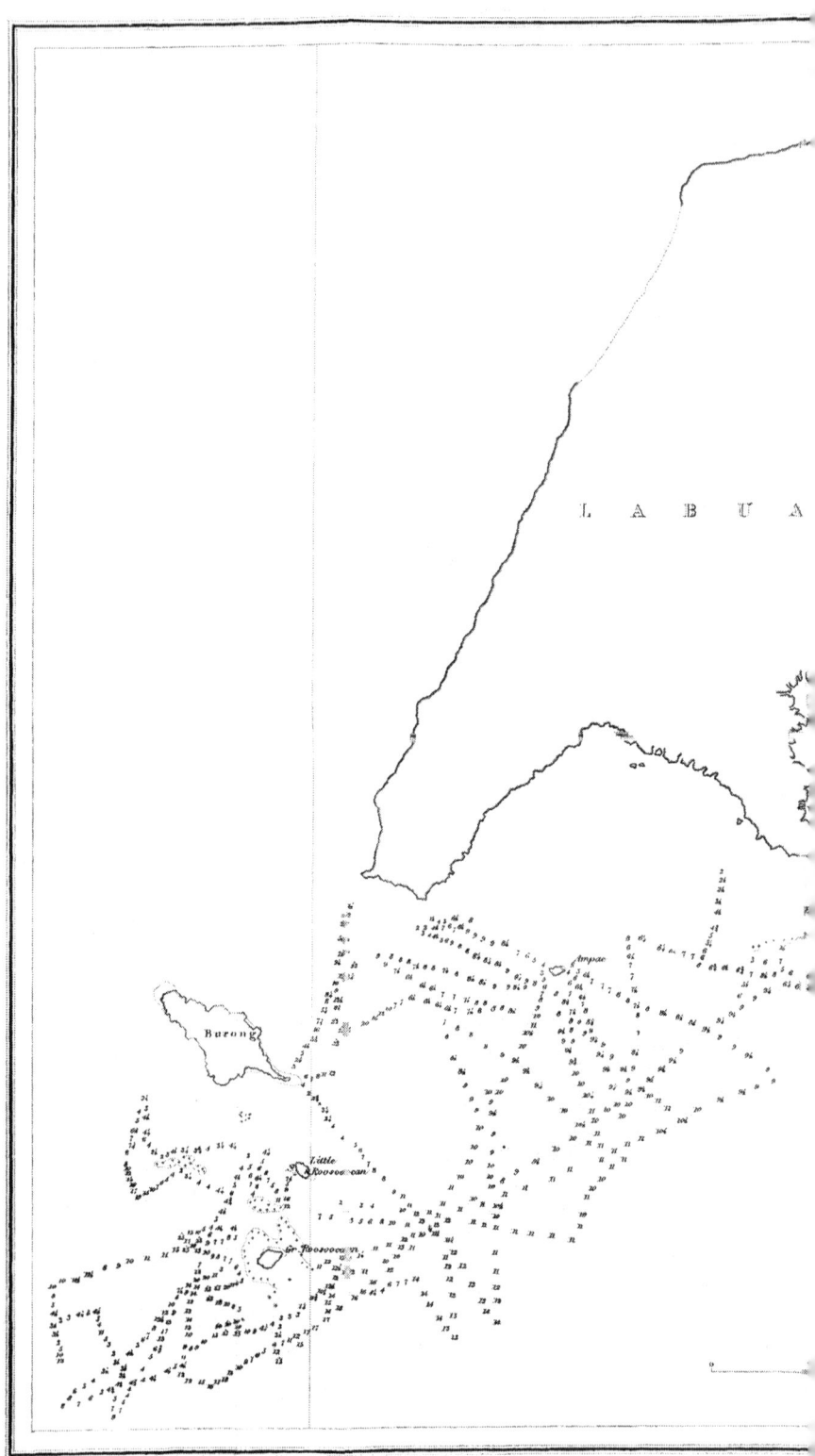

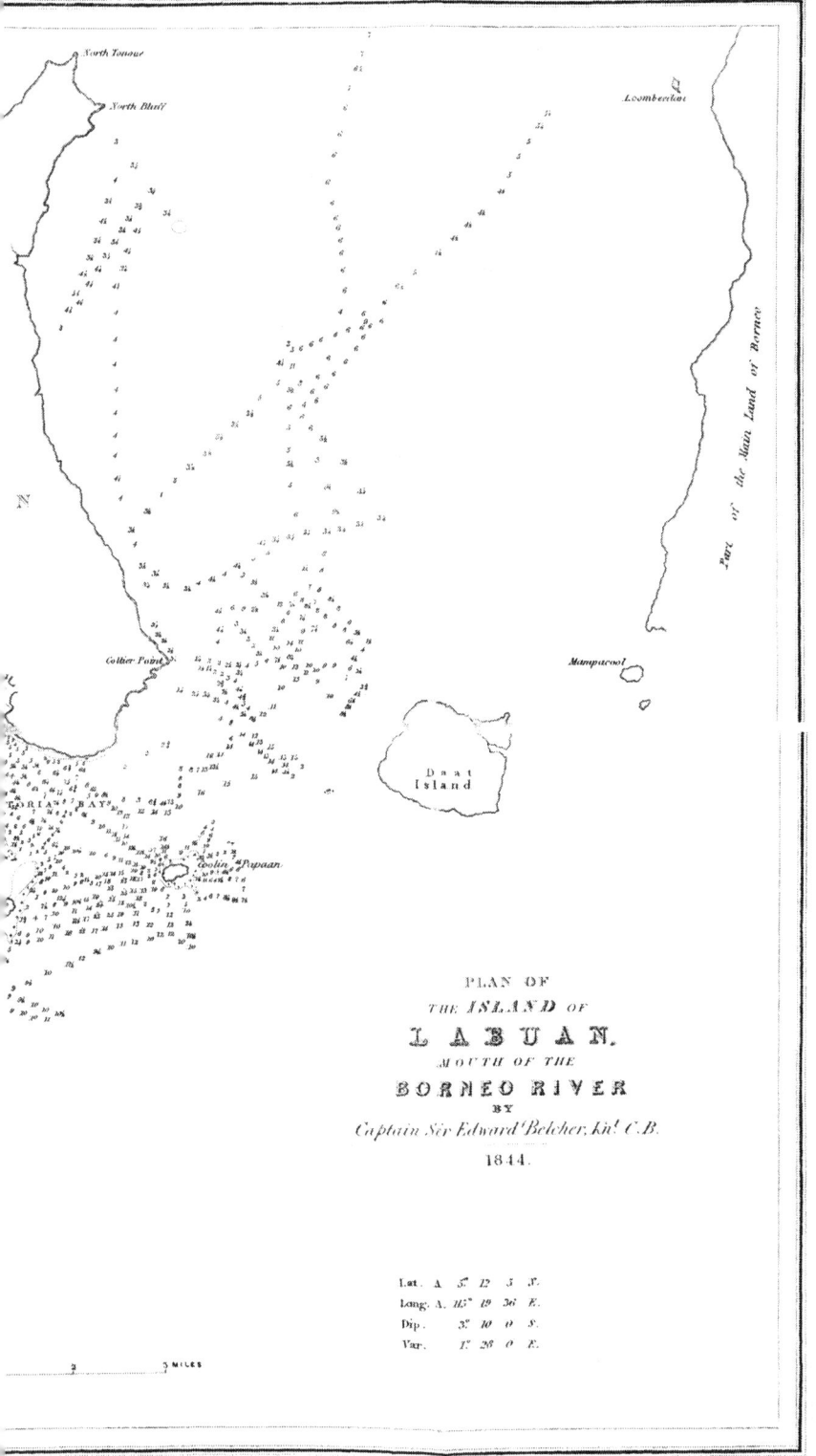

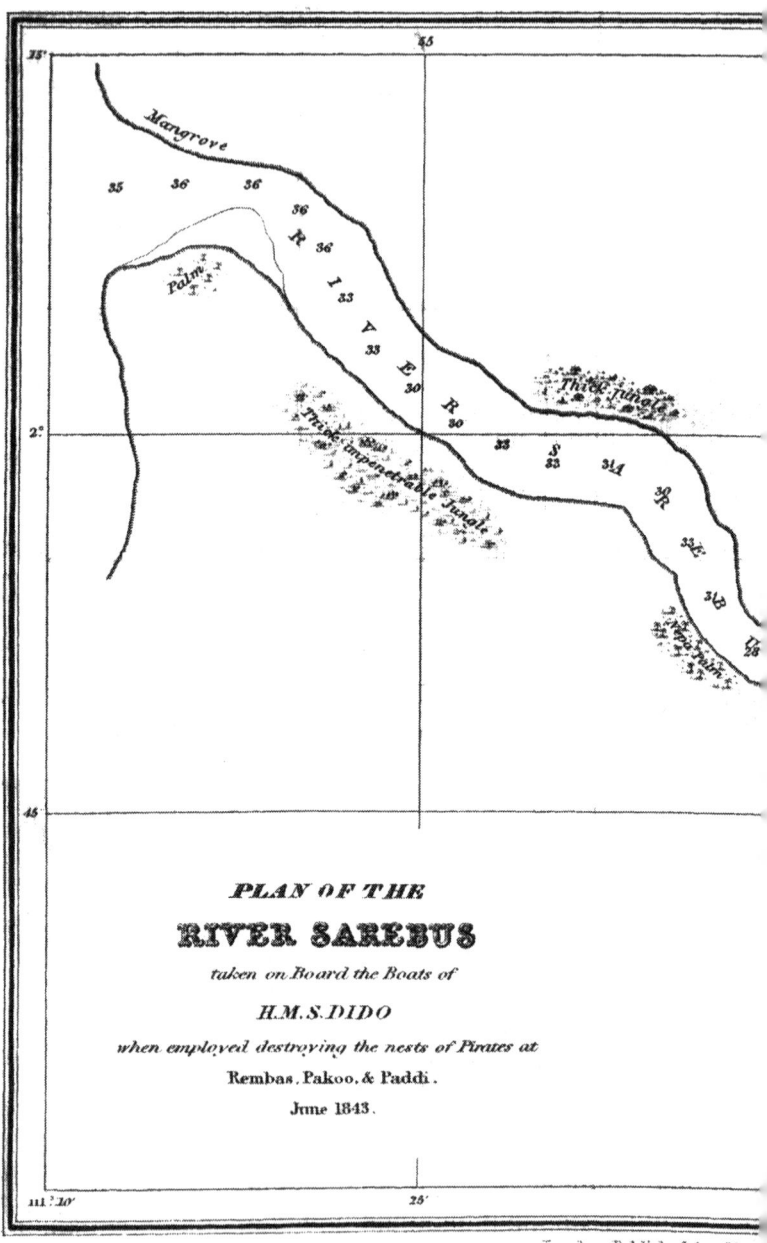

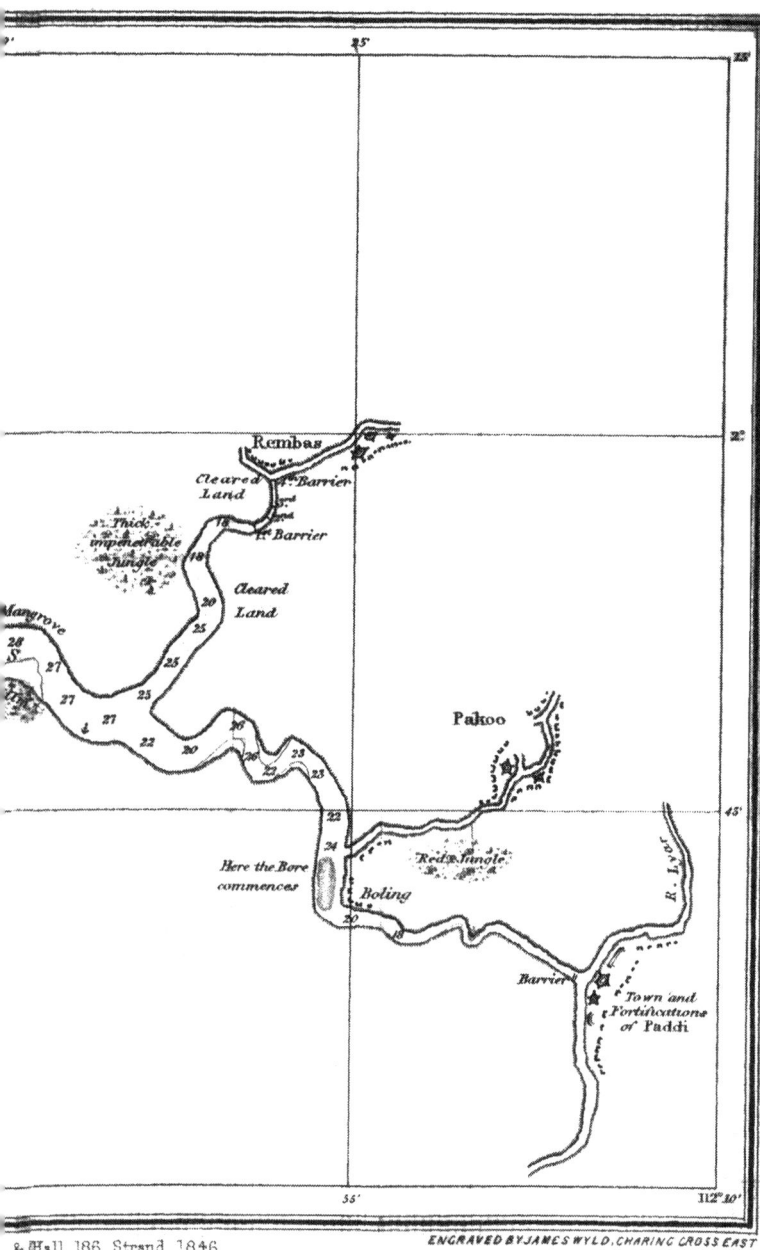

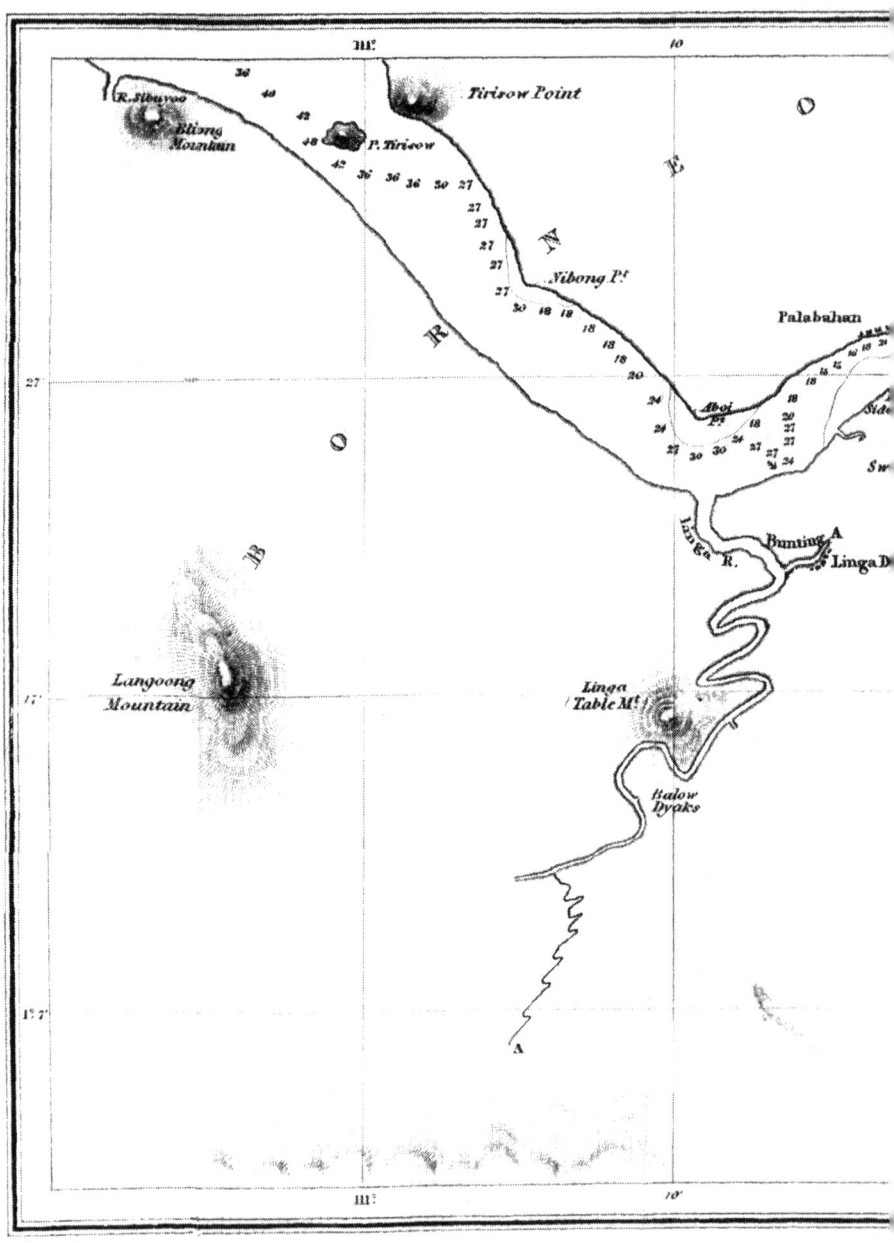

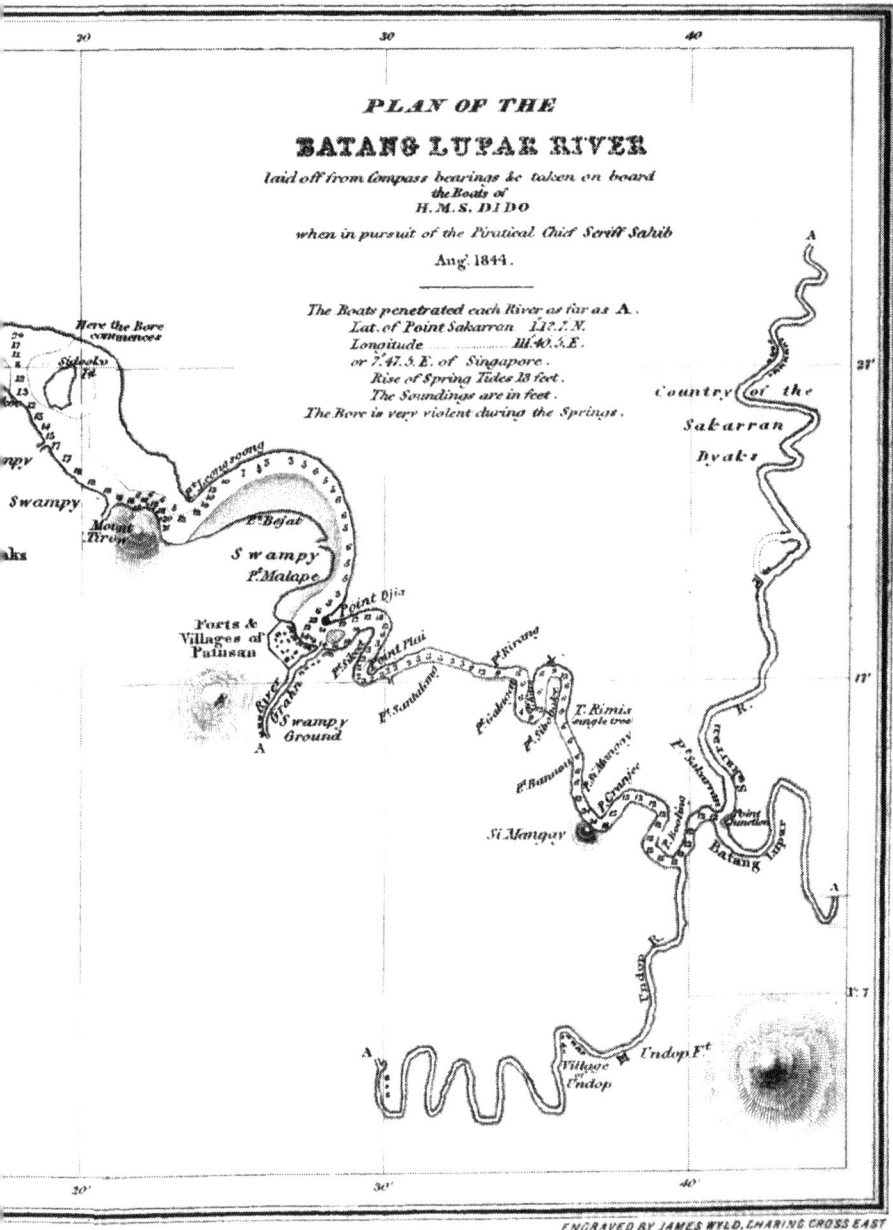

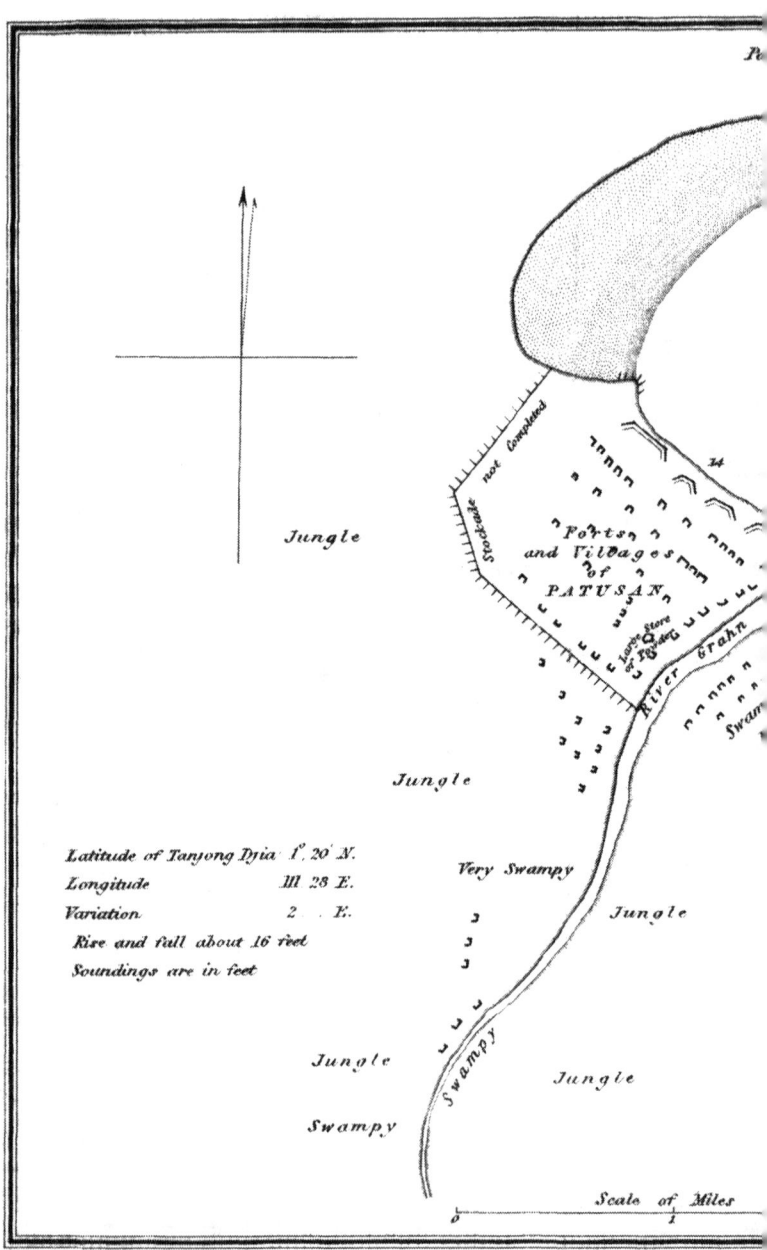

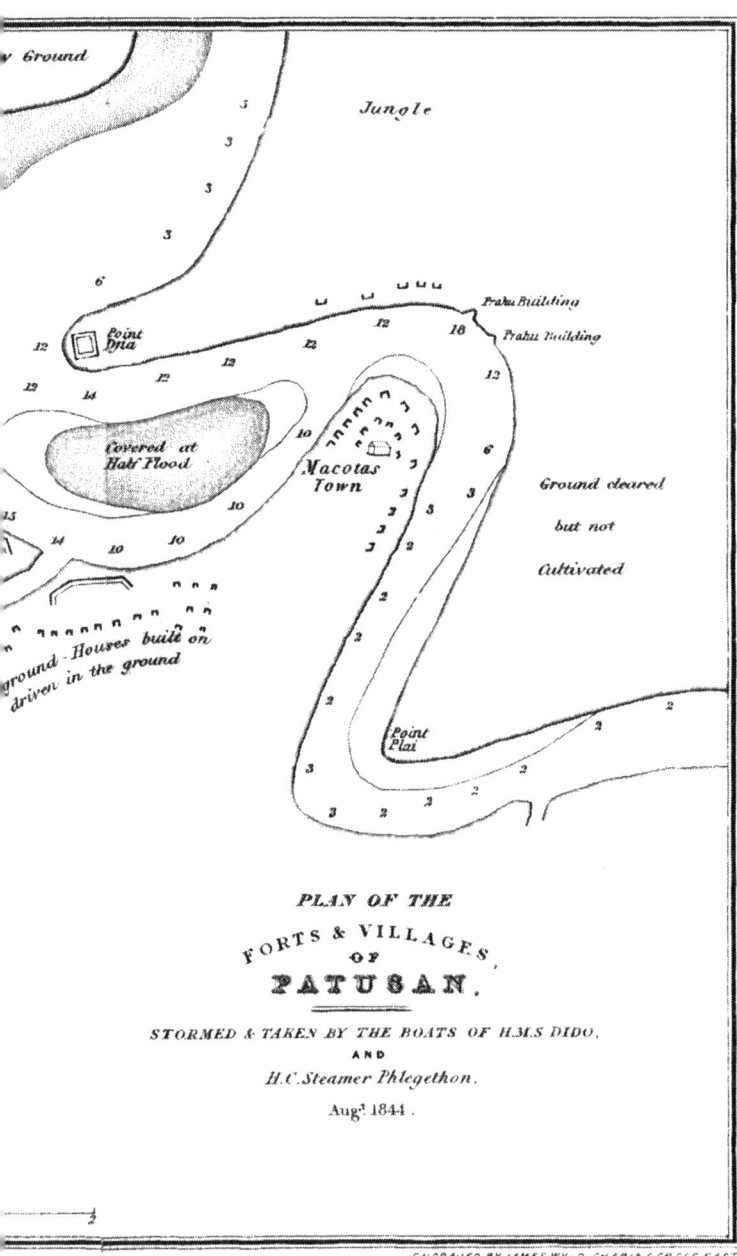